Modern European History

A Garland Series of Outstanding Dissertations

General Editor
William H. McNeill
University of Chicago

Associate Editors

Eastern Europe
Charles Jelavich
Indiana University

Great Britain
Peter Stansky
Stanford University

France
David H. Pinkney
University of Washington

Russia
Barbara Jelavich
Indiana University

Germany
Enno E. Kraehe
University of Virginia

Lord Acton: oil painting by Franz von Lenbach, reproduced by kind permission
of the Hon. Richard Acton

The Reign of Conscience

Individual, Church, and State in Lord Acton's History of Liberty

John Nurser

Garland Publishing, Inc.
New York and London 1987

336141

Library of Congress Cataloging-in-Publication Data

Nurser, John, 1929–
    The reign of conscience : individual, church, and
state in Lord Acton's history of liberty / John Nurser.
        p.   cm—(Modern European history)
    Bibliography: p.
    Includes index.
    ISBN 0-8240-7826-8 (alk. paper)
    1. Acton, John Emerich Edward Dalberg Acton,
Baron, 1834–1902.   2. History, Modern.
3. History—Philosophy   4. Church and state.
5. Individually.   I. Title.   II. Series.
D15.A25N87 1987
909—dc19   87-29230

Printed in the United States of America

To

Arthur John Nurser, 1898–1961

who believed in the truth of good craftsmanship

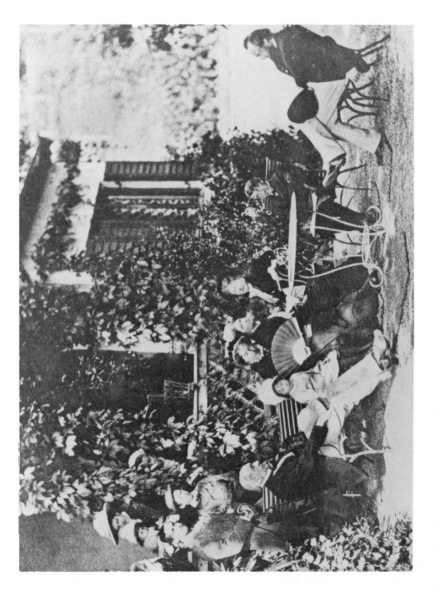

Family photograph at Tegernsee, Bavaria, 1879: (from left) Mr and Mrs Gladstone, Dr Dollinger, and Lord Acton; reproduced from H. Paul, *Letters of Lord Acton to Mary Gladstone*, by kind permission of George Allen & Unwin Ltd.

CONTENTS

Preface and Acknowledgments

Dr Peter Stansky of Stanford University, California, suggested to me in 1985 that the Garland Press might be able to publish the doctoral work I had done in the mid 1950s at Cambridge University. I submitted that dissertation from the other Cambridge, where I began training for the ministry at Harvard Divinity School in 1956 immediately after completing the statutory three years as a research student on 'The idea of conscience in the work of Lord Acton'. In the normally busy and varied life of an Anglican clergyman since then, there has never been enough space and time to prepare the work for publication. Naturally enough I have regretted this. The work on Acton has been influential on all that I have done in the intervening years.

The invitation to prepare a thirty-year-old dissertation for publication was the spur, but nothing could have been achieved without the willingness of my colleagues the Dean and Chapter of Lincoln Cathedral to grant me two months' sabbatical. In this time I have enjoyed the hospitality of Westcott House, Cambridge, and of my friend the Dean of Gibraltar.

It is hard to make adequate acknowledgment of help received when it stretches over such a long period. It becomes a kind of 'thank you' for a whole autobiography. The supervisor and *animateur* of the research on which this book is based was Sir Herbert Butterfield, and he is no longer alive. I received my training as a historian at Peterhouse and my invitation to Acton studies from Brian Wormald, who is in some sense still my 'master'. I was encouraged to see connexions with the social dilemmas of my generation's church by James Luther Adams. At ten-year intervals I have been fortunate, first at Trinity Hall, Cambridge, and then at St Mark's Institute of Theology, Canberra, to have been granted short leaves for reading and reflexion. Above all, of course, I owe to my wife the courage to persist in hope, and gratitude for her professional skill in preparing this manuscript through its various revisions.

At one time I believed publication should wait until the argument of this book about the role of conscience in Lord Acton's thought could be placed in the context of a definitive biography.

Working in the Cambridge University Library on the Acton notebooks and boxes of cards in the 1950s was an odd experience. There was so little definite shape to John Acton the man or to the sequence of his public and private life. It seemed only too likely that even the best efforts of a young research student could only result in the accumulation of notes on Lord Acton's notes – on only a part in fact of his notes – so that inadequacy would be piled on futility.

Here was a man of enormous intellectual application and unquestioned social status, who enjoyed a private income and domestic servants, and who was 'at home' with family in at least four countries of Europe, who travelled incessantly. He made notes on the books he read; he employed amanuenses to take notes on manuscripts in libraries and archives; he drafted paragraphs that seemed never to have been put end to end in any argument; he made lists of names; he wrote down pithy comments (whether his own opinions or those he was arguing against, who could tell?). After he died these largely undated notes seemed all that was left, poignant building blocks of a what-might-have-been that his contemporaries were convinced had a quite special significance. It was as if Moses had fallen and died on the climb down from Mount Sinai: his face still aglow with the revelation he had received, and the tablets of stone fractured into bits. It makes a dramatic but not altogether attractive comparison.

During the last thirty years, however, a quite substantial number of volumes of Acton's writing has been published. The greater part of it is correspondence, and therefore datable. Together with Acton's collected essays and lectures published in the generation after his death, the talks recently discovered, and contributions to the liberal Catholic journals established as Acton's, there now exists a very solid shelf of his writing. His letters are the equivalent of other men's essays. His production can no longer be accused of being 'slight'. And it has been very well edited. The result is that a skeleton now exists for a much more plausible reconstruction of Acton's life and intellectual development, that might even structure the notes in the Cambridge University Library. The argument of this work on 'conscience' can now find its place alongside this skeleton. It draws strength from it, and can itself give significant shape to it.

I am only too aware that I have not been able to read as widely as I would have liked. More than a few of the works referred to – especially those published in the last twenty years – have not been satisfactorily digested. It is a case of the best being the enemy not only of the good, but – in my present life – of the attainable. Acton remains a hard man to catch up with. Nothing however that I have seen has led me to believe that the thrust of my argument is untrue – or, indeed, uninteresting.

Lord Acton still remains one of the very few unquestionably 'great' Victorians of whom there is not even a biography, let alone a satisfactory one. He deserves one. To understand his life in its manifold complications and subtleties would be to solve what has remained an important problem in intellectual history. He exercises a puzzling power over anyone who has lived with him. Gertrude Himmelfarb, in the introduction to her most recently published collection of essays, testifies to that. So much of what he worked for, even when he was mistaken, is still part of the life of our time.

John Nurser

The North Mole, Gibraltar
April 1986

1
Introduction

Lord Acton was a European. At any rate, he was not exactly English: his family was accustomed to speak four languages at meals. His grandfather, Sir John Acton, was prime minister of the Bourbon kingdom of the Two Sicilies between 1790 and 1804.[1] In those years English influence through the Royal Navy – and Admiral Nelson in particular – was actively present, and Naples itself had been for generations one of the principal pilgrimage shrines of any English milord's Grand Tour. The Actons were an old Shropshire family, baronets, with their seat at Aldenham outside Bridgnorth, but had become Roman Catholic and lived abroad for three generations before John Edward Emerich Dalberg Acton was born in the Palazzo Acton at Naples on 10 January 1834. His mother was a Dalberg from Herrnsheim near Worms on the Rhine. The Dukes of Dalberg were the senior family of the Holy Roman Empire of the German Nation – Catholic in religion and accustomed to use French as their first language; indeed, prominent in the service of France both militarily and diplomatically.

Acton's father Sir Ferdinand Richard Edward Acton died in a riding accident when his son was three years old, so the boy inherited the baronetcy and was 'Sir John' from his earliest memories. He was also an only child. His mother soon remarried (1840), this time to Earl Granville, a member of one of the Whig aristocratic families, who became a principal figure in British political life, serving with distinction in Gladstone's administrations as Foreign Secretary. They came therefore to live in England.

The young Sir John was placed in a Catholic school at Oscott, Birmingham, run by the later Cardinal Wiseman. When the time came for him to go up to university, it was Cambridge that came naturally to mind. His uncle Charles (later Cardinal) Acton had taken his degree at Magdalene College in 1823. Cambridge was the more congenial university to Whigs (it is interesting that in that upper-class world no one appears to have considered the newly founded non-denominational University College London).

1

But 1850 was a time of public agitation and indignation at the 'papal aggression', when a hierarchy of territorial Roman Catholic dioceses was introduced into England for the first time. So Acton was refused admission on the ground of the still unrepealed Test Acts, which required members of the old universities to subscribe to the 39 Articles of the Church of England. It was necessary therefore to explore the universities of Catholic Europe. The reputation of the German universities and, in particular, that of their scientific (*wissenschaftlich*) methods was then without equal, and Acton became a student at the University of Munich, the capital of the kingdom of Bavaria and the intellectual centre of German Catholicism. He lived almost as a medieval apprentice in the house in Frühlingstrasse of Professor Ignaz von Döllinger, a priest whose great reputation was as a church historian. There is little evidence that he took part in any social activities with his student peers: his world was that of a very domestic and unpretentious High Table; he was a very model of what a Cambridge 'fellow-commoner' (if a young and properly Anglican lord of such habits existed) ought to have been – but rarely was.

Through the good offices of Granville, the young Sir John Acton was attached to diplomatic missions to the U.S.A. (1853) – where he much enjoyed the experience of American ice-cream while marvelling at Niagara – and Russia (1856). But his experience as an Englishman was profoundly untypical of his generation or class. The fox-hunting squires, the Jorrockses, are on a different planet. Not for him the new college boat races. He shows no sign of ever moving into the traditional upper-class English niche of eccentric amateur enthusiasm. There is no reason to suppose he was familiar with the dark Satanic mills of the industrial conurbations. Even the cosmopolitan network of his family was more characteristic of an ancien régime that was already old fashioned. The marrying-out that became frequent in the next generation was to be more directed to the English-speaking diaspora across the seas than to mainland Europe. The sheer excitement of Prince Albert's Great Exhibition of 1851, for the first time a network of railways enabling a whole people to come to marvel at the modern world, passed him by. When *The Times* spoke of the evident danger that even foreigners would be coming to the Crystal Palace – 'their bearded visages conjuring up all the horrors of Free Trade' – young Sir John Acton was in the library, his latest news fresh manuscripts in a variety of non-English languages, rescued from the archives of no longer autonomous princedoms and sequestrated Catholic monasteries. For Acton at Munich, the connotations of 'science' and 'progress' were not so much – as they would have been at Cambridge – mathematics and the physical sciences, as the sudden opening of obscure languages and secret histories to the light of exact and systematic public study.

Acton lived together as a household with his teacher. They naturally entertained other leading figures of that historical, academic, ecclesiastical, and political world – most of whom were of an older generation than Acton. He and Döllinger soon developed a relationship that remained of extraordinary significance to both men. Acton had never known a father; Döllinger could not have a son. Perhaps encouraged by the development of this close relationship with Acton, another pupil of Döllinger's, Charlotte von Leyden (later Lady Blennerhasset),[2] and then – in a sense – William Ewart Gladstone himself, were drawn into this family of elective affinity.

Döllinger was almost romantic in his attachment to England, and to the Whig tradition. The 1850s were a time when England was quite spectacularly the rising star, the shape of the future. If Japan seems to us peculiarly at home now with computer technology, so did Great Britain then with the applications of the steam engine, and with a network of safe sea-borne free trade whose limits could only be those of the world itself. Obviously enough, it was not then clear that the Yankee manufacturers or the Prussian state machine would within twenty years have taken the leadership of America and Germany through civil war, and drawn alongside Britain and then ahead of her as models of practice. At that time, the Irish who had survived the Great Famine were largely occupied in making a new life overseas, and those sections of society which had given dangerous power to Chartism were not yet clear in which direction to move – so that it was still possible to think that English Whiggism was sustainable – indeed normative – in British political life.

Acton learned to honour Burke and Macaulay with lifelong passion, not in England but at Munich. Yet even these loyalties, so apparently of a piece with the mainstream of English life, had a matrix that was singularly foreign to any self-consciously 'Whig' experience. For Döllinger was a professional, a historian, a Bavarian priest. In photographs taken at Tegernsee of Döllinger with Acton and Gladstone, it is he who looks the foreigner, the guest. He is a slight figure, with the grace (in that company) of a quizzical expression. He never developed social pretensions; his was an almost medieval life story of meritocratic promotion to leadership from *Kleinstadt* origins. He had the integrity, and the sense of limits, that comes from *Amt* and *sacerdotium*, public function and sacred priesthood. For Döllinger, Burke and Macaulay were enthusiasms of the decades and the places of his youth in the 1820s and 1830s, together with and inseparable from such regional heroes as Bishop J. M. Sailer, J. H. A. Gügler, and Alexandre Vinet. However dedicated to 'open' scholarship and to the great issues of public policy and diplomacy Döllinger was, he was by vocation, training, and conviction a churchman – a consciously Catholic priest. English Whigs were not like that.

This made it difficult, when Acton returned to England, for him to make himself as understood as he supposed among either Whigs or fellow Catholics.[3] It was virtually unheard of for a Whig in England (and certainly in Ireland) to be a Roman Catholic, and the public concerns of English Roman Catholics were far removed from those of Bishop Sailer. The descendants of the English recusants tended to be rural gentry from the north, with little interest in academic issues of the faith – they had after all been kept out of the universities for centuries past. The converts from the Church of England via the Oxford Movement had an apologetic intellectual zeal; but it was a conscious reaction precisely against the absence of specifically church self-conscious-ness and sharp dogmatics in religious Whiggery. The hard-pressed Catholic clergy had problems enough setting up a pastoral ministry to the urban settlements of Irish working-class immigrants, and integrating these with the scattered indigenous church community. They were inward looking, and taught to be suspicious of the Catholicism of German universities.

The question of an identity – even if a salary was not strictly necessary – had to arise when Acton returned to London. No posts existed for a historian. In Acton's view, there were no English historians worthy of the name in the German sense. There was not the tradition of working from primary manuscript sources. There was not the intellectual self-consciousness of a distinct discipline with its own autonomous sphere and traditions. People did not apply themselves seriously enough. It was all, he said, 'at a lower level'.[4] It is central to Acton's whole life that, as a student, he chose to be a historian. He remained faithful to that self-image, in the particular guise it presented itself to him at Munich, till he died as Regius Professor of Modern History at Cambridge. Many at the time and since have thought it eccentric

– or even corrupt – that Acton should have been nominated to the chair at Cambridge as wholly innocent of publishing a book as of holding a teaching post. But Acton had been recognised for a generation as the bearer of standards, the English focus of an international community of scholars, and a central figure in the foundation in 1885 of the *English Historical Review*.

If Acton saw his future as the apostle of historical method to the English, he also caught some of Döllinger's sense of religious vocation. These skills, and the fruits they might bring, could be useful to the causes of Whig politics and the Roman Catholic church. He did not at first see his future in politics as merely advisory. However, it was apparent that his future in the church must be a lay one, and this gave a possibility to his service to the church as a lay historian that was different from Döllinger's. He would need to keep a certain distance from the church if he were to be most useful to it. If a historian is to be accepted as a professional, he has to accept a certain disengagement from the cause about which he writes, and must be open to evidence from any source and to the variety of sustainable perspectives.

Acton set about proposing and, so far as he could, exemplifying this stance. He repeatedly claimed that this was the profitable path of apologetic for the Roman Catholic church in the world in which it now found itself. This was not the seminary path, it was the open ocean of the modern university; virtually all Catholic clergy found it unfamiliar and uncongenial, and most judged it dangerous. So Acton was rejected. Not only was his own self-offering rejected, but the metropolitan academic discipline he had mastered and brought with him. He felt perhaps as boffins on ships felt in 1940, whose radar equipment had been installed but whose commanding officers refused to use it. In a life that had more than its share of family suffering and chronic financial anxiety, it is no hyperbole to suggest that he experienced his own Calvary.

Granted that no professional niches existed in England for historians, Acton had to find another platform for his activity as historian of politics and its philosophy. He was elected to the House of Commons as member for the Irish consituency of Carlow in 1859, and moved into the developing world of Catholic journalism. Both Burke and Macaulay had found comparable niches. The great reviews, the *Edinburgh*, the *Quarterly*, were established centres of British intellectual life, each with its constituency. Two Catholic reviews had recently been founded, the *Dublin* and, on the liberal side, the *Rambler*. The story has been well told by Professor Altholz of how Acton committed himself to editorial work on the *Rambler*, and above all to its successor, the *Home and Foreign Review*. In its brief life – and with such a very small natural constituency it had to fight for every subscription – it was one of the most distinguished publications in Britain. Acton was emphatic that he wished no future for the *Home and Foreign Review* that did not allow it both to exercise the proper autonomy and objectivity of academic discipline and to enjoy the confidence of the Roman Catholic church.

The *Syllabus of Errors*, the papal response to the Munich Catholic Congress in 1863, made it plain that this confidence could not be claimed. Other titles less directly related to Acton, the *North British Review* and the *Chronicle*, followed, their dragonfly lives ended by ecclesiastical displeasure.

It is important to stress – given his later reputation for unproductiveness and *accidie* – the quite extraordinary scope and energy of Acton's life before the First Vatican Council of 1869. He ran his estates (and advanced money to his enterprises), he wrote important articles of great learning, he reviewed books, he suggested themes and bibliographies to others, he arranged for printing and distribution, he continued to collect books and manuscripts for a great library, he made frequent visits to mainland Europe, he kept up a remarkable correspondence, he dined out and played an active role in political life, and he actually broke new ground in his studies. Added to which, he established a household.

Acton's marriage to his cousin, Marie Arco-Valley, was celebrated by Döllinger in 1865. This had been his mother's dying wish in 1860. The Arco-Valleys were an actively Catholic family in Munich who had their seat at St Martin near Ried in Upper Austria. The Actons soon had children, and Acton's letters show him to have been a model father – playing with them, staying out of the library to look after them, taking them on walks, and instructing them in the faith. Marie Acton's health became fragile and she preferred to be out of the English winter. The caravan of the Acton family seems to have been on the move almost continually. For someone to whom his working library meant so much, this must have been a real difficulty. There was a sequence of houses in London; there was Aldenham (though used less and less); there was Munich and the Villa Arco at Tegernsee nearby; there was La Madeleine at Cannes – besides the houses of relatives in Italy and of course the family home at

St Martin. The recently established system of European railways made this life style possible, as it did the letter posts – so much quicker than in our own generation, and so frequently used by Acton.

It is extraordinary how many of Acton's letters are preserved, from very early in his life. Those who received them must have been very conscious that they were involved in a correspondence that might come to be thought important. Even insignificant notes were kept so that the collection could be complete. Acton had the joint authority of a prophet and an encyclopaedia, even as a young man, and even at a distance. He wrote vividly, clearly, forcefully, coherently, and – above all – fluently. So much of the intellectual energy that in German scholars produced monographs, in Acton's case produced letters the length and weight of centre-page articles. As it became clearer that he would never write his great books, his letters became longer and more charged. A letter to Döllinger covers fifteen printed pages,[5] and he refers to the twenty-four pages sent to Creighton, setting out his '35 theses' on writing history.

There are three volumes of correspondence between Acton and Richard Simpson, his colleague in editing the journals of the 1860s. There are three unusually bulky volumes of his correspondence with Döllinger. As Sir Owen Chadwick has remarked, Acton seemed to need as well a woman correspondent to whom he could unburden his thoughts and experiences. First his wife, then Gladstone's daughter Mary, and finally his daughter Mamy served this role. Long letters survive to Gladstone himself, to Lady Blennerhasset, to his cousin the Italian prime minister Marco Minghetti, and many others – probably there are important collections still in private archives in several countries.

The various liberal Catholic reviews were glorious, but like the Charge of the Light Brigade (or Thermopylae) they had the smell of death about them from the beginning. It was soon evident in those years that Pope Pius IX – supported by the bishops of the Roman Catholic church in general and of England in particular – was determined to call an Ecumenical Council, the first since Trent in the 16th century, and to use it to proclaim a dogma of papal infallibility. In Acton's eyes, and Döllinger's, this would be a denial of historical scholarship, a false and short-sighted response to the unbelief of the day, and therefore a disaster for the church. So the practical activity of writing, inspiring, and managing the reviews gradually merged into even more intense practical political activism in preparing for the Council. By this time he had become a trusted lieutenant and personal friend of Gladstone's and in 1869, partly to show the confidence he and the policy he represented enjoyed in British government circles, Gladstone offered him a peerage, so that he became Lord Acton, with a seat in the Upper House of Parliament. He was introduced with Lord Rothschild; the first Roman Catholic and the first Jew to be proposed in that House.

By any standards 1870 was an unusual year: Bismarck defeated Napoleon III, Rome became the capital of the kingdom of Italy, the Paris Commune signalled the Socialist International, the Pope lost his Temporal Power. But nothing was more extraordinary than the campaign which Acton, as a 35-year-old layman without official standing in the Council and from a Protestant country, waged at Rome against the proposed Decree of Infallibility. 'Acton ist von einer fieberhaften Thätigheit', Lady Blennerhassett reported to Döllinger, 'und leistet das Unmöglich.' It was his command of languages, his personal contacts, his persuasiveness and moral authority, his knowledge, and his consuming energy which enabled those bishops who were troubled by the proposed decree to become an organised opposition party. At one point it was touch and go whether Cardinal Antonelli would withdraw the proposed decree as inopportune. But in the end the decree was approved over-whelmingly and Acton was defeated. The representative of the British government, Odo Russell, wrote back in his despatches of 18 June 1970: 'Whatever the Liberal Catholic party achieves in the world after the Council will be mainly due to the influential presence of Lord Acton during the Council in Rome: and I feel it is my duty to place these facts on record in the annals of Your Lordship's office.'[6]

Acton and his friends left before the final voting and the proclamation of the decree in the *Götterdämmerung* context of St Peter's in July, thunder and lightning raging spectacularly and the national army of Italian liberation at the gates of Rome. The Council was adjourned abruptly, and only reconvened under the presidency of Pope John XXIII nearly a century later. A good deal of business accumulated, which gave the opportunity to the Fathers of Vatican II, in their decrees, to put infallibility into a notably different context.

It is easy to exaggerate the significance of the proclamation of papal infallibility for Acton. He had something of a breakdown, it is true, but that is normal for those who fight hard and lose. The qualification of the dogma that the opposition succeeded in writing into its definition turned out to be of great importance, and was on any realistic assessment (and Acton had a good deal of the typically Italian hard-headed politician in him) more than could have been foreseen. He regularly replied to those who enquired what he was going to do now the dogma had been proclaimed, that he would do nothing. Everything in Rome before 1870 had not been so perfect or to his taste. Nothing significant had changed. There was never any question of his joining the breakaway Old Catholics. He was very angry when his name was used – without his permission – in one of their manifestos. He accused their apologist, J. Friedrich, of using history in exactly the partisan style which remained the gravamen of proper continuing opposition to Ultramontanism in the Roman Catholic church.[7] He was happy to leave the resolution of the new difficulties for the church's mission posed by the decrees to the natural – and providential – processes of reflexion and argument in the next generations.[8]

He realised that as a layman he would not be exposed to the loyalist mopping-up operation – the question of in or out – that led to the submission of all the opposition bishops. Even the redoubtable Bishop Josef Strossmayer of Djakovo in Croatia had submitted on 28 December 1872.

But it was clearly not going to be an easy world for Acton to live in.[9] The English bishops, and especially Cardinal Manning of Westminster, had been hot for infallibility. One of Acton's most intimate friends among the opposition bishops was Archbishop Darboy of Paris, who returned from the Council only to be imprisoned and shot by the Communards. However he distanced himself, it was well known that Acton's particular associates were close to the heart of the move to set up breakaway Old Catholic dioceses in German-speaking Europe. Döllinger himself had been excommunicated rather than submit to the decrees but did not join the secession. The pope and the curia could ask every ounce of loyalty and sympathy from Catholics now that they had lost all the papal territories; and an accommodation with the anti-clerical government in Italy seemed only slightly more probable than exile. Within a few years, Bismarck launched his *Kulturkampf* against the Roman Catholic church's school system in Germany. It did not seem, to most churchmen, to be the right time for leading German-speaking Catholic laymen to have too sensitive and theoretical a conscience.

One of Acton's principal strategies in Rome at the Council had been to arouse the interest of the European governments in the changes which threatened to happen in the church, and their anxiety at the extent to which they could have political consequences in Catholic countries, not least within the British Empire. Governments had after all played a part at Trent. So the non-ecclesiastical backlash against the infallibility dogma could hardly have taken Acton by surprise. It had a pleasant side. Honorary doctorates were showered on Döllinger by the universities of northern Europe. Acton himself was awarded a doctorate by the University of Munich in 1872 and elected a member of the Bavarian Academy of Sciences in 1876.

This seemed to indicate not just an alternative, but a highly desirable, future for Acton. The last years of hectic activity could be recognised as an interlude, played indeed with distinction, in an academic vocation. It was obvious that in the eyes of the hierarchy he must be vigilant in denying himself incursions into theology, and keep as low a public profile as possible. The more it became evident that the family was to live for substantial periods in Bavaria and Austria, the less necessary – or indeed possible – it was to have definite career responsibilities. So historical research and writing could claim the mature years of a marvellously gifted and prepared scholar. He began to speak – at first in limited and realistic language – about the project of a multi-volume History of Liberty to which he wished to address his energy. Döllinger continued for a few years to appeal to him to produce the volume he had already prepared on the history of the Council of Trent, whose imminent publication colleagues at Munich had been expecting. But Acton always justified his lack of progress on the grounds that there was another collection of materials to explore. Once he had decided that the more grandiose theme of the History of Liberty itself was to be the scope of his writing, it became more and more difficult to bring the volume on Trent to completion.

The situation was given an unwelcome twist and one that was particularly awkward for Acton – given the post-Council strategy he had adopted – when his own friend Gladstone insisted against his advice on publishing in November 1874 his pamphlet, *The Vatican Decrees in their Bearing on Civil Allegiance.*[10] There was still in England a great deal of traditional no-popery feeling. The Gordon Riots were less than a century old. It had all died down, but Acton himself had met the force of this still latent prejudice against Catholics in politics when he decided to give up his Irish parliamentary seat and stand for his home constituency of

Bridgnorth. It was only after a recount that he lost, but his initial triumph was that of the one Catholic in England to get a seat in an open election. There was still a feeling that Catholics were not their own men in politics, that priests and foreign powers could tell them how to act; so that there was always an aggravated possibility of divided loyalties. Guy Fawkes Day was still celebrated with popular enthusiasm as a symbol of deliverance from the dangers to 'English liberties' and the 'Protestant succession' represented at various times by the Spanish Inquisition, the Armada, Louis XIV of France, and the Jacobite Pretenders.

Gladstone chose to take the decrees on papal infallibility as a text for a wide ramble through this minefield, implying that whatever speculative danger there might have been to the safety of the state had become practical overnight. It was clearly a situation in which leaders of the English Catholic community had to react. Newman began to prepare his admirable *Letter to the Duke of Norfolk*,[11] in which he made the classical assertion of the priority of conscience in determining a Catholic citizen's response to *any* call for obedience, even from an infallible pope. Acton wrote the first of a sequence of letters to *The Times* asserting that Gladstone was quite mistaken as to the difference the decrees had made.[12] The upshot of these was that – well after the immediate brouhaha of the Council had died down – he was faced with the most acute crisis. Cardinal Manning had had enough: in spite of Acton's lay state, it seemed that the question of adherence to the decrees would be pressed home against him to the point even of excommunication.

Admittedly Acton's apologia for his church took an unexpected line as an exercise in defence advocacy. His fellow churchmen had an excuse for their agitation.[13] The breakfast tables of the upper classes in Britain that autumn were exposed to long and extremely detailed exposés of how wicked past popes had been. The argument was that this had not affected, and (because it was hard to see how they could become worse) could not in any future affect, the discernment which loyal Roman Catholics had learnt over many generations to exercise in attributing his proper theological authority to the pope.

It was bad luck that Acton should have felt himself forced in honour to take the field in so public a way on this ground. He was damned if he remained silent and therefore associated with what Gladstone had said, and he was damned if he spoke more than the bare minimum formulas of truth (such as he offered to his

11

bishop). His children testify as to his almost obsessive passion for truth-telling.[14] It was certainly an unripe time to begin unveiling how he understood the church might in future interpret the meaning of the decrees, an understanding which experience has largely confirmed.

The overpowering anxiety of those final months of 1874 soon passed. It had injected an element of additional personal tension and vulnerability into Acton's life for which he was unprepared, and which inaugurated a period of unproductiveness, self-doubt, external distraction, and at times almost hysteria, that lasted with diminishing force almost to the end of the 1880s.

It is this period which is the most creative of Acton's life, when he established to his satisfaction the shape of 'universal history'. However unable he was to get to the point of writing a major historical work, he never ceased for any length of time to study, to discuss public affairs, and to worship. There was in him an intense electricity of frustrated promise, and of a continuing identity of preoccupations, that had phenomenal quantities of information at its disposal. Yet he rarely brought together an actual historical argument. Waiting for all the sources to be available meant in practice a devastating fluidity: Acton never wrote a single definitive book. Yet what was forged in the lonely crucible of these years was above all the shape that Acton gave to the historical consciousness of the English-speaking world for nearly three generations in the synopses he set out for the chapters of the *Cambridge Modern History*.

It is perhaps hard to gauge in any quantitative way how far that influence extended. At least in England the Grammar School libraries that had a major reference work of European history at all would have had a well-thumbed set of the *Cambridge Modern History*. The posthumously published *Lectures on Modern History* fleshed out the characteristically Actonian story of how changes in the 13th century church (especially in the papacy) and the emergence of national kingdoms set in train a centrally significant process of constitutional development which was in principle completed when the independent North American colonies drew up their Constitution in 1787. His *Inaugural Lecture* of 1895 as Regius Professor at Cambridge was published with the *Lectures*. It made the same points. The heart of the matter was not only how certain forms of constitutional government came to be accepted by states that were particularly powerful and successful (and defined what was to continue to be 'modern'), but perhaps even more how a drama that was in its early days played out almost exclusively in theological and ecclesiological language had become more and more secular and 'scientific'.

It would be wrong to suppose that these two linked stories of the growth of liberty and secularisation, which Acton created and gave to the 20th century, reflected a diminution of the force of his religious commitment either as a Christian or a Catholic. If ever there was a case of a historian being influenced by the characteristic linear shape of Old Testament history, this was it. His providential history was a *Heilsgeschichte*: God has a salvific purpose in time; this purpose can be evidenced by a historian or a prophet in the experience of a covenanted people (whether the tribes of Israel, or a Catholic church, or a Liberal political party); and the moments above all others when this divine hand can be perceived are when they experience surprising disaster or 'Judgment', or surprising rescue or 'Exodus'. It is a history of crisis, of a choice that determines its subsequent 'period'. Sir Herbert Butterfield was never more Actonian than when he used to commend the strategy of historical study that selects a focus for intense work of the most detailed and textured kind, and then another focus elsewhere, only connecting them by the most general narrative lines.

In the last years of his life Döllinger wrote how deeply he rejoiced to hear that Acton had come to use the word 'theodicy' of his universal history. By this he meant not only, in Milton's words about *Paradise Lost*, to 'justify the ways of God to man', but also to refer to Leibnitz's *Theodicy*, his assertion that this is indeed the best of all those worlds that are possible. The argument against God could be the pervasive experience of sin in the world, or that against Leibnitz could be the random catastrophe of the famous earthquake of 1756 that destroyed so much of Lisbon. In Acton's case, the argument against God that required a theodicy to meet it was what he called 'the devil behind the crucifix'. He never doubted that Christ had indeed committed to St Peter and his successors the keys of the eternal kingdom of God. How could it then be that the cause of truth, the sort of 'sincerity' that might stand even at the Day of Judgment, could be defeated in the most formal and deliberate way before the bishops of the universal church at the Vatican Council?

The crux of Acton's problem in justifying the ways of the God of the historic papacy to men was church-initiated murder. The evidence is massive for Acton's preoccupation with this problem between 1874 and 1889. Not only popes, the line of apostolic succession in the church's hierarchy of *magisterium*, but also saints, her hierarchy of virtue and holiness, were – as he put it – 'guilty' of the worst conceivable human act. Where instructions to kill were not directly given, there was throughout the body corporate a tacit conspiracy to find an excuse, to fuzz the issue and to project other aspects of the life of a 'saint' known to have colluded in killing. He might still be presented for admiration – indeed as a fit intercessor in the courts of heaven. Wherever possible the horrible truth of what had been intended and executed might be concealed altogether.

The case of St Charles Borromeo, the archetypal hero of the Counter-Reformation, played a specially important part in the change in Acton's perspective on his church. Acton had been a genuinely pious young man, willing in principle to accept quite directly the 'rightness' of what the church authorities gave him to believe, and to admire for discipleship. In 1864 he was at the Ambrosian Library in Milan 'to look for the letters of St Charles Borromeo, my dear patron. Perhaps I shall be able to do something in his honour.'[15] Coming to terms with the Borromeo revealed by his historical work of the the 1870s as in conscious solidarity[16] with liars and murderers was a deeply painful and difficult experience which, in the context of family difficulties and deaths in the period 1878–82, goes a long way to explain his sense of desolation and hypertension.

He certainly did not feel close to Newman. Acton suspected that Newman's doctrine of doctrinal development would accommodate too much error. Döllinger (and with him at this time Acton) held in principle to the proposition – the classical Anglican one – that only 'positive theology', the revealed tradition current in the church of the first five centuries, could be owned as the faith of the church. Only in this way could the historian be the arbiter of theology.[17] But above all Acton was outraged by what he saw as Newman's shiftiness in bringing the deeds of past saints into the open. He claimed that he knowingly suppressed Borromeo's condoning of persecution and murder; he was not repelled enough by the St Bartholomew's Day massacre, and so shared that guilt.

It was Acton's ill fortune that his letters to *The Times* in 1874 were written from what was to have been the climax of final immersion in the original sources for his book on the Council of Trent. Acton's correspondence with Döllinger shows that the festering conviction of apartness from his former master that broke surface in 1882 was rooted in this issue of guilt – that popes had killed. He saw his terrible and total aloneness as the fruit of surpassing Döllinger and other scholars in detailed historical knowledge. The truth about the modern papacy became progressively worse – far worse than he had supposed it to be in the 1860s – the closer the historian reached to the particularities of events, and the roots of the system. He found himself convinced by his studies that his church, the Roman Catholic church, was not one church but two. He called Ultramontanism a system of 'conventional mendacity' for it had been developed to poison the wells of historical truth and to murder and cheat for the glory of God. It was not only still extremely powerful, but it was a 'false religion', a worse enemy than Protestantism.[18] 'It is not error but sin,' it makes the channels of grace the occasion of evil. The precise location of this evil is not in ignorance at all, but in the intentional and institutional sterilising of conscience.[19] It was not surprising, therefore, that he could write, 'I cannot obey any conscience but my own .... Apart from dogma, I should feel myself, at heart, nearer to Roth[e] or Vinet or Martensen or Thiersch than to a Church in which nobody agrees with me in the fundamental question of the conditions of Grace.'[20]

It would be foolish and untrue to Acton's own deepest concerns to play down the irreconcilability of his antagonism to what he found embedded in the Catholic church, both in its past and present. As Conzemius has said, his opposition to infallibility was fundamentally on ethical grounds. The Ultramontanes were the mirror image of the socialists: both, as a matter of principle, were prepared to use evil in order that papal power (or the revolution) should triumph. He wrote: 'Just as the people of the Commune seem to me altogether odious, so do the people of the Vatican.'[21] The full perversity of the system is the Spanish Inquisition (or the Crusades), whose 'godlessness' is utterly inseparable from the 'highest' in the lives of holy men – fasting, prayer, sacraments.[22] The same limitlessness is to be seen in absolute monarchy as in democracy. Perhaps the hinge on which the change in Acton's thinking turned was when, in 1882, the insight came to him that it is not people who change, but the conventions under which they live. It was the 'godless Press', the 'Protestant police', of Victorian England that made clergy like Newman act decently: in the age of the Borgias and in Rome, they would have acted differently, and no better than their predecessors.[23] Constitutional government was literally their salvation.

In 1887 Acton reviewed a volume of Mandell Creighton's *History of the Papacy*, in the course of which they exchanged letters. Each was shocked at the other. Creighton, who as an

Anglican bishop may not have been so very surprised to find a history of corruption at Rome, could hardly believe the passionate intensity – the un-Englishness – of Acton's reaction. Acton, who was probably more deeply acquainted with the materials, could not credit that an honest historian (especially a churchman) should not see it as his duty to compensate for the wrongs of the past by being a 'hanging judge'. It was in this correspondence that Acton coined 'all power tends to corrupt, and absolute power tends to corrupt absolutely' – a dictum that has become a folk proverb.

It was necessary for Acton that he should resolve this tension. He frequently used the phrase 'the Whig church', and he was proud to belong to it. It is plain that he transposed on to an apostolic succession of frequently deist or atheist champions of liberty characteristically Christian ideas about the church as a vehicle for the purpose of God in history – indeed, he attributed to them an almost papal infallibility. Particularly after the rift with Döllinger in 1879, his experience of engagement with colleagues in significant enterprises became almost exclusively political and English, and to that extent Whig. But although his religion came to be more private, and remained very traditional, it was consciously and assertively Roman Catholic. There had therefore to be some way for popes to be saved.

Acton seems to have recapitulated in his mind synopses of significant history and noted them on cards. The solution of the problem had to be a historical solution that could be earthed in the political machinery of a real-life society. Mary Gladstone writes of an evening on the lake at Tegernsee and again some days later at Venice in October 1879, and Lord Bryce of an evening at Cannes a few years later. On both occasions, the Acton who so often in company was withdrawn and taciturn found himself almost prophetically inspired; in exalted language he spoke connectedly and at length on the threads of history and God and freedom.

The key piece in the jigsaw puzzle in enabling Acton to reconcile his experience of Whig and Roman Catholic churches as complementary enterprises of the one God was the United States of America. For years 'America' stands in Acton's notes and letters for all that a true Whig would count utopian but practically dangerous. In the late 1870s Acton's growing friendship with George Eliot[24] persuaded him that it was possible to find non-believers who could be relied on to promote a sufficiently shared doctrine of the central significance for humanity of 'conscience'. In the same way his friendship with Bryce in the 1880s helped him trust American democracy and to come to welcome its revolutionary edge. So that, if the world were to grow more like America, the Roman Catholic church could be saved from its private 'devil behind the crucifix'. The pope of a church separated by an insuperable wall from the power of the Caesars would not be corrupted so absolutely that the vicar of Christ could ever again be a killer of men. In effect, it would be a renewed church.

In so many ways, the real argument that Acton had was not about America, but about Italy. It was after all his cousin Minghetti who exercised considerable responsibility for the way in which the nation of Italy with its government now at Rome dealt with the problem of the Holy See. After fifteen hundred years a new solution had to be found for St Peter's 'patrimony'. Cavour had taken the slogan 'a free church in a free state' and applied it to the Italian church. Acton believed the slogan had come to Turin from Lausanne, coined by his (and Döllinger's) hero Alexandre Vinet. Almost immediately after the Vatican Council he chose to appear in public as a prominent local lay Catholic and speak on this very topic.[25] Two months later, in April 1871, Acton expressed the fear to Massari that the application of this slogan in Italy would result in 'an absolute pope in an indifferent state'.[26] He continued to search for the right answer to this question.

However imperfectly by 1890 the relation between Italy and the Roman curia or between America and its Roman Catholic church exhibited the potential for mutual salvation of Whig politics and Catholic religion, there is little doubt that Acton was persuaded that this was indeed the way of the future and that his fears had been exaggerated. From this time, he believed he had reconciled the elements of what might fairly be called a system. It was very different from any tradition of 'system' in theology, and there have been whole decades when Acton's working definitions of the life and consciousness of the Roman Catholic church must have seemed the self-delusion of a desperate man, and untrue. It all looks a far more plausible interpretation since Pope John XXIII: events have given it a coherence and resonance. The fundamental value attributed *sub specie aeternitatis* to human life in this system was the free exercise of conscience. It is uniquely where man and God come to know each other.

Acton had from his early days at Munich given a high place to the notion of conscience. What he came to believe was that the evolution of constitutional structures by which the free exercise and experience of conscience might in actual practice be protected, and indeed encouraged, was the object of whatever providential progress the historian could, however tentatively, perceive. It was therefore the heart of 'scientific' Christian theodicy.

It has often been remarked how little political advantage Acton gained from his friendship with Gladstone. They admired each other enormously. Gladstone's Irish policy owed at least something to Acton's advice and Gladstone went to considerable trouble to arrange with Andrew Carnegie that Acton's great library and papers should be purchased in a way sensitive to Acton's financial difficulties and made available after his death to Cambridge University Library. But Acton hoped in vain for a place in Gladstone's last administration, and had to satisfy himself with appointment as a Lord in Waiting to the Queen at Windsor. It was Gladstone's successor Rosebery who nominated Acton to the Regius Chair of Modern History at Cambridge in 1895.

Perhaps it was an odd appointment, but it was soon clear that it was abundantly justified. Acton had after all played a leading role in founding the *English Historical Review* in 1885, and he had been a trustee of the British Museum, active in securing archival collections for its library since 1871. It was said he 'knew everybody', whether abroad or in Britain. He had remarkable personal authority, so that when he addressed himself to the unfamilar task of giving oracular public lectures, they immediately attracted general attention. It was a decade of climacteric change in the transition to a 'modern' *Weltanschauung*. The cult of nationalist violence and the rising tide of working-class discontent were causes of anxiety. It was the decade of settlement into a 'liberal establishment' based on London and Oxford and Cambridge, whose consequences are still so dominant in England that most educated people find it hard to see they are not part of the nature of the universe. In Acton, Cambridge found it had a man whose whole being asserted that history is the natural discipline to study for those seeking to understand leadership and administration, and use them for good. What Acton taught was readily accessible, convincingly academic, and rather more subtle and complex than it appeared. He attracted a shoal of disciples. Crowds of Cambridge ladies came to his public lectures.

In a curious way Cambridge played to Acton's strengths. It is not convincing to say simply that he was a frustrated writer of definitive monographs. Doubtless he believed he should have been. But what he actually did as a young man – and rather more than most men ever are he was free to choose – can broadly speaking be divided into three parts. First, he was a collector – of gossip, and people, and books, and primary sources. Second, he was a highly successful editor of quarterly reviews; a writer of essay-length pieces of considerable intellectual depth on issues of the day, who was also able under pressure to turn his hand to short notices on any subject under the sun. Third, he performed with so much *brio* at the Vatican Council as a political organiser that he must be regarded as a natural. If we take these *seriatim*, we can at least see analogues in his life as a professor: he loved the dining element of Cambridge life, and became famous for the generosity with which he lent books and gave bibliographies for others to use; to give lectures was very like writing essays; the promotion and structuring of the Historical Tripos in the university and the organising of the *Cambridge Modern History* required someone with political skills.

It might even be claimed that he was the morning star of that characteristic 20th-century university figure, the mid-Atlantic scholar. Though not himself an example, he required of writers for the *Cambridge Modern History* that they should locate themselves at longitude 30 degrees west, midway between London and New York.

Acton died at Tegernsee in 1902 after a year of progressively more crippling strokes. No published title was in print at his death, though he had written many articles, most notably the pioneer English study in the history of ideas ('German Schools of History') in the inaugural issue of the *English Historical Review*. Characteristic of the man who had failed to publish on the Council of Trent,[27] on English constitutional history, on the History of Liberty, and on the life of Döllinger, he had not succeeded in writing his introductory chapter – on the 'Legacy of the Middle Ages' – to the first volume of the *Cambridge Modern History*. The obituaries indicate how widespread was the immediate awareness that an important life had ended. It was difficult to gauge whether it was of a successful Great Victorian or of a failed academic historian.

In the years after his death, the world in general was suddenly able to read something of the work that might justify the reputation of such a famous and yet elusive historian. In quick succession the first volumes of the *Cambridge Modern History* began to appear (1903 onward), 'planned by the late Lord Acton', but now – in smaller type – 'edited by A. W. Ward, G. W. Prothero, and Stanley Leathes'. Other principal disciples among the young Cambridge historians, J. N. Figgis and C. V. Laurence, edited a sequence of selections from his writing and lectures: *Lectures on Modern History* (including his inaugural lecture 'The Study of History'), 1906; *The History of Freedom* (which included the two Bridgnorth lectures of 1877), 1907; *Historical Essays and Studies*, 1908; *Lectures on the French Revolution*, 1910; *Selections from the Correspondence of the 1st Lord Acton*, vol. 1, 1917. A selection of *Letters to Mary, daughter of the Rt Hon. W. E. Gladstone* (1904; enlarged 1913) was edited by Herbert Paul. F. A. Gasquet edited (perhaps more accurately 'massaged' in precisely the style of Catholic window dressing most abhorrent to Acton) a selection of letters from the earlier period, *Lord Acton and his Circle* (1906).

This effectively remained the canon of known Acton work for over half a century. During this time, he was a highly significant figure in the teaching of history in Britain, and a dominant one at Cambridge. Sir Herbert Butterfield's *Whig Interpretation of History* (1931) is inexplicable except in the context of his lifelong dialogue with Acton. Sixth-form students came to university for entrance examination and interview even after the 1960s having been advised by their teachers to take a last quick look at the *Lectures on Modern History*. It continued to be included in bibliographies for the Modern European History paper. The structure of the history degree course itself remained largely as Acton left it, with a strong emphasis on the broad sweep of European history, on English constitutional history, and on political thought, at least until the Tripos revision of 1967.

It was the reaction to experience of Hitler and Stalin that led to new centres of interest in Acton. Ulrich Noack wrote in Germany (1935–47) and F. E. Lally in New England (1942); while G. E. Fasnacht at Oxford (1952) collected Actonian fragments into some kind of pattern and published them. Bishop David Mathew published a study, *Acton: the Formative Years* (1946), which in much expanded form was revised as *Lord Acton and his Times). Butterfield published his Historical Association pamphlet (1948); and together with A. Watkin (1950) produced a devastating critique of the liberties Gasquet had taken in editing Acton's early letters. Gertrude Himmelfarb (the wife of Irving Kristol, he editor of Encounter)* edited with an introduction a further collection (1948) of Acton's essays for the liberal Beacon

Press of Boston, that included the first serious analysis (by Bert Hoselitz) of what material in the reviews edited by Acton had been his work. These *Essays on Freedom and Power* in a more popular edition have often been reprinted and are much used in American colleges. Douglas Woodruff edited a further collection of Acton's early essays, *Essays on Church and State* (1952). Miss Himmelfarb's monograph *Lord Acton: a study of conscience and politics* (1952) has been the single most important contribution to the interpretation of Acton; and in 1954 Lionel Kochan wrote a study of Acton's work as historian.

This was the situation when the work behind the present study was done in Cambridge (1953–6). The second volume of the *Selected Correspondence*, with Döllinger, promised a whole generation previously, had not appeared. The notebooks and the many thousands of cards and boxes in the Acton Collection of the Cambridge University Library were listed but had never been systematically studied. As so many are undated and not in their appropriate boxes, it was difficult to know their location in relation to Acton's work and plans.

During the Second Vatican Council H. A. MacDougall published an essay on *The Acton–Newman Relations* (1962), and followed it up in 1973 with a collection, *Lord Acton on Papal Power*.

However, the most important new element in the resources now available for Acton studies is the full edition of Döllinger's correspondence with Lord Acton (3 vols., 1963-75) and with Charlotte Lady Blennerhasset (1981) edited by Victor Conzemius and published, appropriately, at Munich. The delays in making this vital material available had been quite accidental, and it makes an extraordinary story.[27] In the event, however, it may have become a case of *felix culpa* for it is hard to see the various subsidiary collections of letters coming together earlier, or being given the masterly and meticulous editorial treatment they have received.

The second major new element since the present author published his paper to the first meeting of the International Society for the History of Ideas in 1960, 'The Religious Conscience in Lord Acton's Political Thought', has sprung from the interest of Acton's family in making his papers available for study. Douglas Woodruff had married Acton's granddaughter Mia and was editor of the *Tablet*. It was through their generosity and care that so much more material has now become publicly available. More manuscripts have been deposited at Cambridge, which, alas, there has not been time to consult for this study.

At the time of the Second Vatican Council, a young American Franciscan, Fr Damian McElrath, was studying under Professor Roger Aubert at Louvain, and from his work on the reception of Pio Nono's Syllabus of Errors (1964) came to Cambridge to work on the Acton papers there and in the care of the Woodruffs. In 1962 Professor J. L. Altholz of Minneapolis published his *Liberal Catholic Movement in England* which dealt in some detail with the reviews with which Acton had been involved. Out of these shared interests came the three-volume edition by McElrath and Altholz (and, volumes II and III, with James C. Holland) of *The Correspondence of Lord Acton and Richard Simpson* (1971–5), splendidly published by the Cambridge University Press, and, from Louvain, McElrath's *Lord Acton: the Decisive Decade, 1864–74* (1970), an edition of further Acton talks, articles, and correspondence with a substantial introduction. Yet another collection of Acton letters had been found at Aldenham in 1965. Fr C. S. Dessain has continued to publish *The Letters and Diaries of J. H. Newman* (1961—). *The Wellesley Index to Victorian Periodicals 1824–1900*, vol. II (1972), edited by Walter E. Houghton, gives what is now virtually a definitive list of Acton's contributions to his own and other reviews.

All in all, the primary materials for work on Acton published since 1960 have revolutionised the scope for using the notes in the Acton Collection, and have made the full-scale intellectual biography of Lord Acton, whose absence has been so long deplored, both imaginable and dauntingly massive. It seems most probable that an American Catholic priest might undertake it. If so, he will need special qualities of historical imagination, for Herrnsheim and the Palazzo Acton are at some distance from a parish in the 'secular city'. But there could not be a more appropriate tribute to that particular *History of Liberty* whose outlines were so clear to Acton in his lifetime, but which he early despaired of ever himself writing. In 1879 he wryly called it, following the title story of a volume by Henry James that had just been published, his 'Madonna of the Future'. The artist, in James's story, dies with his canvas still blank. In Acton's case, however, there remain two very recognisable figures in the composition already blocked in. On the one side is the tradition and the 'givenness' of the Catholic Church. On the other is the American Constitution – so peculiarly a civil religion. They act as heraldic supporters for a central space designated as Liberty.

This work cannot be more than another partial and tangential contribution – a complement to the biography that needs to be written. But it does claim to assert what was the central preoccupation of Acton's life, to adduce the historical evidence he used, to establish that there were distinct changes in its evolution, and to delineate in a fresh way the nature of the coherence within the man Acton of Roman Catholic, Liberal, and academic historian.

The picture here presented is of Acton's own world-view and is drawn – where possible in his own words – from his published lectures and essays, correspondence, and notes. If published even as late as the 1950s, it would (as regards his interpretation of Roman Catholic faith and church history) have invited an adjective more forceful than 'idiosyncratic'. That is no longer the case. In the broadest sense, Acton becomes the heir – in a newly 'scientific' world – of those 'jansenising' Catholics of the 18th century whose pre-eminent concerns were with the ethical well-being of their society and the pastoral activity of their church.[28]

This book falls into three parts. Chapters 2, 3, and 4 attempt to dissect Acton's language of 'conscience', and to investigate the consequences of a doctrine of the centrality of conscience for the relation of church and state, and for politics, respectively. Chapters 5, 6, and 7 set out the highly creative and unusual shape that Acton gave to his 'universal' or significant history; firstly with regard to the role played by the United States (and especially the Quaker state) at the crisis of that history, and then to the origins and course of 'modern history'. These are fleshed out with evidence from his work. Finally, there follows a chapter, Chapter 8, that attempts to evaluate Acton's standing as a Victorian 'scientific' historian and as prophet of the Second Vatican Council.

2
Acton's Language of Conscience

It is no novelty to suggest that conscience was a word which Acton used unusually frequently and to which he attached special significance both in its public and private senses. Among the commentators immediately after his death who noted its centrality for him, J. N. Figgis wrote, 'It is the preaching in season and out of season against the reality of wickedness and against every interference with the conscience, that is the real inspiration both of Acton's life and of his writings.'[1] Even in his published works there are many passages where the intimate relation between conscience and liberty is pointedly expressed. Acton's notes for the projected History of Liberty now in the Cambridge University Library provide evidence for the pervasive influence of the idea of conscience on all that he considered significant history.

There are two principal tasks in exploring this apparently idiosyncratic preoccupation: to trace the sources of Acton's idea of conscience and the development of his usage of it, and then to consider the consequences of Acton's applying it as a 'leading idea'. It soon becomes clear that 'conscience' carried implications for Acton's thinking about progress, the church, and liberal institutions which bring them together into an unsuspectedly organic whole. He defined conscience in such a way that it became the delicate fulcrum on which his Catholic and Liberal faith, his scientific and providential history, were held in balance. The penetrating criticism of Dr Paolo Alatri, that Acton's thinking falls between nature and super-nature,[2] would have been met in Acton's own mind by the conviction that it is in the conscience of the individual man that the two meet and – if they can be distinguished – mingle. The world of German universities in Acton's lifetime was very much under the influence of Hegel's unwillingness to divide them.

Conscience was of such importance to Acton that in his later years he repeatedly asserted that its history was the 'Whig Theodicy', the justification of the ways of God to Man. Yet it was an assertion that can hardly claim to be historical in any

24

academic sense. Rather like the Pentateuch in the Bible, it told a story that could give consciousness and significance to a present-day community and shape its corporate life. The 'community' of Acton's history was what he called the 'Whig Church', our Western secular state-system. Acton's neo-Pentateuch could provide no coercive evidence for Whigs who denied a divine providence, or for Tories.

What was Acton's particular definition of conscience and the context out of which he developed it? Like 'nature' and 'reason', 'conscience' is a word which by itself gives little indication of its meaning. In popular usage it can have the sense either of a nagging moral ulcer or of a citadel of the moral personality – almost that interior castle of the soul where God dwells, of which St Teresa speaks. In a mind of Acton's breadth of reading, the possible variations on the theme of duty, remorse, and moral knowledge were as many as the cultures and philosophies in which they arose. Conscience was an idea current throughout the Victorian period not only in serious writing, but in journalism, sermons, and conversational usage, and it is not easy to discover how precise Acton was in his own usage of either the word or the idea. An indication of the centre of Acton's meaning is given us when his old friend and fellow enthusiast for Dante, Mandell Creighton, wrote in his introductory note to the *Cambridge Modern History* that 'modern history begins with a struggle for liberty on the ground which was the largest, the right of free self-realisation towards God'.[3]

The massive accumulation of the manuscript notes in the Cambridge University Library ought to be uniquely valuable for this enquiry. There are, however, two serious difficulties in using them. It was Acton's habit to express the various possible points of view about a topic on different cards; and also, among such a large and inadequately organised collection, there occur the changes of opinion only to be expected in the thirty industrious years he spent compiling it. It is consequently dangerous to say that a card necessarily expresses Acton's own opinion at any particular time. Nonetheless the criterion of general coherence can be applied, so long as assertions that an opinion was in fact Acton's is buttressed by a quantity of references. The importance of such cumulative quotation has been repeatedly demonstrated by its neglect, and in many cases the manuscript material is of such intrinsic value in clarifying Acton's pattern of thinking as to justify its inclusion. It is for this reason that quotations from Acton's writing have been made in this work on a scale that may seem repetitive and superfluous.

In understanding conscience as an essentially cognitive faculty, Acton was taking over some of the most powerful ideas of his generation, and especially of the generation of liberal-minded academics in southern Germany amongst whom he was educated and formed.[4] It was the systematic authority which Acton gave to his notion of conscience rather than the idea itself which was his original contribution. It would be hard to find a trio more significant for their influence on Acton than Döllinger, Newman, and Gladstone, yet all three held Butlerian doctrines about the conscience which were scarcely less absolute than Acton's. The period in Germany around 1825 which Acton called that of 'Ideal Catholicism' placed almost as much stress on conscience from the Catholic side as continued to be put on it from the Protestant side under the influence of Kant, who in Acton's '100 Best Books' stands for 'Infallible reign of Conscience a substitute for God'. These were Döllinger's formative years, when men like Sailer, Chéverus, and Möhler set the tone. Acton cites Gügler, whom he describes as 'an obscure schoolfellow of Döllinger's', as claiming that it was only with the coming of Christianity that conscience could be perceived as directly mediating the word of God.

Döllinger considered the Lausanne pastor, Alexandre Vinet, as perhaps the most sympathetic of all his Protestant contemporaries. The Église Libre du Vaud, which he led, has in our generation given the world Roger Schutz, the founder of the Taizé community. Vinet was the principal interpreter of Kant to French-speaking Protestantism, and made conscience the sole forum in which man might meet God. The dogmatic and philosophic standing of conscience was clearly one of the great questions of the day, and one in which Döllinger's friends had been protagonists.

When Acton returned to England, the terms of the argument were different, but 'moral science' was, again, one of the most characteristic preoccupations of the time. In England, however, the idea of conscience was less fashionable. The utilitarians had rejected it, Butler had ceased to be rated so highly, and it came to be associated in popular usage with the political issues that mobilised the 'chapel' classes, such as sabbatarianism and temperance. Most significant for Acton was the intellectual pilgrimage of George Eliot. He thought her so honest, open-minded and well-read that she was a kind of microcosm of her time, and the fact that he saw her as building a masterpiece like

Middlemarch around conscience can hardly be overestimated.

Acton believed that men were converging to give authority to a high doctrine of conscience. In a card (Add. MS 4901/187) he wrote: 'Idea of conscience which Butler, Rousseau, Kant have made so familiar to the modern nations. Sovereignty. Not so clear formerly. Not even to the modern Whig.' By virtue of an apparent consensus which might blossom into unanimity, Acton was encouraged to suppose that it could claim to be a discovery of 'ethical science' and that it was perhaps the way in which providence was to by-pass the incurable rancour and schism of theological argument by making clergy and churches *pastoral* necessities. It was generally agreed by the 19th century Idealists, whether within or outside the churches, that the coming age would be of the 'spirit', and that it would spell a world brought together in peace and justice. To Acton, for whom the idea of conscience was 'filled with the Holy Spirit', the biblical prophecies gave a sharp expectancy and certainty to the elaboration of a synthesis based upon it.

These are general considerations. There can, however, be little doubt that Acton's specific experience in fighting and losing his battle against the Infallibility Dogma in the Vatican Council of 1870 gave a special insistence to his development along this path. Even before 1869, when the problem of obedience took on a personal significance for him, Acton frequently expressed the conviction that 'A Christian must seek to extend as much as possible the field where he is responsible only to his conscience, and free from Governmental authority.'[5]

'Conscience as political disobedience' was already a concept familiar to him, when the pressure of the political and dogmatic crisis at Rome in the 1860s forced him to explore more urgently the authority which his own conscience could legitimately claim, not so much against the state as against his own church. In the change that took place, it seems that Vinet, whom Acton and Döllinger re-read together in 1864, provided the bridge from Butler to Kant.

In this crisis there were three areas where Acton felt conscience was involved. First, like most of his English contemporaries, he could not accept the priority given by Pope Pius IX's curia to the Holy See's continuing to exercise the tradition of a Temporal Power based on Rome. Nevertheless he did go out of his way to show he accepted the duty of any Catholic to help secure a proper solution of the problem. There was indeed a need in conscience for the Pope to be seen by the national churches as exercising his role

27

independent of any state. Acton spoke on the subject in Parliament in 1860 and again gave a public lecture to his local Catholic community at Kidderminster in 1871.[6]

Second, he felt that the direction of authority at Rome was towards a supersession of the individual conscience of the believer by the corporate conscience of the Church. In the Quirinus letters, for instance, which express Acton's views, great significance is attached to Manning's claim on the Pope's behalf that he is 'the Supreme Judge and director of the consciences of men .... I am the sole last Supreme Judge of what is right and wrong.'[7]

That to view this as a real danger was not eccentric is shown by Newman's *Letter to the Duke of Norfolk*, which was written to re-emphasise the ultimate claim of conscience. Acton's reaction to what he clearly believed was the intention of the Ultramontane party was characteristically sharp. He wrote to Gladstone in 1872 that he did not know of a 'religious and educated Catholic who really believes that the See of Rome is a safe guide to salvation'.[8] The opposition party, he said, was forced to regard the Ultramontanes as 'insincere Christians' because they planned the Infallibility Dogma. Out of this maximalist assessment of the intentions behind the Vatican Council, an assessment which put the preservation of the independent rights of the layman's conscience at the heart of the discussion, sprang the whole fevered enthusiasm of Acton's political activity among the bishops at Rome.

Third, there was the question of science. The *motif* running through much of Acton's writing in the decade before the Council is the offence of most Roman apologists to what he called ethical and historical 'science', but which might be more appropriately called the *wissenschaftlich* conscience. He wrote from Rome in 1870, 'The root of the matter lies not simply in the relation to be maintained towards the chief authority in the Church, but in the right relation to science; it is not merely freedom but truth which is at stake .... A contest has arisen not of dogma but of a theological opinion against history, that is against truth .... Not only was history falsified, but the rules of Christian morality were no longer held applicable where the credit of the hierarchy was at stake. The very sense of truth and error, right or wrong – in a word the conscience – was thrown into confusion.'[9]

It was here, primarily, that Acton could follow Döllinger in his opposition to the Infallibilists. For both of them, the authority which ecclesiastical tradition could claim was subject to the prior enquiry of history, and history must be 'disinterested' in the Rankean sense. To employ special arguments on behalf of one's own historical faith which could not be applied generally, or to conceal its warts, was not only 'unscientific' but 'insincere'.

Thus, the anti-Infallibilists believed that their campaign was crucial for the establishment of a Christian scholar's right to come to his historical or political conclusions in freedom, independent of church authority. Duty of the highest kind, Acton believed, had induced him to stand out in opposition to the Infallibilists, and it is perhaps from this root that there grew his integral association of conscience with risk-taking and revolution.[10] However, he found that his opponents too claimed to be working under a high doctrine of conscience, and he was forced to find some invalidating factor in their motives. He concluded that abstract moral knowledge is freely available in the conscience of every man, but that under certain systems (and he spoke not only in general about the Roman tradition but especially of the Inquisition) this knowledge is 'perverted'.[11] The process by which such 'perversion' could take place in the consciences of even the most holy men is almost his leading idea in the 1870s, and the preoccupation out of which his systematic development of a constitutional structure of protection for conscience arose. Perhaps the only safeguard against hierarchical churches was for them to work within a secular society.

Presupposing that conscience was the 'direct opening of the soul to God',[12] and therefore the most direct knowledge of the source of ethics, Acton could write, 'Conscience. NB that with us we can test conscientious conviction. It is not faith if it is not moral. For we deem faith an act of grace.'[13] In order, therefore, to provide a criterion capable of taking religions into its net, he went on to say that morality is not only the fruit of faith but, for the purposes of the historian, its *raison d'être*: 'One must apply principles that cut either way in politics. If you are guided by any object, then that object must be the highest. Men may then say, the highest object is religion. Therefore persecution is the right thing. To counter that, you must have some object higher even than religion. That is, either politics an affair of morality or the purposes of religion transcend it. If politics transcend religion, that is, if you are Liberal, it is because the ethical purposes are supreme.'[14]

Holding this belief, it is clear how congenial George Eliot's ideas became to Acton. F. W. H. Myers tells the story in *Essays Modern* (1883) of how he walked with her one rainy May evening in a college garden at Cambridge, and the conversation turned to God, Immortality, and Duty as 'three words which have been used so often as the inspiring trumpet calls of men'. She 'pronounced, with terrible earnestness, how inconceivable was the first, how unbelievable the second, and yet how peremptory and absolute was the third'. Acton wrote that 'the making of something non-dogmatic the centre of history is a postulate of science',[15] and noted what Herbert Spencer had written in 1880: 'Now that moral injunctions are losing the authority given by their supposed sacred origin, the secularisation of morals is becoming imperative'.[16] According to Acton Eliot was similarly trying to find a non-dogmatic yet absolute centre for ethical behaviour.[17] He believed she had found such a centre in the conscience, but that she saw conscience primarily as moral pain and cited the case of Bulstrode in *Middlemarch*.[18] In the light of Leibnitz's importance for the Munich circle, it is interesting that Acton interpreted his doctrine of conscience in the same way: 'Leibnitz's doctrine of Providence – punishment within. The soul bears the burden of its faults. Therefore he makes conscience the seat of justice.'[19] By means of this he thought Eliot had established, as in 1877 he asserted Grotius had in his generation established,[20] a moral *'modus vivendi* – to subsist if all religion should chance to evaporate, the forms of society shall remain – to lose nothing that centuries of Christianity have won, but to support those results by means independent of the power that won them'.[21]

This taking over by secular political institutions of the fruits of religious struggle is Acton's characteristic understanding of historical process and is the heart of his interpretation of the English Revolution and, via Pennsylvania, of America. Yet at this point he seems to have been curiously uncritical. His notebooks show him aware that Eliot gave no support to revolution, that she leant very hesitatingly on the conscience as a guide to action; for instance, 'Does she think that a man ought to think for himself? No, if he has only common lights. Yes??? if he has trained himself.'[22] Acton's own later position was similar: 'Conscience says, do this, as it is thy duty, and is infallible. But to discover my duty is a work of the intellect, which is not infallible.'[23] He doubted whether Liberalism was possible without a primary duty to God.[24] But in spite of this, there can be no doubt that he identified with her. He believed that the problems they perceived and – rather naively – the way they sought to solve them were akin.

However, Acton more and more sharply recognised the

distancing of his own thinking about conscience from George Eliot's: 'To form the character as a man trains his ear for music. Not her view – Never begin anew.'[25] Acton sees a necessary role for a distinct *spiritual* discipline, in a way not dissimilar to the practice of religion commended by the Anglican theologian Don Cupitt, even in an apparently Godless universe.[26] It is clear that here Acton is propounding a view of the conscience which makes it the dynamic centre of the personality (what in the Old Testament is called the 'heart'), not a phenomenon of the personality's experience. He saw a conscience as the *sine qua non* of the equipment of a Carlylean hero. This was a crux of his consciousness that he and Döllinger had grown apart: 'D[öllinger] disbelieved in the power of men to shape their own minds.'[27] In his Cambridge Inaugural Lecture in 1895 Acton made this radical distinction clear. He said, 'A man of ordinary proportion and inferior metal knows not how to think out the rounded circle of his thought, how to divest its will of its surroundings and to rise above the pressure of time and race and circumstance, to choose the star that guides his course, to correct and test and assay his convictions by the light within.'[28]

Bishop Butler would not have recognised this usage as referring to 'conscience' – it is more like Nietzsche's 'superman'. Behind the exalted language of the 1895 passage lie a series of definitions in the box Add. MS 4960, which are almost certainly from that immediate period, and which apply Acton's special concept of conscience to such issues as progress, democracy, and learning. This box of cards contains perhaps the most explicit exemplifications of the way Acton's mature pattern of thought centred on conscience.

Typical of these cards are: 'Escape from heredity and milieu – from the voices of man – to the voice of God. We require in an honest man not submission, but resistance and independence – ask what place his particular time and country holds – what other things are to be considered – that he shall look about and within',[29] and 'Conscience – perception of evil and desire of improvement. That is, the disposition to seek what ought to be, rather than what is, makes for progress',[30] and 'Conscience. Idea of an irreducible stronghold – within which a man accomplishes the formation of character, and develops the power of resisting the influence of example, and the law of multitudes.'[31] Subsumed in Acton's ethical use of the word 'conscience' were the concepts of Romantic genius, the mystical soul, the Holy Spirit, and the heights of mathematical reason.

If we look for a particular point of reference by which to locate Acton's development, we might find it in the Scholastic concept of *synteresis* with which – it appears from the manuscript notes – Acton became increasingly familiar. St Jerome translated it 'scintilla conscientiae' at its first occurrence in Christian literature, and defined it as that part of God's Paradise which Adam retained after the Fall; indeed the fruit of his contract with the Serpent that he should 'know good and evil'. St Bonaventure gave it its highest expression; he identified it with the inward divine spark, the conative energy which all the time worked to pull man's will back into conformity with true morality and, more importantly, with the eternally triune God – creator, redeemer, and sanctifier. The Quaker William Penn used it in the sense of 'do as you would be done by' with the force of a Kantian moral absolute. This is the Actonian spectrum of conscience.[32]

It would be unrealistic not to see the relevance of Acton's personal religious experience to this central strand of his thought. He came from a tradition where self-examination was the principal religious exercise of the faithful – he himself was accustomed to go to confession once a week – and in which visions were commonplace. He claimed 'that visions occupy a regular place, not only in the hagiology, but in the daily life of Catholics. Something supernatural expected'[33]; and asserted a 'belief in direct action of God upon the soul. Not through men or outward things. This secret action is personified, dramatised, in the legends of visions and dreams.'[34] Thus although he tended to reject the idea of miracle, visions were a more immediate form of the general action of God upon the 'inward eye' or through the 'inner light' of conscience. Acton's mystical sympathies find expression throughout his later work.

These concepts are very far from George Eliot. Yet Acton believed that in the quest of an 'ethical science' based on 'conscience' they were engaged in what could meaningfully be called a common activity. At a critical moment in Acton's thinking about conscience, he quoted Whewell: 'This idea of Conscience as the basis and principle of Morals has not yet been completely and rigorously worked out into its systematic form and consequences.'[35] It is clear that this task was the one he set himself, and which he thought Eliot had set herself. In this task he saw them both as working under the shadow of Kant,[36] and consequently over against the great majority of contemporary Utilitarians and Catholics. Acton was acutely aware of the great number of arguments which could be levelled against the universality and authority of conscience.[37] Its supersession by revelation on the one hand and the variable social origins of conscience on the other were the two principal ones he had to face. Like Thomas Arnold, however, and in the same stream of English thought, Acton rejected these as expressing 'the two great opposite forms of all human wickedness .... Priestcraft and Benthamism.'[38] But he was unwilling to explore the difference as well as the similarity between a nonconformist lay Christian and a confessed atheist in their approaches to what actually happens in conscience, because to do so would reduce the element of the universally applicable (or 'scientific')[39] in their conclusions. This was a mistake. It was a curious one for him to make, because of few people could it be claimed that their Christian faith made a more observable 'difference' to their thought, and indeed their life.

3
Conscience, Church, and State

Toleration and ethics

Acton's world was not one where the great non-Christian religions affected daily life or the newspaper headlines he read. In an academic sense, he could be said to have been more than commonly aware of these religions. He commonly quotes Max Muller and Sir Henry Maine, while Sir Peter Renouf[1] was a personal friend and a lay Catholic colleague in the publishing enterprises of the 1860s. But the concept of a religiously plural society was, with the exception of imperial India, unfamiliar to him. In retrospect, this may seem regrettable, for his reflexion on the possibility of a secular or 'scientific' system of values for a state, giving and receiving its character in its political constitution, in effect took in only Christian church members and the atheists and agnostics still powerfully marked by their Catholic or Protestant antecedents. Even the Orthodox world was in the twilight at the circumference of his vision: he described Russia as for the most part 'inert' in Universal History. Acton was really only concerned with the 'religions of the Book' that were accustomed to play a proactive role within history. But in principle he held that all religions should be tolerated.

His 'Whig church' was, however, 'established' over all others. A religion's 'right' to toleration was a granted one, and only on the basis of the prior claims of the community's moral well-being, and of the liberal constitution itself. Acton was at war with any church that was dedicated to the extirpation of other churches or, like one wing of the medieval Cathari, engaged in devil worship, or, like the Syrian Assassins (the Old Man of the Mountains is a familiar figure in Acton's notebooks), murdered as a religious obligation. The practical limits of a toleration bred in Victorian England can soon be reached.

Yet, for an active Roman Catholic of his time, this was a radical position. It was at the heart of his view of the history of liberty. He wrote c. 1890, 'You must prefer heresy to unity, if you prefer liberty. It can only be had that way. What we owe to Socinians, Latitudinarians and Deists.'[2]

Vinet had been a figure in that outbreak in the 1830s of

movements among Protestants in Europe to separate the life of established folk churches from land taxes and state power. He was influential on the Scottish 'Wee Frees' and, Acton claimed, through his pupil Melegari, on Cavour in Piedmont. There is no doubt of the powerful authority of Vinet's writings for both Döllinger and Acton. It was perhaps through him that the principle of both the separation of church and state and anticipation of the fruits of free denominational competition were so attractive to Acton.[3] Vinet had talked of the social goods that followed such bidding by denominations for esteem in a liberal state. He had talked of these goods as the answer to the scandal of Christian disunity. This 'theodicy' language may even have been the germ from which Acton developed his own interpretation of the Reformation in providential history.

The prime advantage to Acton of such free competition between denominations was the sovereignty it gave to 'the ethical standard'. Always ready to play down the dogmatic in favour of the ethical aspects of religion, Acton appears to have regarded the churches in a Liberal state as competing for favour in an arena where the conscience of the intelligent layman would judge. He wrote, 'Toleration weakens action of dogmatic motives – strengthens purely ethical motives, apart from denominational considerations.'[4]

He also regarded toleration as especially natural to Christianity, because St Paul had taught that a coerced faith is sin, the opposite of faith. When Fénelon said, 'La force ne peut jamais persuader les hommes; elle ne fait que des hypocrites. Quand les rois se mêlent de la religion, au lieu de la protéger, ils la mettent en servitude. Accordez a tous la tolérance civile',[5] he expressed what Acton simply called 'Religion'.[6] It was this that Acton meant when he said that the men of Döllinger's generation had to choose between the Church of Fénelon and the Church of Ximenes. He wrote, 'The old order which had not succeeded with the aid of force could not succeed without it. Religion could not prevail under Liberal Rule with the principles of intolerance. The idea, long renounced – to revive it, was suicide.'[7] There was, after Napoleon, an either/or in which it was impossible to disentangle ecclesiology from politics. It was one of the principal reasons for Acton's advocacy of such a 'Liberal Rule' that he believed it carried within it the impossibility of the 'Church of Ximenes' ever resurrecting itself.

Tolerance is a word which Acton used in the context of two favourite words: scientific and sincere. In 1870 he wrote, '[Pope

Pius IX] wished of course that Catholicism should have the benefit of toleration in England and Russia, but the principle must be repudiated by a Church holding the doctrine of exclusive salvation. The meaning of this intimation, that persecution would do as a substitute for infallibility, was that the most glaring obstacle to the definition would be removed if the Inquisition was recognised as consistent with Catholicism.'[8] Acton was criticising Pio Nono on two grounds: first, that it was a religious mistake to translate any doctrine of exclusive salvation into political consequences, and second, that to deny the principle of 'do as you would be done by' was prudentially wrong. This moral judgment of imaginatively universalised behaviour, which is fundamentally the Kantian doctrine of conscience, was also the ground on which William Penn had proposed toleration in the 17th century.[9] Acton claimed that toleration, if it is a principle, must be both universal (i.e. scientific) and implacably even-handed (i.e. sincere) in its application.

Acton was able to live in a normally schizophrenic way; on the one hand he took St Peter's power of the keys seriously in his instruction of his son Richard, and on the other, he was a notably 'Broad Church' man,[10] for whom no persecutor can be 'sincere'. Vinet and Penn both maintained that persecution is the practical recognition of a bad case in argument. Early in his life Acton quoted the Stoic philosopher Lactantius: 'Religion is to be defended by exhorting, not by slaying, not by severity but by patience; not by crime, but by faith:— nihil enim est tam voluntarium quam religio.'[11] A card of *c.* 1878 spoke of the example of the early Christian church: 'Christianity appealed, not to authority, but to opinion, to the masses. It recognised the right of each man to resist all government, his nation, tradition etc. How this changed afterwards when the Teutonic nations were converted by their kings, never by spontaneous motion. It was the first appeal to public opinion against authority and law.'[12]

Another card of the same period runs, 'Early Christianity. The Church claimed only one liberty among many. L[iberty] of conscience. But all others followed – *solidaires*. It promoted them in the source, not severally.'[13] It was Acton's contention that this liberty of conscience so characteristic of classical Christianity had again in the 19th century become normative – for the first time since the fall of the Roman 'Imperium'. In an unusual use of the adjective, Acton describes the 'inorganic Europe' destroyed by Napoleon[14] as the prelude to an open society. The post-1660

English Catholics, 'without the State, without intolerance, conciliatory, reunionist',[15] had become a model for all contemporary churches. Perhaps not surprisingly, there is an attractive lyricism about the letters Acton writes from Italy to Marie Arco-Valley in the months before their marriage. He compares the admirable qualities of the Roman Catholic community when it is in a minority or socially unpretentious – as in contemporary England – with the more shop-soiled ethos of traditionally Catholic nations.[16] He hoped – rather optimistically – that this 'Christian' spirit could be imagined as spreading from these centres of 'reformed Catholicism' and from what in the 19th century had already become the established atmosphere among academics[17] into a general ecumenism.

There is therefore a logical connection when Acton wrote in the same notebook, 'Persecution began against heretics, not against pagans'[18]; and 'That no persecutor can be sincere. That the denial of sincerity must accompany persecution. Accordingly that theory followed the other. NB. S. Augustine'[19]; and 'Liberal Catholics. The Catholic revival – necessarily liberal. So far as it was sincere. Görres. Lacordaire.'[20] Acton's judgments of the 5th and 19th century climacterics in the development of Christian liberty thus depend in great part upon his rational and objective interpretation of religion and of moral knowledge. It was at this time that he became conscious of his break with Döllinger on the question of the severity with which church heroes who persecuted should be judged by Catholic historians. Assuming that unity would follow from dialogue, Acton hoped that suppression of divergent belief might become as outmoded as it was ethically unthinkable.

In a notebook of 1880 about the same time, he wrote about medieval nominalist philosophers and the Reformation: 'Idea of Abelard, Scotus, Occam ... that good and evil are arbitrary distinctions. God might upset them – and make it good to lie etc. (being the God of Truth, but not deriving His commands from His nature). So the Church can explain the will of God – This makes all morals uncertain, dependent on the Church',[21] and 'Ref[ormers] long avoided ethics. Treatises on politics before treatises on morals. When they did, they differed. Examine this closely. If morals come from auth[ority], then Persecution.'[22] Acton stood in a different tradition. Like Penn and the Quakers, he deemed every man to have access to the common source of morality independently of his teachers.

There is a profoundly mystical and platonic character to a great deal of Acton's thought. It is not surprising that in later life he became a friend of von Hügel.[23] His rationalism is a fruit as much of the ascetic tradition as of argument. The Munich circle in which he was trained was open to mystical writers; in particular, Döllinger was 'a great reader of mystics',[24] and in his hands mysticism was 'a solvent of dogma and a converter of philosophy to religion'.[25] It is no accident that when he came to write of the effect the proposed *Cambridge Modern History* should have on its readers he required that it should 'illuminate the soul'. It is language that is taken from the traditional description of the mystical way, from purgation through illumination to union with God. The same mystical type of rationalism was expressed in another form when Acton drew connections between virtue and peace.

On these not altogether proven assumptions, the kind of behaviour which requires to be repressed is in itself the result of sin on the part of those in authority, and so – on the premises of many post-Vatican II church prayers and organisations for 'Justice and Peace' – a perfectly just government will need no armed forces: for instance, 'Fewer criminals in Ireland, if fewer Conservatives in England'[26] and '[after St Bernard] the voice of tolerance dies away. A German of the XV century says – You burn people because of the opposition you provoke. Reform yourselves, and you need not burn anybody.'[27]

Acton's horror then at heresy and crime has to be expressed as horror at those who were in authority at the time. A revealing insight into the way these matters were connected in his mind in 1878 is given in the following soliloquy: 'If the Church was despotic, esp[ecially] by the Inq[uisition], did not the rel[igious] opposition become pol[itical]? did not the friends of religious reform become also friends of pol[itical]? Wicliffe. Hus. Bohemian Brethren. Waldenses. To save one's soul is more important than to govern the state. Ergo, Indiv[idualism]. But to save souls in the future, it is well to influence the State – one does that by the Church, literature, and State.'[28] This was an important argument and estranged him from Döllinger, both in what he said about the Reformers and about the church's contemporary vocation. It is also the context within which the history of the Quakers of Pennsylvania became so pivotally important. In effect, it was only where the church did not exercise political power that movements of heresy could gain strength so that those in seats of spiritual authority could be prompted to the self-examination which the situation demanded, and perhaps mend their ways.

Acton advocated toleration then, very largely, by arguing that it was salutary for the Church itself. He believed that an atmosphere of freedom forced a church to act ethically. The Cambridge University Library notes show Acton haunted by the paradox of public crime and private sanctity within the same church. The card, 'The central prob[lem] of Cath[olicism] – by what influence men of innocent and religious lives – glad to suffer death for religion, were also willing to inflict it, with every conceivable aggravation of torture and despair',[29] is typical of many references to the problem of what we would now term sado-masochism. The church might only excise it by welcoming tolerance as a constitutional right of freedom of religion.

About 1879 Acton came to the view that the authority and respect in which the saints of the Church are held must vary directly with their ethical character. He expressed this obsession to Lady Blennerhassett: 'To me, it is a question of morality and nothing else.— Satisfy me as to that and no objection remains. All the auth[ority] com[patible] w[ith] recog[nition] of murder I accept. All the poison is taken out when that is gone. The limitation which that involved is enough for me.'[30] And, 'The Church (i.e. when persecuting) as much working for sin in ethics as for truth in dogma. Not only independent or superior, but hostile. — To be regarded as Old Man of the Mountains, and treated as such. Respect is qualified. none at all. a sort of derision. Auth[ority], however ack[nowledged] in theory, only fit to be curbed.'[31] Thus Acton was prepared to buy liberty at the expense of heresy: it would have the paradoxical effect of strengthening orthodoxy by forcing it to become morally acceptable.

In this field, Acton was much influenced by Vinet's conceptions of the nature of a true Church. 'Vinet is not thinking of what he calls "les églises de masse ou de hasard". His theory does not apply to them. He cannot imagine a Christian nation. He means a chosen minority, an invisible Church of the Elect.'[32] It is easy to see that Acton was never greatly attracted by the routine and often uninspiring requirements of the vision of church life exemplified by the Church of England. He pursued this often sectarian notion of a set-apart 'people of God': 'Sects. Early Church exerted a splendid discipline. Picked men. This vanished afterwards. They would restore it, so gave up a State Church, where there is no picking and choosing'[33] and, 'Sectaries — generally, superior in morality to larger churches – virtue in minorities – even in comparing churches.'[34] But Vinet was also a strong believer in the necessity of a morally acceptable state and the eventual reconciliation of the various churches in a form which, however inadequate in the present, could be anticipated by those whose sympathies were sufficiently generous.

Acton held that the various Christian churches operating in a Liberal state might remain divided but at the same time be able on certain issues to apply an effective consensus of moral force. Sometimes it seems that Acton's way of thought requires division of the churches as a positive advantage in the formation of spiritual minds: 'Religion. – It may be wild, savage. When men believe it because they know no other. Never learned to think the thoughts of others, to live their experience, to see others from within, their own from without. No sense how their own was formed.'[35] There is a need, for the sake of faith itself, for it to grow in the opportunity to experience other faiths. He wrote that the Whigs 'reacted against that notion of religion which degrades men into partisans — and weighs down in the scale of dogma until the scale of virtue kicks the beam.'[36] And Acton described himself as a Whig. For him, too, the 'scale of virtue' was primary, but it would be a mistake to imagine that it sprang from a carelessness about faith. His supposition that toleration would produce a quality of unity may derive from his discovery in the late 1870s of the blend of consensus and the individual 'inner light' that characterised the building of Pennsylvania.

The relation of church and state

The idea of toleration thus depended on a direct argument from his fundamental position. It had clear consequences for his thinking about the position in the state of the various ecclesiastical organisations which, together, might be called the Christian Church. The relationship which Acton demanded should exist between this 'church' and the state is subtle to the point of implausibility as a model for widespread practice. It can perhaps be expressed as 'disestablishment without separation'. Within a very particular state, the present-day status and functioning of the Anglican Church of England may, paradoxically, be very much what Acton posited. Although Acton's views on 'church and state' were influenced in various measure by Döllinger, Vinet, and Gladstone, his great theme was always the interpretation of the text *Render unto Caesar*, and it is significant that it was with such an interpretation that he brought to a close his lecture on 'Freedom in Antiquity' at Bridgnorth in 1877.[37]

It was this which, in Acton's opinion, finally broke the identity of church and state which had made any real civil liberty impossible before Christianity. He closed his lecture on 'Freedom in the ancient world' with these words: 'But when Christ said, "Render unto Caesar —", those words, spoken on His last visit to the Temple, three days before His death, gave to the civil power, under the protection of conscience, a sacredness it had never enjoyed and bounds it had never acknowledged: and they were the repudiation of absolutism and the inauguration of freedom. For Our Lord not only delivered the precept but created the force to execute it. To maintain the necessary immunity in one supreme sphere, to reduce all political authority within defined limits, ceased to be an aspiration of patient reasoners and was made the perpetual charge and care of the most energetic institution and the most universal association in the world. The new law, the new Spirit, the new authority, gave to liberty a meaning and a value it had not possessed in the philosophy or in the constitution of Greece or Rome, before the knowledge of the truth that makes us free.'[38]

It is easy to show the attraction which the idea of disestablishment had for Acton. It recalled the earliest days of the church. It was the most powerful cry of the early Quakers and the Independents, and perhaps most vividly, it was the major innovation which the Americans had made in their constitution. It was the ark of the covenant of the neo-Kantian Christianity that Vinet exemplified. A card carries a quotation from Vinet, 'La protection est déjà une négation', to which Acton appended, 'This is how liberty and faith went together, so closely, in his mind and in his career.'[39] It appears that Vinet and both Gladstone and Acton considered such separation from the state as a necessary safeguard against the absolute power of democracy and, in particular, of socialism. Acton quotes Gladstone in 1875 as foreshadowing a political campaign for disestablishment whose 'arduousness ... would itself terrify the lazy and emasculated minds of our generation',[40] and himself reflects, 'Vinet means that Democracy is a danger to consciences and ought to be deprived of the power of oppressing them. It is a new danger, to be avoided as it is in America. The power of oppression is supplied by the connection of Church and State. — What Vinet signified to the Catholics was this: when it comes to be a democracy, do not rely on it, do not trust it. Deprive it of the ecclesiastical power and prop[erty].'[41] The interplay of democracy with a corporate church or churches is the very stuff of Acton's interpretation of the Liberal Tradition.

Yet there is another side to the picture. When Acton wrote,

'The Catholics claim certain rights as due to the Church by divine command. There is no such claim in the Protestant churches. Therefore the same rule cannot satisfy both. The only solution is, separation of Church and State. When they demand the same for all – they demand what others do not demand, and cannot enjoy'[42], he gave an insight into the difficulties of his position. For, although he comes to the conclusion there that complete separation is the only just and equal answer, he recognises that a Catholic church is not living the fullness of its own tradition when it does not enjoy political recognition as the apostolic witness to the nation, or when it does not exert direct influence over what most liberals would term purely political policy, e.g. family law and education. It would perhaps make Acton's position more understandable if we were to assume that, having abandoned the overt rights of any one church by welcoming the 'wall of separation', he was able to reassert those rights and the essential concepts from which they arose by claiming them for the society of Christians-in-general, led – naturally – by the Roman Catholic church. In America something like this has till recently functioned as a three-legged 'Christendom' of Catholic, Protestant, and Jew.[43] However rich and varied these particular ingredients have been, they are still all within the biblical family.

It is one of Acton's recurring epigrams that heaven is to be won as much in the life of politics as in the life of prayer. Eternal 'life-in-Christ' is the fruit – in Christian language – of an individual's response to God's grace in active vocation, so that Acton's 'as much as' signifies not so much an alternative as a polarity within the life of the person. A great corpus of Acton's writings could be collected to show the way in which he repeatedly elaborated this concept. He connected this necessity with the medieval notion of Christendom, out of which the doctrines of constitutional polity and political conscience flowed down to contemporary Liberalism: 'There was [the Council of] Constance, and there was conscience, a system of ethics would be a mere fragment without a system of politics. Savonarola indicated this at the same time. This has been a growing force in politics – Rousseau, Vinet, a very great force indeed.'[44] In so far, then, as Liberalism is to be understood in these terms, it is clear that it is to be understood as a function of the inheritance of Christendom: 'Liberty has not subsisted outside of Christianity. — that freedom should be religious, and that religion should be free.'[45] For Acton, Liberty and Christianity were in practice descriptions of the same house.

This house was the creation of the Middle Ages. Acton held that it was the medieval papacy which had introduced the notion of a Christendom and (like many of his contemporaries) the German races who had introduced that of limited, 'organic' power. It was these two elements together which distinguished the 'open society' of the Apostolic church from the 'open society' of the 19th century. This second period of freedom for the church was shot through with the ideas of political resistance and social responsibility which had been the great achievement of medieval Christendom, the churches so summarily dismissed by Vinet as the bearers of un-conscientised 'folk' Christians. The medieval image of Christendom as a garden in a wilderness, a castle in a hostile country, implied that within this limited space the Christian religion was also a state in the same way that, in later times, the colony of Pennsylvania surrounded by virgin forests was also in a peculiar sense the exemplification of a religious vision or paradise. It was called the Holy Experiment.

In his lectures on the French Revolution, Acton wrote, 'To us, in an age of science, it has become difficult to imagine Christianity without the attribute of development and the faculty of improving society as well as souls. But the idea was acquired slowly.'[46] Fénelon, whom Acton regarded as the pattern of 'Ideal Catholicism', had written in 1710, 'Dieu se contentera-t-il d'une dévotion qui consiste à douer une chapelle, à dire un chapelet, à écouter une musique, à se scandaliser facilement, et à chasser quelque janseniste? Il s'agit encore de rendre au-dedans du pain aux peuples moribunds, de rétablir l'agriculture et le commerce, de réformer le luxe qui gangrène toutes les moeurs de la nation, de se ressouvenir de la vraie forme du royaume et de tempérer le despotisme, cause de tous nos maux.'[47] It was a specially Christian character, Acton believed, that stimulated this concern, and connected it with Liberalism. He wrote, with a broadness of assertion that had no evident roots in the world's experience of much, if not most, Christianity in previous centuries: 'Influence of Religion. It is the home of general propositions. Christianity essentially alien to place and time. Adaptable to many races. So it accustoms men to sweeping theories – applicable to man as man, no matter what sex, or colour, or age. So it promoted doctrinaire thinking in politics. Calvin.'[48]

The Calvinists were but especially vigorous exponents of this abstractness of argument. The medieval experience of European *territories* that were 'Christendom' had laid the foundation. Acton believed that it was now a general Christian duty to secure certain human rights for all men everywhere, even at the price of revolution. This made Christianity 'scientific': it extended the *hortus inclusus* (the enclosed garden) until it covered the world. It expressed the genuinely Catholic – if not the curial – tradition, and established that 'politics are an affair of conscience, not of policy and expediency'.[49] The edge of true Christianity for Acton is its capacity to sustain the duty of conscientious revolution: 'Puritan Tolerance. Important, because liberalism founded on taxation does not go far. It substitutes majorities for authorities. It ensures no protection for the minorities. When you have got, by fair means, an evident predominant conviction and resolution, it must be obeyed. A republican has no idea of resistance or insurrection. — Religious liberty provides a very different notion of state.'[50] The reproach of Christianity is its actual record of falsely perceiving passivity and quietism as holiness: 'Christianity and Liberty. It has struck external observers. From Celsus to Strauss. Their gravest reproach. How asceticism told that way – and mysticism. Joy in suffering. — only Baxter a strong politician. only St Martin [Baader's old teacher] among mystics.'[51]

When it is examined a little more deeply therefore, Acton's emphasis on separation of church and state nowhere reduces the responsibility of the people of God for what the state is and does. The institution of services of coronation for early medieval kings expresses this most clearly. This is the essential idea of historic Catholicism, and it is perhaps at this point that it is most clear what Acton meant when he said, 'Vinet's liberality comes to the verge of Catholicism.'[52] Granted that the church is concerned to watch over and inspire the policies of the state, it would seem to Anglican heirs of the English Elizabethan Settlement that the state might be similarly concerned to watch over the church – both, of course, remaining administratively distinct. This conclusion was repugnant to Acton, at least until the 1880s. He wanted to trust to the invigorating effects of a free press and academic enquiry to check the corrupting tendencies at work in the church, rather than to any formal state intervention. He was not averse, however, to using every ounce of influence during the Vatican Council in order to mobilise the governments of Europe to exert pressure against the decrees, partly on the grounds that it had been the tradition for the Catholic powers to participate in Councils of the church.

Catholicism and the Liberal state

A considerable number of cards in the group of boxes which Acton used to collect material for his proposed biography of Döllinger are concerned with the problem of how far the 'Church of Ximenes' could be trusted to wither away in a milieu such as the United States, where all churches were divorced from state power. These cards are of great interest, for they show Acton developing a line of thought which does not occur to the same extent in his earlier notes, and up to which time he had perhaps considered the safeguards of public opinion and disestablishment more adequate. Nonetheless, anxiety about the possibility of a 'free church' being the more open to takeover by bigots and autocrats is evident as early as the Council. Acton had noted the compliant behaviour of bishops from missionary dioceses in European colonies, under the direct administration of Propaganda Fide. He remained anxious about the possibilities for papal absolutism in its new-found separation from the politics of the Italian nation.

The following card of *c.* 1892 shows this dormant concern had revived. 'The Church not allowed to govern herself by her own laws. That must be interfered with. Liberty depends on division of powers. Government by the hierarchy, uncontrolled, would be absolute government. It is only by the interference of the State that liberty exists. The Church, left to herself, to her own laws and penalties, her own legislative and judicial powers, will govern by fire and torture. The very principle of liberty is: the Church curbs the State, and the State the Church. Propaganda, churches governed by Rome only. without the State.'[53]

This is in clear contrast with the attitude he had maintained in his youth, when he had criticised a state where, 'religious profession is free, but Church government is controlled. And where ecclesiastical authority is restricted, religious liberty is virtually denied.'[54] But in 1862, the date of this quotation, he was primarily concerned to show how necessary the machinery of Catholic organisation and law was to act as a bulwark against the state. This was the position of Döllinger who had said in 1848, 'Die Katholische Kirche — begrüsst die Freiheit als das eigentliche Element ihres Lebens.'[55] According to Acton, what Döllinger meant by this was primarily freedom from the old monarchical absolutisms. He commented, in the same box, 'Governments mainly were absolute – The salvation of religion lay in independence. Its ruin lay in subjection. The main idea — of his [Döllinger's] life. – The danger comes from the state.

45

Against that, Catholicism possesses a security which Protestantism does not.' And again, '[Döllinger] wished to remove the
constraints which, in the preceding ages, had reduced religion to
so low an ebb.— The danger was in the checks and obstacles, not
in the Church itself. At first, he saw no farther than this. __ [But]
if the limiting and restraining forces are removed, what remains
is unlimited and unrestrained authority. Freedom and self-
government of the Church lead to absolute will of hierarchy.'[56]

Acton held that, in distinction from his own position, Döllinger
'believed that Catholicism could live and thrive apart from
Liberalism'[57] because his formative years had been spent at a
time when the escape from local absolutisms seemed to lie in the
negotiation of concordats by the state with the papacy.
'D[öllinger]'s admiration for Pius VII and his system of
concordate. Under that regime he had witnessed the religious
revival of his youth, a revival accomplished without violence or
intolerance, by conciliation and compromise. without traditional
instrumentality.'[58] This, Acton argued on the same card, was why
he 'did not prefer the American model'. Acton saw objections to
the concordat type of formal relationship: 'The modern state could
not accept the ecclesiastical law as presented by the Church, or
acknowledge her official claims. It had to determine for itself the
limits and conditions, and to impose them upon the clergy. It fell
to laymen, to jurists and statesmen to select these things in which
the Church might exercise her rights and those which she might
not. D[öllinger] never made this reflexion. He saw no such
danger.'[59] The experience of Bismarck's *Kulturkampf* made these
questions acute.

It is thus an extremely complex task to disentangle Acton's real
views on the position of the church *vis-a-vis* the state at this time.
He was perhaps clearer as to what he wanted than how to get it.
He wanted the church to be quite free of connection with the
state, and yet to be kept pure and reasonable by it. He envisaged
the entirely paradoxical situation of an 18th century Gallicanism
set in an American context. This is attainable only in very
civilised circumstances and can hardly be made into the
doctrinaire and universally applicable kind of statement about
the relation of church and state which Acton desired to formulate.

Nonetheless, Acton was easily persuaded that Catholicism was
the form of Christianity most suited to a Liberal state. His vision
of its ideal form combined the principles of unity and federalism,
and stemmed essentially from the ideas which had been
propounded at Constance. He wrote, 'Catholicism. The one

political idea is that there is a power beyond the state. Not coterminous with it (which is S. Augustine's idea, no longer true). How great is this power? That increased later, until it destroyed the original idea. It absorbed power instead of checking it. Down to the Gregorian age it only checked it. Never absorbed it. So that is the genuine Catholic action: a Church inside and outside – vaster than the State, bringing general influences to bear – a force of public opinion, of international law, or arbitration.'[60]

The advantage, therefore, of Catholicism was its power. This power, which arose both from its organisation and its doctrines, gave it the necessary point of leverage outside the state to be an effective check. The same power carried within it the possibility of a cancered absolutism.

The concern that Acton felt for drawing the teeth of absolutism in the Catholic church is shown in several rather hypothetical sketches in the cards. He writes: 'America. The dread of influence directs itself against Catholic clergy. By renouncing marriage, they are thrown upon power. For them there is no surrender of power possible. To acquire power is the object, the consolation, of their lives.'[61] 'Sects. Against abuse of royal power Middle Ages set up the full doctrine of revolution. But how against abuse of spiritual power? In the long run they would always hold it right to yield. One pope might be opposed or disregarded – not all popes. — How could they shift the seat of spiritual power? That is what the Councils tried and failed to do. How then, would it be without papacy? Was there not more security in rejecting so uncontrollable a power?'[62]

But this power in Catholicism was of special value for checking democracy. Acton wrote, 'All Catholics agreed that some offices of authority are planted on earth by God. Episcopate. So they could not accept the idea that all authorities are created by those for whose sake they exist. The theory which builds up authority from below encountered an obstacle in the Catholic doctrine of orders.'[63] The kernel of the question was summed up in 1880, at a crucial moment in the formation of his 'central idea': 'Catholic Politics – Notion of a checking power. That is the essential element. Therefore opposes Democracy. Promotes Federalism',[64] and 'Liberty dissolves Protestant churches – but favours the Catholic church. By its organization, independent of state. By its continuity and development.'[65]

In addition, Acton saw Catholic dogma as intransigent, not subject to the vagaries of fashion and scholarship: his 'Out of religion, a man must be always ready to change. An economist who was deaf to Adam Smith etc. The reluctance of French to accept Newton etc. ridiculous. But in religion you want people you are sure of, who will not be influenced by arguments'[66] contrasts with Döllinger's perspective of the 'dissolution of the Protestant churches'. All in all the Roman Catholic was well fitted to survive in the context of a Liberal state.

From the moral point of view, too, Acton believed the Catholic church would quite naturally assert its pre-eminence. It not only had a more elaborate casuistry, and a larger-scale machine for teaching the moral law, but its aims and methods could be more directly appreciated by an intelligent unbeliever as tending to good in this, as well as another, world: 'If morality dependent on religion, is useful to the State; most useful is that religion which has most means of est[ablishing] morality and most agents. so Cath[olics] superior to Quakers',[67] and 'Idea that the State prefers a Church that has strong means of promoting virtue, and a body of men trained for it – This failed in Middle Ages, by dispensing power etc. the influence of religion on society was weakened. The priests ceased to be of use for virtue – Everything served only for the other world. So for this also contending competition was wanted.'[68]

Like Bishop Butler's method in the introduction to his *Analogy*, Acton was eager here to find evidence that, however indecisive might be the proofs of the Catholic dogma, its solid advantages here and now were sufficient to convert any benevolent man to its practice. He noted a passage in Leibnitz where Catholicism is spoken of as 'the most natural religion'. He rejoiced in George Eliot's finding in Catholic liturgy and Anglican cathedrals and Jewish morality the satisfaction of her religious impulses.[69]

Commending the church

There is another very deep strain in Acton's religion. Throughout his life he showed himself aware of the poverty and misery which remained for the Christian church to alleviate. This too he undoubtedly believed to be an especially Catholic preoccupation. St Francis is a figure to whom Acton was devoted to a degree only equalled by his admiration for St Thomas Aquinas and St Thomas of Kempen. He embodied the practical side of the general efflorescence of conscience in the 13th century. St Francis led the Jesus-life in the ordinary world, and perceived that this meant renouncing all power. He was: 'the greatest Catholic Reformer.

First, he gave up all property. Next: he lived, not for the convent, but for the people. He sought, not the domination of the clergy, secured by wealth; but the conversion of the laity, by renunciation. Not, they said, a new reform – only a return to the primitive life of Christians. For the depravation, worldliness, came by property – not so much because it gave ease and luxury, as power. He strove to carry the sanctity of the cloister into the world.'[70] This emphasis is perhaps a necessary corollary of relogous liberty. If persuasion is the only road to men's souls, it is important not to overlook the necessity of speaking the gospel to the hungry as yourself hungry in the manner of the Abbé Godin and the post-war French worker-priests.

In spite of his recurring emphasis that 'the great thing' in Christianity 'is the care for the poor',[71] Acton was never prepared to take the *Magnificat* so seriously as to contemplate any capture of the state machinery by the poor as socialists. The Catholic tradition, at least until the Second Vatican Council, has emphasised the voluntariness of charity: philanthropy rather than justice has been its keynote. When Acton wrote, 'So Christianity demands that the strong give way to the weak. The strong govern, but not for themselves',[72] he stood in the paternalist tradition of St Louis, and Fénelon's benevolent King of Salente. This tradition fitted well into the individualist pattern of the Liberal state and into the ethos of service so characteristic of English public schools and colleges in the 1890s. An important aspect of Acton's life – and one in which he found considerable satisfaction – was as a Shropshire squire.

To conclude, it would be possible to sum up Acton's position in two sentences he used of Fénelon. He 'dreads the excess of power, both in Church and State, but most in the State' and 'The right is above the law – or the interest of religion.'[73] As early as 1861, Acton set out his position clearly: 'In modern times [the church] can only demand the self-government due to every legitimate association .... In politics as in science the church need not seek her own ends – she will obtain them if she encourages the pursuit of the ends of science, which are truth – and of the state, which are liberty.'[74] Yet he perceived, especially after *c.* 1880, that in the historical past these values had pre-eminently been lived and commended by the sects. He wrote of the Independents, 'Unity must exist in a Church. But in all numerous bodies, it does not exist, unless by force. Now compulsion is wrong. To be of one accord, a community must be small. — The Independents, wiser than almost all their imitators, wished to deliver the individual, not to create an irresistible force for the collective individuals. Our democracy sets no limits to the general will. The Independents set the most definite limits.'[75]

The more extreme heirs of the Reformation had set the terms of the struggle and seen the goal. But, for the future, Acton believed the Catholic strength of Order could most effectively achieve this same aim. The dangerous lust for power in the professional leadership of the Catholic church could meet its match in the growing light of the democratic Leviathan. 'We restrain the intolerant as long as we have to fear them – but not when liberty becomes strong. In other words – Restrain majorities, not minorities',[76] and again, in 1878, 'Liberty of the conscience and liberty of the Church check and qualify each other. The state must neither sacrifice the Church to the individual, nor the individual to the Church. To secure liberty of conscience, the state must limit the liberty of churches. That is the principle of the Prussian legislation.'[77]

The last years of the 1870s, the period of the *Kulturkampf*, was the time when Acton developed his way of fitting together his two value-systems as a Whig who was also a Catholic. In doing this, he found that the one idea of 'conscience' could serve as a keystone in the language of both systems, and that a particularly significant contribution to the future of the modern world (and therefore to its providential past) had been made by the Quakers.

4
Conscience and Politics

Liberty defined as the 'reign of conscience'

One of the few facts we know about Acton's projected *History of Liberty*, the work which was to be his *chef d'oeuvre*, is that he hoped at one point to open it with a chapter on the varying definitions of liberty. In a notebook of July 1878[1] he collected seventy-nine such definitions: it was probably a few months later that he made the choice that was to define his system, and noted, 'Definition. Liberty is the reign of conscience.'[2] He went on to one hundred and then to two hundred definitions. This attention to a definition of his central concept is significant. It shows that Acton was aware that, by seeking to exhibit liberty as the central chain of history, he was embarking on a quasi-theological argument where precise technical distinctions were indispensable.

Although there is a broad consistency in Acton's use of the word 'liberty', and although – as we shall see – he conceived of its application in terms of 'science', it is hardly surprising that he nowhere succeeded in using it in this technical way. Indeed it appears that Acton's usage of it changed during his career.

By the 1890s Acton wrote, 'Liberty. – Reign of Conscience. Reason commanding reason, not will commanding will. Safety of minorities'.[3] This was a fuller range of definition than that to which he had been accustomed in his youth. In his early writings, he was less pragmatic and more German and philosophical in his approach to the nature of liberalism than later. The freedom to do one's duty was its dynamic requirement. This figured prominently in the columns of the *Rambler*; for example, in 1860, 'Liberty is not the power of doing what we like, but the right of being able to do what we ought'[4] and two years later there is the pontifical note of a *Times* leader writer in 'If we take the establishment of liberty for the realization of moral duties to be the end of civil society ...'.[5] When he came to deliver his lectures on the history of freedom at Bridgnorth in 1877, he defined this 'freedom' as the 'assurance that every man shall be protected in doing what he believes his duty against the influence of authority and majorities, custom and opinion'.[6]

The distinction between the two definitions is important. In the

51

earlier one, 'what we ought' may not be our own discovery. In fact, the words lend themselves to interpretation in the light of the German tradition of 'forced to be free'. In the later instance, the emphasis was placed on the certainty we can have of protection, and on the phrase 'believes [to be] his duty'. Certainty of protection can only be the result of a political apparatus working on known principles, such as are embodied in a constitution. The protection was argued as for the individual 'conscience'. Only the individual, the owner of a conscience, can be the subject of the phrase, 'believes his duty': 'Liberalism is Individualism. It loses its supreme importance if there is no soul.'[7] There has to be some kind of individual micro-theodicy in allowing the sovereignty of erroneous duty within society. It is significant that it is only after the Bridgnorth lectures that Acton began to place so much stress on the American Constitution and that cards which link liberty and conscience begin to occur. For instance, 'Liberalism admits the dominion of Conscience. Less impeded by authority, reputation, and time.'[8]

Another change of emphasis in Acton's thinking about what constituted political freedom took place even later. A card of the early 1890s runs, 'Is liberty the power of governing others? It is not only negative. Not only the minority preventing the majority. It is a share in the work of the majority – a part in the government – not the negation of it. A mode of action, not of restraint.'[9] This is now only a logical extension of Acton's insistence on the Liberal's duty to maintain the character of the state in a particular pattern.

Two principles which Acton had early identified as the Christian contribution to political thought remained the key principles also of liberty. These were the 'Division of Power' and 'Care for the Poor'. As early as 1861, Acton quoted Calhoun as saying, 'I care not what the form of government is: it is nothing if the government is despotic, whether it be in the hands of one, or of a few, or of many men, without limitation.'[10] Then, again, in the 1870s a card runs: 'Monarchy, aristocracy, democracy not question of good or evil, right or wrong, but only of time and place. The question is limitation. Each tends to exaggerate its principle.'[11] Late in life, in 1896, Acton spoke of 'that principle of division which is useful for stability, and for liberty is essential'.[12]

The principles of social justice had rational as well as charitable implications for Acton. He wrote, in terms which present-day Third World countries have endorsed in their contribution to Human Rights thinking: 'There is no liberty where there is hunger. — The theory of liberty demands strong efforts to help the poor. Not merely for safety, for humanity, for religion, but for liberty.'[13] Liberty depended on the extent to which personal and group interest could be counter-balanced in taking political decisions. While men were starving it was obvious that their political motive would be food rather than duty. Only when that had been achieved could the dialogue of rational judgment and duty, which both Gladstone and Acton expected from extending the parliamentary franchise, be anticipated. Acton wrote, 'Liberty is the minimum of will over will. — Lib[eralism] desires the reign of law in which all concur – and the subordination of the executive'[14] and 'Why Democracy? it means liberty given to the mass. Where there is no powerful democracy, freedom does not reign.'[15]

The political machinery of the Liberal state having drawn the teeth of greed, lust for power, and deception, Acton believed the way would then be open to the freedom of Universal Reason for all citizens and all souls. This was what he meant by the 'reign of conscience'. This view was to have its later main-stream proponents: the leading Catholic political philosopher of the inter-war period, the neo-Thomist Jacques Maritain, asserted that the question of political structure is not indifferent to the church, and that she chooses liberal democracy.

Politics as 'science'

In talking at Bridgnorth in 1877 of freedom in the ancient world, Acton said: 'The Laws [of Plato] and the Politics [of Aristotle] are, if I may trust my own experience, the books from which we may learn the most about principles of politics.'[16] The 'principles' which could be derived from the two classic Greek authors were essentially indications of how to preserve the state from change, and consequently from decay. There was a 'right' political order, which was the correct relationship between different social groups in the state. Once found, this political form being proportioned to the nature of man and the nature of a *polis*, it was reasonable to suppose that its application would lead both to happiness and success. This form was also an abstract thing, and *in potentia* universally relevant. It is abundantly clear that Acton, too, considered the history of states as the expression of an inner health or disease which depended on their constituent form. Throughout his life he transcribed notes from contemporary medical works which would indicate a relation between physical health and ethical living. In 1868 he wrote – perhaps in that context inviting comparison with the language of 'sound money' and IMF loans – of the Mexicans, 'They formed a republic after the model of their more fortunate neighbours, and accepted those principles which are so inflexible in their consequences and so unrelenting in their consistency.'[17]

He was particularly prone to consider the development of the French Revolution in this way. It came so near to the correct form, but was diverted into the 'pathology of revolution' by the weight of the past error in French history. Even in 1878, he perceived the Jansenists as ruining the chance of 'health' in 1792, a fruit of the oppression they had suffered in the past.[18] It is in this context that we should see Acton's frequent usage of the word 'repentance' of a 'monarchy' or 'papacy'. A statesman might be someone who by acknowledging and righting an ancient wrong, as for example Gladstone attempted to do with the Irish Home Rule Bill, cleared the ground for future healthy and creative relationships.

It is with this background, therefore, that we must approach Acton's usage of the phrase, 'political science'. Imported from the current natural sciences were notions of law, simplicity, experiment, and, above all, coercive demonstrableness. It was the certainty, and not the humility, of science which Acton always had in mind. In effect, his 'science' was like the archaeology of, for example, an already substantially excavated Viking ship. As early as 1866 he wrote of 'that political science which resides in serene regions, remote from the conflicts of party opinion; a science whose principles are clear, definite, and certain, and not more difficult to apply than the principles of the moral code'[19]; and then, in the 1870s, 'Burke. In his time it was found that some parts of government can be so certain as not to depend on national influence – Adam Smith. Bentham'[20]; and 'Idea that there is such a thing as political science. that it is clear and certain. that it is sacred as morality. that it is imperfect, progressive, and increasing. As essential to the welfare of society as religion or private morals – and as demonstrable as the truths of science.'[21] Indeed, 'politics acquired a certainty as different as astronomy before Copernicus by the rise of statistics'.[22]

It was not only from the Greeks that he inherited the desire to make of politics an ideal structure. The Kantian influence also helped to make him conceive Liberalism in universal terms. He wrote, 'Liberals Kantian. look for a general pr[inciple]. see how it applies in a variety of cases. Tory content with present problem.'[23] This was a less wooden approach. In his later years, his choice of constitutional prescription became less of a Procrustean bed or – acknowledging its American flavour – a black Model-T Ford. A card of the 1890s runs, 'Laws and institutions are local – Ideas are universal.'[24] The experience of Britain in the 1950s and 1960s in endowing colonies at the granting of their independence with Westminster-style consitutions of impeccable liberal – indeed Cambridge – ancestry and short life expectancy is evidence of the wisdom of that gloss.

The fact, then, that Acton believed political thought had reached the stage where it could be spoken of in the same breath as Victorian science was important in two ways. It meant that techniques were available with which to attain chosen ends, that the norms of political science (which were equated with political liberalism) were abstractly demonstrable and in principle universally applicable, and also that, by definition, the failure to apply them argued wilful sin.

Döllinger, it seems, had refused to recognise these techniques, and had consequently demanded very little from government. 'The science of politics, the bulk of political literature, were foreign to him – unknown.'[25] Indeed, he 'admired Indian empire, the lowest in aims of all governments. — as long as a government secured peace, order'.[26] Acton was confident that a complex and humane society could be built by applying the findings of political science. 'We think much more of the rights which protect our duties than for the protection of our enjoyment. They need to be secured, as well as proclaimed – and they can be secured only by a complete system of polity.'[27]

In this way, it appears that Acton conceived that a comprehensive constitutional framework was an absolute necessity for a state based on the sovereignty of conscience. Such a state was not to leave everything to the free play of events. Acton was a paternalist as well as a liberal. His conscience would not allow him to countenance the sacrifice of the masses to laissez-faire economics.

If the object of one's political conscience is that all other citizens should enjoy the maximum opportunity to engage with God in *their* consciences, the possible implications include the following: that they can be expected to be able to use their reason and sympathetic imagination, so that they will not be starving, will have had a secure upbringing, and will have been educated; that there is no overwhelming temptation for them to embark on behaviour that will coarsen or destroy their moral identity; that

55

they will have an experience of 'owning' the legal and political system under which they live; that the society they live in will give space and recognition to the human individual as against the corporate mass; and that they will be inducted into a tradition of religious language. Such are the practical fruits required by Acton's 'reign of conscience'.

Thus a political philosophy whose sovereign value moves from the mere freedom of the potential exercise of conscience to concern for the quality of its happening, will either have to limit its critical concern to religous experience, or else proceed some way towards a careful allotment of responsibility which is proportioned to the maturity of a myriad of particular con-sciences. This must result in only a limited commitment to atomistic individualism and liberty for the great majority in any societies we know. Acton's subtlety of historical insight broke through the mechanical rigidity of 19th-century 'political economy'.[28] The authority he continually sought to gain by associating himself with contemporary science worked paradox-ically – as it has with many since – to undermine the real effectiveness of his teaching.

The second point which follows from the proposed scientific and sovereign character of liberalism is its capacity to absorb all political institutions into its disposition. In Acton's usage, this relates to the word 'sincere', which has connotations of 'unprej-udiced', 'clinical', 'secular'. In 1862 he wrote, 'Liberty alone demands for its realization the limitation of the public authority, for liberty is the only object which benefits all alike and provokes no sincere opposition',[29] and later, in the 1870s, 'Medieval politics not sincere – No idea of right apart from religion. Did not supply a method for various societies. No provision for mixed religions. The distinction between orthodoxy and misbelief was as broad as in paganism that between Greek and barbarian.'[30]

It was essentially what Acton analysed in his Cambridge lectures in the 1890s, when he commented on Cardinal Baronius's denunciation of the new and damnable 'political heresy' that had appeared and was the characteristic of the modern world: 'By that was meant the notion of a science of politics limiting the ecclesiastical domain: an ethical and political system deriving its principles elsewhere than from the Church, and setting up a new and rival authority yet to be defined, ascertainable in no book, and not accepted by the nations. Those amongst us who deny the existence of a political science and believe that ethics cannot be made to include politcs, have ardent supporters in the Roman clergy of three centuries ago.'[31]

The aim then, was to find a political pattern which would have a moral claim upon any society, religious or non-religious. Like George Eliot, Acton conceived himself as 'legislating for a society without religious conviction'.[32] In this activity, which became one of the most significant of Acton's preoccupations, he was quite out of sympathy with Döllinger. Acton believed that it was possible to cast atheistic societies into a moral mould, which although it was divorced from the church, could only in the end be explained and defended by reference to the Christian tradition. He also believed Christianity to be the gift of the *logos*, the rational creator-God, and therefore not only 'true' but in some sense 'natural' and therefore efficient and health-giving. He did not see the problems in extending his term 'scientific' to include this sub-Christian or Christian-derived ethical framework.

There are two adjacent cards in the *History of Liberty* collection which discuss political conservatism (and the argument applies as much against socialism), and make it plain that Acton opposed it on religious, not practical, grounds. They run: 'Conservative case. Liberty is a luxury, not a necessity for all men. The poor, ignorant people cannot enjoy it. Give them first all other things. Use their power for their welfare, and sacrifice liberty to security, to morality, to prosperity. These have a larger space in the lives of common men, a larger share in their happiness. Their happiness depends, if at all, on the appearance, not the reality. So give them delusive forms, consistent with the strong hand, with guidance from above.' And 'Conservatism. there is no answer to their case, apart from religion. If happiness is the end of society, then liberty is superfluous. It does not make men happy. It depends on the other world. It is the sphere of duty – not of rights. Suffering, sacrifice, for an end beyond this life. If there is none, there is no object to sacrifice to.'[33]

Acton, as we have seen, wished Liberalism to be considered as scientific and universally acceptable. But if Liberalism depends completely on a religion whose origins are in a particular tradition and scriptures and whose rewards and meaning are not limited to this world of sense experience, how can it be recommended to those outside that religion and whose judgment is based on other traditions and other criteria? Not as a science, certainly. Doubtless a religion can and does develop, but it is at this point that the absolute centrality of the idea of conscience in Acton's scheme becomes explicit. For he came to assert that, at least in language and convention, 'conscience' could function as 'scientific' in this way.

Liberalism and religion

Acton laid special stress on unbelievers and Christians coming 'from all sides' to an idea of conscience. It is a question whether in order to do this, he had become either intellectually naive or completely eclectic and relativist in his use of the word 'conscience'. Even if it could be agreed that conscience is so valuable a bridge between systems that it should be accepted as a central value for practical political reflexion within our culture, it is only a conscience set in the framework of a particular religious language that can be given the transcendent authority that comes from being used as a vehicle of the Holy Spirit. Perhaps only within the framework of such language can 'conscience' properly exact the sacrifices Acton proposed. It is here that Acton's pervading difficulty lies. At the level of inter-faith secular discourse, is there any answer, on Acton's terms, to 'conservatism'? Acton tries to use the suppositions of religious doctrine to apply to political arguments in which – if it is used at all – the term 'conscience' has completely altered its meaning.

When Acton said that Whiggism was 'morality applied to politics', what did he mean? It is clear from his attitude to the English 18th century[34] that he did not only mean liberty. The question was one of those that arose in his interior dialogue with George Eliot. Some cards from the box relating to her[35] run, 'Her motives are the elements of conservatism. Reason is the element of liberalism. A tribunal above tradition – the reign of the living', 'Progress by public opinion. Sustain that. Increase it. That is liberalism. Not her idea', and 'Liberty. To be free from outward compulsion, the state can do this. From inward it cannot. Religion and education can. So the state must promote education and free religion. Only checks it when it finds religion not liberating.'

The morality which Whiggism is to apply to politics is the corpus of principles of 'adult' or 'continuing' education: to be accurately informed about the current affairs of the world, to be able to reflect upon experience, to evaluate in a critical way one's own culture and its traditional religion, to associate with others in political pressure for change. S. T. Coleridge's vision of a professional 'clerisy' – a focus of both religion and learning – which was close to the role of the late-Victorian Oxbridge 'don', is congenial to Acton. Overarching any discussion of Whig morality in politics in Acton's mind must be the primary imperative to establish and maintain constitutional government itself.

The gospel which Acton so peculiarly preached was the ethical character of public action, and especially the fact that one political tradition, that represented by the Liberal party, was the bearer of ethics in political life. The alternative was claimed to be Machiavellianism: 'When we say that public life is not an affair of morality, — that the code shifts with the longitude, — we carry obscurely tribute to the system which bears so odious a name.'[36] It is clear that the force of this stance is derived from an amalgam of two criticisms. Acton thought that the opposition to the Liberals was a criminal opposition: it was wrong, both in the sense of having got the wrong answer, and in the sense of moral blindness and malevolence. He really did talk of Disraeli as criminal.[37] This makes it difficult to see how a two-party system can work whose values are only defended, understood, and exemplified by one party.

There is considerable evidence that Acton was an ideologue, able only to see 'us' and 'them'. A card of *c.* 1896 runs: 'Much national sentiment prevents men from seeing that the essential issues are only two – Liberal and illiberal, others are not scientific.'[38] Döllinger was one of those dismissed as unscientific. He 'preferred free government to absolute, but never believed that they were divided by anything like the chasm that parts truth from falsehood, purity from vice, or that sin can be defined in politics, with the same exactness as in morals'.[39] In fact, 'D[öllinger] never was a Liberal and was not influenced by the problems which arise when a Whig politician is a religious Catholic.'[40]

However, it was Louis XIV and Machiavelli whom Acton regarded as the archrepresentatives of illiberality, and he was sure they would be damned. Such men were indicted as 'wrong': 'Party does not mean that one set of men are specially able, always right, virtuous and wise. But that the others are profoundly wrong.'[41] In consequence, Acton lines himself up in the most explicit way with those in the 20th century who have preached political commitment as a corollary of religious vocation. Acton's is indeed a Liberation Theology in every sense: 'If there is a right and wrong in politics, the Church ought to proclaim it, and to take sides.'[42]

Thus political allegiance was a matter where lack of interest or attention was almost as grave as admitted error. Acton was accustomed to use the phrase, the Whig Church. This was no coy metaphor: there is no doubt that he thought of party loyalty and doctrine with the same commitment as religious loyalty and doctrine, for 'party is above country, as principles are above interests. We cling to our country as a passenger to a ship, whose safety is his own. We cling to our party as to our religion, because we deem it true.'[43]

At the point conscience came on stage, it contributed the element that made Acton's 'party' function as a 'church'. It was the point where compromise stopped and prudential this-worldly considerations had to give place: 'The moment Conscience became the issue, opposition became a crime. It became a conflict with wickedness, not with another opinion.'[44] A card from the box lying behind the Cambridge lectures reveals the nub of the matter: 'there are no public, as distinct from private, objects worthy to be purchased at the expense of souls. Consequently, the interest of the individual is above the exclusive interest of the state. The power of the whole is not to be set in the balance for one moment with the freedom – that is, with the conscience, of the subject. and those who act on the other principles are the worst of criminals.'[45] Some of the young men who heard Acton lecture may well have found such an argument cogent for them twenty years later when the question arose of conscientious objection to military service in the First World War. Acton knew the cost of the value he put on conscience.

This *sanctity* of conscience was the crux of the history of significant reflexion about the values of public life: 'Whether politics are a question of might or a question of right. It took centuries of earnest and combined thought to institute anything like a code of political ethics, and the rights of man. Grotius. Selden. Harrington. Penn. Locke. Fénelon. Montesquieu. Rousseau. Turgot. Leibnitz. Wolff. Smith. Burke. Holt. Adams. Hamilton. Jefferson. Mill. These men were long feeling their way – and the result was even then not universally accepted.'[46] The best armed champions – because the most recent – to add to these lists of challengers to Machiavelli were, it appears, Jefferson and Mill. They claim that politics is after all a question of right, but neither would have spoken readily of the 'expense of souls'.

The absolute value of conscience

Acton's Inaugural Lecture of 1895 states his whole *Weltanschauung* in a compressed form. He expressed his conviction that the history of liberty is a history of conscience, and this was confirmed when he delivered shortly afterwards the first of the lectures in his course on Modern History.[47] The earlier exposition is especially interesting, however, because there he annotates his own words with two quotations which, as was the purpose of many of these notes, set and limit the sense of his terms. He had said, 'I know not whether it will ever fall within my sphere of duty to trace the slow progress of that idea [liberty] through the chequered scenes of our history, and to describe how subtle speculations touching the nature of conscience promoted a nobler and more spiritual conception of the liberty that protects it, until the guardian of rights [the free government] developed into the guardian of duties which are the cause of rights, and that which had been prized as the material safeguard for treasures of earth became sacred as security for things [conscience] that are divine.'[48]

Appended to this passage are the two following notes: 'In this sense, Freedom, self-developing moral Reason, and Conscience are synonymous. Only in so far as he develops Conscience within himself, is man free' and 'From the unending and eternal value of the historical personality before God, from the conception of the person who is Free-in-God, also follows the title to justice itself in the secular sphere, to municipal and political freedom, to conscience and freedom of religion to free intellectual enquiry, etc., and especially the demand that no one should serve merely as an instrument for another.'[49] There is every reason to suppose that both these represent Acton's own view.

The most complete and succinct exposition of the inter-relation of Acton's thought here is provided by a remarkable card, which illustrates the degree to which he brought together concepts of 'law' and 'inspiration' (voice of God) in the experience of 'conscience'. It is headed 'Individualism': 'Idea of Conscience. Man has a soul. Society has not. Therefore it is the highest purpose. and he has a conscience – He knows the law, and does not surrender his knowledge of it to any outward authority. For Conscience is the voice of God. authority is the will of man. on this I found the revolutionary idea.'[50] Similarly (for that last phrase identifying himself with the revolution's break from the past is an integral part of his system), 'Liberalism thinks that you must let God work – not restraining His action with fixed barriers. It is the Liberty of Providence they demand. God's chief means of action on man is Grace. And Grace is individual. Expose the individual to that alone. Parle seule à mon âme – Do not bury the Conscience beneath the ruins of crumbled ages and set the throne on sepulchres. Snatch the sceptre from the grasp of the dead.'[51]

Thus the practical assumptions of Acton's theory of conscience include habitual openness to God in meditation and prayer, with the expectation of receiving a prophetic 'word' that will supersede existing authorities and structures. Like St Paul in the early chapters of his letter to the Romans, this is all set against a background of the universal morality of natural law, so that – as Acton puts it – we 'know the law' in our conscience. Vinet was accustomed to regard conscience in terms of confrontation with God, while the medieval Schoolmen were accustomed to think in terms of natural law. To think of conscience in both ways simultaneously, it was necessary that Acton should assume a continuity between Grace and Ethical Science – the supernatural and the natural, the voluntarist and the rational.

Indications of the way in which conscience worked in Acton's mind toward expression in political liberal states can be found in the cards. There is more than a hint of Kant and Vinet (and the word 'infallible' does have a particular overtone and history for Acton) in: 'The doctrine of the sovereignty and the finality of conscience. The doctrine of its infallibility. The first prompted toleration. The second all liberty.'[52] But it is in a box that was labelled (perhaps for a previous usage) 'Inquisition' that we find brought together the most compelling and coherent indication of Acton's position.

These cards probably date from his first years at Cambridge, from 1895. He writes, 'If man has an immortal soul to save, the public interests are subordinate to it, and if he has a conscience, he must not be prevented from obeying it. Therefore the state powers are limited. strong enough to protect the rights of man – not to oppress – That set up the state against the Church – not subordinated to it.'[53] 'Equality from conscience. wherein all are alike'[54]; and 'Conscience, the point of junction between Divine and Human – the one security on earth for right against might – mind against matter. not always clear as to conduct – as to principles of conduct.'[55] Also, 'Conscience. If God speaks to the soul, it must touch politics as well. The idea of law becomes distinct from the insurance of interests',[56] and 'Conscience persistently shocked by things as they are. The world as it appears to a conscientious observer, fills him with horror. The desire to convert it, the duty of trying to improve it, is constant. Conscience is always making for change, seeking leverage to effect it with.'[57]

The fabric of Acton's whole political system was woven outward from the inviolability of the initiative of each individual conscience as it interacts with the natural laws of public human existence, which that conscience must itself recognise.

Historically, the dependence of liberty on a theory of conscience is shown clearly by the example of Hobbes. 'Hobbes rejects conscience for the sake of arbitary monarchy. The two went together. So that Butler's restoration of conscience is a preliminary to the establishment of freedom.'[58] The same lesson is taught by Acton's dissatisfaction with the forms of liberty in which conscience is not the centre. He often distinguished, in the way pioneered by the American Bancroft, between the liberalism of Penn and Locke as the difference between value systems based on conscience and on property. It was in this way that he believed Döllinger's liberalism to be inadequate: 'D[öllinger] once said that representation must always depend upon property. — Ignores the very essence of Liberalism, that man owns something besides property – Spiritual instead of material basis of politics.'[59]

Adam Smith, too, in spite of his 'scientific' contributions to the liberal creed, was seen to be inadequate in the same way. Acton wrote, 'A. Smith's political ideas. Essentially liberal, because directed against despotic state. But not ultimately liberal. For it teaches only what makes a country rich. That wealth must be sacrificed to liberty, that the moral purpose of liberty is superior to the material purpose of wealth, he cannot admit.'[60] George Eliot went so far as to 'base her politics on persons, not things', but to Acton, this was an example of glorious illogicality. She could not accept the idea of a soul[61]; so that 'the deepest if not the most energetic principle of Liberalism: duties to God superior to human authority – was unknown to her.'[62] And yet she was prepared to 'sink the ship to save the passenger'. It is plain from Acton's article on her in 1885 that her mixture of traditionalism, conscience, and sacrifice fascinated him by its improbability. Acton was convinced that, for ordinary men, the choice of values was between the state (and welfare) or the individual (and morality). 'The Sabbath was made for man, and not man for the Sabbath, applied to politics. The State was made for man – not man for the State.'[63]

At various times, Acton even played with the idea that conscience required community expression (after all the Quaker experience is nothing if not corporate), and was perhaps given its freest reign in an enlightened autocracy. He wrote, 'The state an organism. It follows that it is self-governing and has a Conscience'[64] and 'Concentrate responsibility. That is the idea of Imperialism. Responsibility concentrated where it meets Conscience. Bring responsibility and Conscience together'[65] and, 'Theory of Conscience favourable to Monarchy. For a monarch has a conscience, a force within working for good. A body of men has no such force, as the individual responsible is less, so conscientious influences are less, an association has not got a soul.'[66]

But this argument was checked by the consequences which spring from the eternal and equal value of souls in the sight of God. Acton wrote with an almost poignant modesty and practical courtesy: 'Conscience. Not to assume responsibility. Never take too much on oneself. It is not only a sense of one's responsibility to God that makes us demand liberty – but also a sense of others' responsibility. a dread of assuming that, that makes us grant it. No man is truly conscious of his own responsibility, truly fearful. who wishes to increase it'[67] and, in a way that lays the foundation for the ideal of what is perhaps more a 'sensitive' than a 'participatory' society, 'Our conscience exists and acts for ourselves. It exists in each of us. It is limited by the conscience of others. It is enough for oneself not for another. It respects the consciences of others. Therefore it tends to restrict authority and to enlarge liberty. It is the law of self-government.'[68]

The influence of Vinet keeps returning. Acton copies a long quotation from which he analyses in more detail the contrast between the conscience-related and society-related life of the individual: 'La société se compose seulement de ce que les hommes peuvent mettre en commun entre eux, des éléments identiques de leur nature ... un élément dans l'homme qui est strictement individuel, qui n'est point identique dans tous, qui, par consequent, ne saurait entrer dans le fonds commun, bien plus, dont le propre but est de ne point appartenir à l'individu lui-même, de ne point relever de sa volonté, mais de la verité seulement et de Dieu, et qui, par conséquent, ne saurait absolument être aliénée, se soumettre, se sacrifier à la communauté, sans renoncer à sa nature essentielle; c'est la conscience. L'état, c'est donc, si l'on veut, l'homme moins la conscience. Mais la conscience, c'est l'élément de la personnalité morale, c'est l'essence de l'homme, l'homme même.'[69] It is surely out of this pattern of thinking, which Acton called the 'culmination of the whole modern theory of conscience',[70] that he labelled Vinet in 1880 with the word 'Individualism'.[71]

We may well judge that Vinet's psychology and sociology were inadequate, or at least that the qualitative distinction he attempted to draw between the life of the conscience, or of the self-conscious moral personality, and social relationships was excessively sharp. But this is the tradition which Acton chooses as his standing ground, and his springboard. He wrote that 'Liberalism grew out of Religion, and Religion is its best safeguard. – See Vinet',[72] and in a card of the 1890s: 'Individualism or, as I would rather call it, the supremacy of the individual conscience.'[73] This gives a particular dynamic to his repeated assertion that the 'reign of conscience' is how he would choose to define liberty.

Conscience the fruit of mature culture

Perhaps because of his hypothesis that liberty is the aim of progress, Acton was extremely tentative about any expectation that it might be widely observable in the world as it was. He wrote, 'At certain times Liberalism makes no progress, because society is absorbed in those things which precede Lib[erty] and enable it to exist. Religion. Social Condition. Conquest',[74] and 'Liberty implies many other things – Depends on many conditions. When we say that it is the aim of Progress – and essence – we mean that it is the result of other things. It cannot be separated from the things it depends on. There must be independence, culture, prosperity, literature, religion, a healthy public opinion – powerful – a high standard of morality – a long historical training. That is why so many elements contributed.'[75] There were not only these physical and structural conditions to be satisfied; he began his Bridgnorth lectures in 1877 with the elegantly phrased proposition that, 'Liberty is the delicate fruit of a mature civilisation' and went on, 'At all times sincere friends of freedom have been rare, and its triumphs have been due to minorities, that have prevailed by associating themselves with auxiliaries whose objects often differed from their own.'[76]

Thus, it was a rare and recent – perhaps accidental and fortunate – event to come across an achieved liberal state. Like the Greeks, Acton feared that any good society might not survive for long. These 'auxiliaries' of whom he spoke (and perhaps he might have thought of George Eliot and her agnostic colleagues) could also be actively destructive.[77]

Although Acton wrote of liberty depending on religion, or on the social condition having reached a certain level, the theme to which he recurs most frequently is the dependence of liberty on a general level of individual morality. 'How moral defects lead to the loss of liberty. So we say that it flourishes jointly with conscience. Decay of the one brings decay of the other. Democracy undermines conscience by making men prefer what others think

65

best to what they think best themselves. So it demoralizes like excess of authority. It relieves men from the sense of responsibility and the duty of effort.'[78] When Acton, in his Inaugural, was detailing the conditions of liberty,[79] the notes which he selected are concerned with individual virtue. He quoted from Ihering and Butler: 'It is well known that Freedom is not a gift of the gods, but a good that every people must owe to itself, and whose quality is proportionate to its moral strength and merit', and 'Liberty, in the very nature of it, absolutely requires — that people be able to govern themselves in those respects in which they are free; otherwise their wickedness will be in proportion to their liberty, and this greatest of blessings will become a curse.'[80] He quoted Benjamin Franklin, 'Only a virtuous people is capable of freedom.'[81] Similarly, in his own notes: 'Keep liberty as close as possible to morality',[82] and 'Liberty depends on so many things besides laws – civilization, morality, knowledge. that the question is, what a country will bear.'[83] It is clear that Acton was unwilling to extend liberty to those from whom an adult response could not be expected.

In the training stage of human development, therefore, liberty could only be partial and conditional. Acton stated that the criminal law and the prison system first need to be made 'scientific'.[84] 'Public opinion' is the heading of a card that runs, 'No public conscience as long as laws are at variance with Morality.'[85] Again, and significantly in the George Eliot box, 'A class unable to act against its own interest for the sake of ideas [is] unfit for political power: as a juror unable to act against his own class or party is unfit to be a juror.'[86] If a society was at a stage of cultural immaturity, Acton could see – at least in his earlier years – its conquest by a higher civilisation as a beneficent process.[87] Only a very remarkable society was equipped to sustain a fully fledged Liberal state, though it was possible for associations of like-minded persons, e.g. a religious community, to constitute themselves in a form that anticipated it. This ideal, however, was the goal toward which Acton believed all societies ought to strive: 'There may be a denial of free trade, on a lower stage. So also of liberty in general. But we take the normal, complete, mature condition. The theory of Liberty is the summit, the supreme law.'[88]

Acton believed that this 'mature condition' of political society had only come into existence in the generation after the American Revolution, to be adopted in due course by the rest of the world as the nations came to realise the preconditions of virtue and prosperity. This does not seem a strange notion in 20th-century western societies, but it may be quite mistaken. It is certainly not 'in the nature of things'. If it were to happen it would require purposeful political stimulation, of the kind which international communism first preached in Acton's generation, and still teaches.

It is hard to exaggerate the importance of Fénelon for Döllinger and the Munich circle. His letters were first published in 1828, and together with the sketch of an ideal – but not self-consciously Christian – state which he provides in *Télémaque*, they seemed to offer a basis for the behaviour of the renovated, 'ideal', Catholicism of that generation. Acton contended that Fénelon was the direct spiritual ancestor of Rousseau, and thus of the American and French revolutions. He said of him, 'He does not resign the hope of making men good by act of parliament, and his belief in public institutions as a means of moulding individual character brings him nearly into touch with a distant future. He is the Platonic founder of revolutionary thinking.'[89]

If we are to take 'Platonic' seriously, it was in the context of avoiding change that Acton recommended revolution. It would be of a kind that laid down the foundations of a form of government which would be just, and therefore natural and stable. Acton wrote, 'The object of revolution is the prevention of revolution. It supplies a security against the use of violence. Absolute government can only be checked by force. Revolutionary government has a pacific redress.'[90] A 'revolutionary government' in this sense is open, where reason and conscience enjoy free play within consitutional structures for change. He spoke of 'what makes governments legitimate and averts revolution'.[91] It was a thoroughly ideological programme: 'Politics ideal. That is, endeavours to realise ideas – doctrine of right. Not to make the best of what is the reality. This is revolution. Not the good of the majority. Not material aims, arising from the facts.'[92]

When Acton recounted the doctrines of the 18th-century economists in his first lecture on the French Revolution, it was a confession of his own belief. As an undergraduate lecture, it must have been almost unintelligibly compressed. He said, 'Political truths can be made so evident that the opinion of an instructed public will be invincible, and will banish the abuse of power. To resist oppression is to make a league with heaven, and all things are oppressive that resist the natural order of freedom. For society secures rights: it neither bestows nor restricts them. They are the direct consequence of duties. As truth can only convince by the exposure of errors and the defeat of objections, liberty is the essential guard of truth. Society is founded, not on the will of man, but on the nature of man and the will of God: and conformity to the divinely appointed order is followed by inevitable reward.'[93]

Almost every clause requires exegesis. Apart from noting its translucent and biblical 'feel', this passage is important for its unequivocal assertion of human rights – admittedly in a particular form – as the basis of political science. God exists, and he requires a response from every man and woman capable of it. That is the over-riding reality of human life on earth. Social and political organisation is subordinate to it; and only has value in so far as it recognises, protects, and encourages this response, which may be termed duty, or obedience, or vocation, or simply a very this-worldly holiness.

The duty of revolution

The perception of this 'divinely appointed order' was the aim of political science. It must result in an upheaval of the kind we call 'revolution'. Acton's sense of the word, though, is perhaps better conveyed by 'conversion'. Its central thought was reorientation as much as restructuring. It certainly involved the renunciation of self-interest. He wrote, 'Copernicus – order, harmony, simplicity. It is the beginning of Revolution. That is, reducing complicated ideas to simple and general ones.'[94] For Acton, this simple and general formula, such as Newton's concept of gravity, was based on 'conscience'.

It was Acton's contention that the principle of a revolution in order to safeguard a normative *status quo* was a medieval invention. It was on the principle of Magna Carta. The function of a good king was to live within his own rights and protect the rights of his subjects and of the church. In defence of this, 'The right of insurrection was not only admitted, but defined as a duty sanctioned by religion,'[95] and 'The medieval theory arrived at this – that the man who stood in the way of true freedom was a culprit worthy of death. that freedom was an object to be attained by bloodshed.'[96] But, 'That it becomes a religious duty to overthrow an unjust ruler, but never to murder him – was the thing required – but never distinguished.'[97] Acton saw this adoption of a theory of resistance, and the consequent liberation from the spirit of the early church, as the teleological *raison d'être* of the otherwise abominable involvement of the medieval church in the exercise of temporal power.

Acton believed the state should be made the instrument of religious morality and that this was an idea derived peculiarly from the 'liberty' of the church in medieval Europe. He wrote, 'The pagan state determines its own purposes and power. Christianity determines them independently of the state. It fixes the lines and aims for itself. The state submits and accepts them. It is no longer a law to itself, nor assigns its own powers. The state recognizes an authority above its own.'[98] 'Christianity' is thus a sleeping watch-dog. When it is passive, it is to be so from contentment rather than from principle. The fact that Acton chose to use 'Christianity' rather than 'Church' as the subject of this meta-political role is interesting. His tradition if not common experience would have alerted him to the need for an institution to carry out a role of this kind, but in his own generation it had perhaps become clear that one church could not carry such responsibility. In the religiously pluriform modern world the problem is more acute.

Many cards show how eager Acton was to reject the tradition of holiness as passive obedience. He wrote, 'Man owes it to his children, to his neighbours to secure their future and rescue their lives from impediments to holiness and happiness. Therefore he has no right to acquiesce in tyrannical or immoral government. Passive obedience not enough.'[99] Acton does not explore the question of *how* immoral a government must be, or the conventions by which resistance might be licensed and organised. His thinking at this time is anchored in the War of American Independence.

Similar ideas recur in a notebook dated February 1878, under the heading, 'All men responsible for the state'. It begins: 'Aristotle introduced the idea of free-will and responsibility, denied by Socrates and Plato. As long as that was unknown [Acton probably means until St Thomas], there was no basis for liberty. It was no hardship to obey, under the vicarious responsibility of the State. Fundamental idea: At first, the State is responsible – determines right and wrong, and commands actions, and regulates worship and prayer. At the other end of the process of history, everyman is responsible for himself: and also for the state. It is not enough to disobey, to resist passively, for the state may still do great evil to others. Not enough to feel safe. You must make others safe. When you have this power, and use it, you possess freedom.'[100]

It is clear that in this argument for the ordinary citizen's responsibility for humanity Acton did not have Döllinger's support: 'Men like Washington and Wilberforce he could admire without stint or question; but he looked for something more sordid than duty in the motives that direct a policy and make men act together.'[101] Acton's argument has had considerable attraction for many theologians of the World Council of Churches and for Roman Catholics since the Second Vatican Council. But it is also an argument that can easily be in tension with the sense of awe and humility at being responsible for another person, which, as we saw above, was part of Acton's commitment to individualism.

It is easy to exaggerate Acton's practical commitment to make the whole world safe for liberalism, if necessary by force; but such a disposition was certainly present in his far from simple mind, and he perceived it as in tension with the example of the early church. Acton took his distrust of New Testament methods to a high pitch. He spoke of the Jewish Zealots as 'a party of political patriots, the zealous liberals, [who] were the men who murdered Christ. Hence the strong feeling among early Christians, the desire not to be confounded with these. This long prevailed, being set in the NT.'[102] Again in February 1878 he wrote in two notebooks about the work of Christ, 'My definition [of liberty] – Liberty secures us against the state. Else Our Lord was rightly put to death. Liberty is the doctrine which denies the rightfulness of his death, and would have prevented it',[103] and in the other, 'Christianity. Revolutionary element. It overthrew very ancient authorities. It destroyed the theory that a power must be obeyed because of its antiquity, of its beneficence, of the greatness it has assisted, of the divine sanction it has enjoyed. It taught men to enquire, not of their country, but of themselves. It required them to believe that they had lived and prospered for thousands of years under an imposture. that their people had grown great, had conquered its enemies, under the protection of wickedness – that all their prayers, their sacrifices, their heroic deeds, had been offered up to an unclean spirit.'[104]

The implications of these are far-reaching. The Cross became an avoidable disaster; and if Christianity thus 'required' the Old Testament past to be thought of as alien and 'unclean', how much more must not the non-Christian world after his death be thought of as unclean too? And in that case, perhaps its rights of conscience were weakened.

It is possible that Acton's view of the role of Christ can be illuminated by the analogy of an academic journal. Such a journal must be kept a neutral stage: it must be available to everyone who qualifies for admission to its pages, and opposition to the notion of such a journal cannot be, as Acton would say, sincere, or properly scientific. Secondly, this journal will occasionally carry articles which revolutionise their whole field of study. These articles, although they appear strange and unwelcome, have a right to be published in complete safety. Their value will be judged, as, in the course of time, they are compared with the preceding corpus of thought on that subject, and perhaps shown to be a more satisfactory working hypothesis by professionals in the field. Thirdly, there will be some who do not test this newer and more satisfactory hypothesis. These men will be living 'on a lower level', and it is by no means incumbent on the editors of this journal to allow them space to ventilate their outmoded opinions.

The Liberal State is the journal: Christ's proclamation of the reign of conscience in the new covenant the revolutionary interpretation of the purpose of God. The prejudiced contributors are those who will not budge from the securities of local traditions and conventional power and prestige – the Tories in church and state.

To fit Christianity into this particular scheme of a growth into Truth by means of new perceptions is difficult to reconcile with credal orthodoxy. Christ must be considered as primarily a teacher, a bearer of the Word of God, whose death – even if followed by resurrexion – is a misfortune rather than the normative act of self-revelation by God in the history of the universe he created. As Acton acknowledges that Christianity first 'taught men to enquire, not of their country, but of themselves', and therefore of their reason-in-conscience-in-Spirit, the analogy supposes that the journal's scientific character derives from this particular revolutionary article. The liberal framework becomes a Christian gift. For this 'scientific' framework is an expression at several removes of a faith tradition that in other contexts is perceived as aggressively partisan. Maybe therefore it depends on that faith tradition having gained power. If Christ was to be saved from Calvary, it would only be by men whose hearts have been moved by the tradition deriving from Calvary.

Thus, Acton, in spite of his insistence on the factual, historical character of the life of Christ, was nonetheless led by his emphasis on rational 'knowing' rather than 'willing' to underestimate the significance in Christianity of the crucifixion both as an act of God, and as a pattern for the continuing life of the faithful 'taking up their cross daily'. While Acton was more Hebrew than normal in his view of history, in its linear and

71

this-worldly teleology, he was more Greek than normal in his identification of God with Reason. When the Kingdom of Heaven is promised as to be experienced in this life, Acton understands it not so much as a relationship with God as an inclusive society in which men can share in this world. It is a situation of *shalom* where the relation of man to God, to nature, and to his neighbour is harmonious, just, and above all, demonstrably reasonable. In so far then, as men introduce reason into their life together, they introduce the Kingdom of Heaven. When the Quakers created a state for conscientious and reasonable men in Pennsylvania – admittedly in peculiarly fortunate circumstances – they could be thought of as bringing into existence, and at the same time discovering, part of the promised universal Kingdom.

In this context, revolution can admittedly be conservative, but the vocation of the Church is not so much to witness by Christ-like suffering in its pilgrimage through the wilderness of a fallen world as to encourage and consolidate a converted Kingdom on earth. Good men are able to recognise these anticipations, for they 'know the law' in their consciences.

A free polity: conscience and federalism the checks on democracy

One of the most frequently recurring thoughts in Acton's work is that those who are able to see most clearly live as 'resident aliens'. He often asserted that 'pure' liberalism or conservatism (and indeed 'pure' Catholicism) is only to be found among those who live in a society where the opposite principles govern. For instance, 'a Conservative, to be worth looking at, must be a Republican'[105] and 'Conservatism in men who have no monarchy, established church, aristocracy or tradition. no army. Hamilton, J. Q. Adams, Webster: Liberalism in deeply religious men – not in a recreant abbé or a studious unbeliever, [not] Jefferson or Sieyès, but in Vinet, Rothe.'[106] Likewise, 'a Liberal must be where there is no fundamental antagonism to institutions – a royalist, a churchman, a man of property. The Liberalism of an outcast is useless – or of an unbeliever, a pauper, an uneducated man. a man with education, property, positive religion.'[107]

It is therefore not surprising that Acton should have been so sympathetic to the stream of conservative American political thought which goes back to Hamilton, to the revolutionary generation itself; and there is considerable evidence to show that, even in British politics, he at times supported the conservative, as distinct from the Tory, position. His life style, his inherited status and family network, so far as one can tell his own religious practice, were all 'naturally' conservative.

There is a card in the George Eliot box entitled 'Resistance to Democracy': 'A man could not be a conservative without being a revolutionist of the deepest dye. Resistance for the sake of duties more than rights. The theory that resisted tyranny for the sake of duties more than rights, held good against the tyrant people. The link of principle was, liberty of conscience.'[108] Other cards show that 'liberalism' as a political structure comes only second. The imperative is 'liberty of conscience': 'Most things depend on circumstances – only liberty of conscience suffers in limit or control – therefore it is the centre of all.'[109]

He defined his terms in the spectrum of political stances as follows: 'Progress without violence – Conservative. Progress with violence – Revolution. Progress with violence if necessary – Whigs. No progress – Tories.'[110] It is not clear where he places himself in this analysis from the the History of Liberty cards: 'Not absolute contradiction between liberal and conservative. It is a question of time and place and expediency. Liberals admit that men are not always ripe for freedom. Conservatives wish to preserve it, lest it be imperilled. But Whigs and Tories really mean contrary things, excluding each other. One wishes to preserve things for their own sake. The other will sacrifice every institution that does not stand the test of liberality.'[111] Thus Acton could reveal a surprising sympathy with everyone except a Tory, and Acton branded him a criminal only because he opposed the whole enterprise of intellectual and political progress. Such a man was perversely and invincibly ignorant.

The influence of the American Burke on Acton was profound, and he shared Burke's attitude to human rights: 'All human laws are, properly speaking, only declaratory; they may alter the mode and application, but have no power over the substance, of original justice. A conservation and secure enjoyment of our natural rights is the great and ultimate purpose of civil society.'[112] In the achievement of that purpose, which is normally best served by a balanced system of government, it is only this 'ultimate purpose' which can be erected into a principle. 'Burke's intolerance in 1773–91 amounts to this – don't tolerate those who would establish intolerance. It is perfectly true.'[113]

Yet there can be little doubt that Acton believed that in his own generation the Liberal party was the bearer of the right ideas, the ideas which could best secure liberty of conscience. This applied in the religious sense to Ireland, and the principle of Disestablishment; and in a more general sense it even applied to the rationalising Benthamite tradition. In a society where laws and interests were not taken as given, but had to answer the challenge of utility, Acton believed there was much more scope for the play of conscience. Men took responsibility for themselves and their future – their politics were 'intentional'.

'The power of the dead' is a constant threat. In the Cambridge lectures Acton roundly declares, 'The Whig seeks that which ought to be elsewhere than in that which is. His standing purpose is to effect change, for the past is essentially Tory.'[114] In the box labelled 'Party' are two cards: 'The permanent and universal question is whether the living shall govern or the dead; past or present; acquired rights or aspired rights; accident or design; the will of man or the will of God; morality or force' and 'The conflict between wealth and poverty is the same as that between the past and present. Defence of property is defence of past labour. Property and tradition are the elements of conservatism.'[115] He judged that where traditions of customary or common law still governed, there was an unrecognised power tending to perpetuate the authority of the past over present insights. 'Law is the instrument by which the past holds us. If embodied in a code, it becomes the expression of present will. Therefore, they (the legal conservatives – esp. Savigny) resisted Codes, in order to prolong the power of the dead.'[116]

Thus, no question of who-owns-what or of convention should be closed on account of its antiquity. If we assume a consistent progress in intellectual equipment, in moral no less than in physical science, every question can benefit from periodic re-examination, for the world-picture in which it is set is constantly changing and better techniques are continually being invented. As it was in the history of political thought that Acton saw providential progress operating most purposefully, and as he held that politics were primarily a moral enterprise, it was a duty of every man in his conscience to be quite self-conscious about his political position. If, as Acton said, souls can be won or lost in politics, self-examination in fear and trembling must precede the adoption of any course of action. To plead tradition or material interest was to reduce the moral stature of man to that of a child or an animal.

In common with the rest of his generation, Acton was brought up to regard democracy as the description of a political disease. Reared on the classical authors, they were ready to see in the reports which Lowe brought back from Australia and Tocqueville from America the corroboration of the working out of an age-old process. Bagehot, in Paris, reflected that it was only national stupidity and the arts of stage-management which preserved the deference, and hence the ancient polity, of the English people. Acton shared this sentiment to the full, and his first reaction to the American Civil War was that of a doctor watching the *dénouement* of a known and inexorable disease.[117]

In the late 1870s however, his association with Gladstone working upon the earlier influence of Lamennais and Newman,[118] Acton came to attribute a quality of judgment to the people in the mass which made their participation in government a source of health. A very important entry in the notebook dated February 1878 runs, 'Gladstone now says the people are generally right against the upper class.'[119] Tennyson's poem, *Locksley Hall*, illustrates how the contemporary understanding of progress involved a more and more democratic society. Acton found himself forced to modify his conception of democracy as an evil in itself. He never ceased to be aware of the dangers of democracy, but he came to see its possible benefits.

Acton was the disciple of Burke, Vinet, and de Tocqueville. All of these had been apprehensive of democracy. Tocqueville was, according to the Acton of the 1890s, 'a Liberal of the purest breed — deeply suspicious of democracy and its kindred, equality, centralisation and utilitarianism'.[120] Vinet had said, 'Les Barbares viennent, pas du Nord, mais de dessous nos pieds,' and 'Le libéralisme est en décadence pour le moment dans toute le Suisse. Le radicalisme, son contraire et non son excès, l'a chassé de partout.'[121]

Acton, himself, in his first Bridgnorth lecture on Freedom, had spoken of Athenian democracy as one of the main hurdles which liberty had had to surmount. In the context of the decay which attends the 'possession of unlimited power ... there is a reserve of latent power in the masses which, if it is called into play, the minority can seldom resist. But from the absolute will of an entire people there is no appeal, no redemption, no refuge, but treason.'[122] This was where, he said, 'if I may enjoy an expressive anachronism, the vice of the classic state was that it was Church and State in one. Morality was undistinguished from religion, and politics from morals.'[123]

In this situation, Acton saw only two factors sufficiently powerful to provide leverage against centralising state power or against populism. They were conscience and federalism. He wrote, 'Democratic theory really against [the Liberal] Revolution. It tries to bring out into power the common will of all – to make that the source and test of power. Against that, there are no rights, no appeal – apart from it. But we affirm that there is another source of rights, to be defended against it.'[124] In the question of revolutionary resistance to a mass tyranny, the plots against Hitler which culminated in the attempt at his murder on 20 July 1944 are exemplary. In the writings which survive, it is clear that conscience was intended to be the watch-word of the post-Nazi German state which might follow, and that it would be organised on federal principles in order to give effect to this.

These two safeguards were necessary to each other. Federalism provides the frame which gives the possibility of checks and balance to power, and provides units of government small enough for the individual conscience to play an effective part. Conscience is the only ground of action whose rhetoric can be rooted outside the society, and which in its nature is able to draw upon the irreconcilable energies of the individual. It is therefore the spring and platform of resistance.

In his lecture on the French Revolution, Acton said, 'The true natural check on absolute democracy is the federal system,'[125] and spoke of 'the Republic one and indivisible' (that is, not federal) as being the 'most rigorous and sterile' of political forms.[126] It was partly for this reason that Acton opposed so strongly and for such a long time the position of the Northern states in the American Civil War. He thought that it was an expression of the incessant forces which worked in an egalitarian society toward the centralisation of power.[127]

The resistance to this process required the strength that only conscience could give. In a notebook of 1879 Acton discussed this relation between opinion and conscience. Having distinguished between government by force and government by opinion, and rejected the former, Acton seeks the limits of opinion. He writes, 'How as to religion? That cannot be subject. The state may decide how property is held or distributed, etc. But it cannot force me to do what I deem a sin – to curse God etc. For that, Religion or Conscience is the thing that cannot be changed or overcome. Absolutist – Democrat – goes as far as that. that is the great American security.'[128]

In his lectures on the French Revolution, Acton discussed the danger that liberty of consience might become only 'liberty of opinion',[129] and that therefore without God it became unsatisfactory as a 'scientific' meeting place for securing the liberal state. Reflecting on this in the 1880s, he writes, 'Kant says the right of resistance is a sin against logic. Apply this to Dem[ocracy]. No breach of contract. No disobedience to law; for it makes the law. So the old argument failed. — Who shall reverse the judgment of the Court of appeal? L[iberty] of C[onscience] basis of all liberty, in constant collision w[ith] the Democracy.'[130] Slightly earlier, he had written, 'Free will the basis of liberty. — In the middle ages there was generally unity of religion. The greatest incentive to freedom was wanting. Contending interests, opposing fores – but the strongest of all intellects and forces, the conscience, did not resist the state.'[131]

So it is clear that Acton was coming to demand a state that was set over a variety of actively religious groups, and that he was thinking of conscience as the primary source of political resistance. It is by canalising the power of conscience into ecclesiastical organisations that powers are erected within society, which are in their nature able to resist the state because their citizenship is elsewhere. The intense interest in the American Constitution, with its combination of these safeguards, which Acton developed at exactly the time he was following up his thinking toward the sovereignty of conscience, was of crucial importance for the way in which that thinking developed. The characteristic shape of Acton's system was forged out of the elements he assembled for his Bridgnorth lectures on the History of Freedom in 1877. As it became articulate, it produced the break with Döllinger, the awareness they no longer shared the same values, that dominated Acton's consciousness for at least five years. The isolation and anguish of that period were the furnace in which he felt himself forced to rethink and establish the whole range of his thinking. It was after this that his reading became more English.

Acton's thought about the actual practice of democracy was, however, largely formulated in company with Gladstone. They came to believe both in the 'uncorrupted conscience of the masses' and in the duty of the statesman to follow *his* prophetic conscience when it conflicted with that of the same masses. These principles were both consciously taken from an analogy with the Old Testament Jews. In 1878 Acton wrote of ancient Israel, 'The monarchy itself was limited by the same absence of a legislative power, by the submission of the king to the law that bound his subjects, by the perpetual appeal of prophets to the conscience of the people as its appointed guardian, and by the ready resource of deposition.'[132]

77

Gladstone used the analogy of a court of justice and a jury for parliamentary elections. He believed in the universality of a moral faculty to which the politician could appeal the more purely, the wider was the composition of the court. At the beginning of the century, Thomas Jefferson had said, 'Independence can be trusted nowhere but with the people in the mass. They are absolutely independent of all but moral law.'[133]

Acton was cautious in following. A jury is only allowed to say 'yes' or 'no', and Acton approached the electorate in exactly the same limited, technical and authoritative manner.[134] He was always quite clear that a representative should never be a delegate. He wrote, 'Doctrine of clearness necessary for popular action. Masses only understand what is quite clear. If they are to decide, things must be made clear – and only such things submitted to them. Hence, limitation of the Whig doctrines. Science goes on clearing things up. The domain of certainty extends – and of evidence.'[135] And, more sharply, 'American idea that we must wait for a wind. Easily leads to believe that the people must be obeyed —. The truth is that we must absolutely disregard, and resist, popular convictions opposed to our own. The seat of conscience is within.'[136]

In general, Acton intended his theory of conscience to work in a way quite unsympathetic to modern democracy. This was cloaked during his lifetime by the fact that Acton approved of Gladstone's approach to politics, as they both approved of America, and both of these objects of approval were regarded by their enemies as democratic.

Like Henry Adams, Acton was an intellectual brahmin in a democratic world. His conception of conscience lost a great part of its meaning when it was detached from a background of scholarship and the conventions of civilisation. It was perhaps only from over the distance of the Atlantic that Acton could ever have appreciated the ideal virtues of a society and constitution that was founded on the sovereignty of the democratic conscience. At home in Europe, living in a cosmopolitan and established milieu, Acton was in himself rather more paternalistic than libertarian. His sympathy for socialism, for instance, was expressed very much under the influence of the German *Kathedersozialisten*, especially Roscher. He wished to use the idea of the conscience as political absolute as much to restrain state power as to give the freedoms of existential morality to the newly industrialised masses.

Acton was accustomed to say himself that his ideas were of an earlier generation. Döllinger, Macaulay, Gladstone, Ranke, Bancroft, and Newman – the most potent of those who influenced Acton – all passed their formative years between 1810 and 1830. It was from this period that Acton's characteristic enthusiasms spring. Partly through his unorthodox education, Acton never found himself in a group of his own generation. His intimates were either older or younger than himself, and it is a consequence of this that he served as a link between the first and second period of Kantian thinking in Europe.

Many of the cards can be brought to support this interpretation. For instance, 'Liberty – independent judgment. But that comes with education. The lower you go, the less people are able to form opinions, the less individual value belongs to them, the more they follow in the ruck',[137] and 'The great purpose of civilization, the upward progress of mankind, only to be got by the predominance of moral and intellectual superiority – not by average opinion – not by the judgment of the uninstructed. By a process of sifting, competition etc., they bring the best men to the top. — just as the best doctors at the hospital, the best scholars at the Univ[ersity].'[138]

Acton concluded that it was impossible to purify public opinion in a democracy of 'prejudice', the reign of men on a 'lower level', the 'reign of the past'.[139] 'Public opinion can never be so finely trained as to follow ideas and not things or persons.'[140] 'Men who lead, the flower of a nation, set by complex motives. The people judges by simple ones. Its notion of character is poor.'[141] 'Prejudices have their *raison d'être* that people are unconscious of. They are the nearest approach to reason of people incapable of it. The fortification of authority. Reasoning divides, where prejudice unites.'[142]

It does not appear, therefore, that either as a Liberal or as an advocate of the claims of government by 'right reason', Acton was starry-eyed about modern democracy. He was prepared to submit to it, however, and in so far as he did, he followed Gladstone. Together they were influenced by American developments.

5
Conscience in America: the Holy Experiment

In the years around 1880 Acton came to believe that 'scientific' answers to the old problem of church and state had been found and made explicit in the 'conservative revolution' that marked the birth of the United States. His Cambridge *Lectures on Modern History*, the shape of his mature thought, begin with the formulation of a political idea of conscience in Aquinas, and conclude with the achieved majesty of the Federal Liberal State in America. It is abundantly clear in Acton's notes and correspondence that the example of American politics was every bit as attractive for him as it had been for Raynal in the 18th-century Enlightenment, and as ultimately meaningful to him in terms of Providence as it was among 19th-century American idealists. For instance John Nevin at Mercersburg, Pa. (with whom Döllinger corresponded) wrote in 1867, 'Here now [i.e. in America] it would seriously seem, are to be settled and solved the great questions — the mystery of the last days, the ominous approximations of the present order of the world to its full winding up in the second coming of Christ.'[1]

This is important in three ways. First, it provides us with a workshop case of how Acton interpreted his leading ideas in the practical manifestation of history. Nowhere are the 'scientific revolution' and the 'federal safeguard' – two of Acton's leading ideas – asserted more clearly, and shown at the same time to be derived from the basic postulate of conscience.

Second, this exemplification of the clear connection between the 'theology' of Acton's 'Whig Church' and the interpretation of history which resulted from it can be used as a criterion. If Acton's picture of American history has to be dismissed as without any substance,[2] we dismiss the historical basis of such a central element in Acton's whole *Weltanschauung* that it cannot be a plausible option.

Third, Acton came to hold his characteristic views about American history only in his mid-forties. The change was rapid and fundamental, and indicates a shift in Acton's ideological standpoint. This can be correlated with particular influences. The traditional assumption that Acton's views were substantially the same throughout his adult life can no longer be maintained.

A survey of Acton's writing about America up to the mid 70s[3] shows only slight development. While the memory of his only visit there in 1853 was still fresh, he was far from 'the unwavering sympathy and admiration' of which Lady Blenner-hassett spoke at his death.[4] What had struck him as surprising when he attended the debates at the Boston State House on the revision of the 1780 Constitution of Massachusetts was the attention paid to mere abstract principle. This remained in his mind. In striking contradiction to his later view of freedom stemming directly down from the American sect-states, he wrote in 1861 of an 'intolerance and religious tyranny — equalled only among the Puritans in America.'[5]

He wrote to Simpson, 'Their state is absolute, their sovereign-[ty?] despotic, and irresistible. There is no immunity, no exemption from supreme control, no corner of the pie in which the state has not got a finger. All this is the clear opposite of our ideas of independence, jealousy of interference, of certain spheres and relations of life being beyond public inquiry. Not so much afraid of control as eager to exercise it.'[6] Even in relation to Tocqueville, and to his views on the future of the Catholic church in America, he remained passionately suspicious of American politics: 'observe that America has not solved the problem of reconciling democracy with freedom, for it has not reconciled power with law – or will with duty, which is the moral aspect of the same thing'.[7]

When the Civil War broke out, Acton saw no special import-ance in the question of slavery, and everything in the preserva-tion of States Rights. These were the last defence against democracy, and their disappearance would make crystal-clear the insubstantiality of a democratic constitution. It was at this point then, when America began to offer a laboratory exposition of the principles of Greek political science, that Acton's interest became focused on American history.[8] In 1866, Acton said, 'The North has used the doctrines of Democracy to destroy self-government. The South applied the principle of conditional federation to cure the evils and correct the errors of a false interpretation of Democracy.'[9] Lady Blennerhasset wondered why he had become so overexcited.[10] He reviewed a biography of Hamilton in 1864: 'Time has shown that there was no security against the arbitrary force of the people's will; and the regulation of the central and the local jurisdiction, the delicate problem of federal government, ultimately failed.'[11]

What is so interesting about his attitude to what he deemed the incompatibility of democracy and federalism at this time is the regretful tone in which it is expressed. 'If America could give the light without the shade of political life, then I believe that the venerable insitutions of European polity would go down before that invincible argument',[12] and, to the people of Bridgnorth in 1866, 'the spurious liberty of the United States is twice cursed, for it deceives those whom it attracts and those whom it repels.'[13]

His opinion advanced swiftly on the ethics of slavery. In 1862, Acton 'readily' subscribed to the idea that 'All history teaches us that no people has ever been retained in bondage if they were fit for freedom.'[14] In 1863, he wrote, 'It is the duty of the Americans to legislate for the real welfare of the Negro, not simply for the relief of their own eccentric consciences.'[15] But by 1866 he wrote, 'All those laws which are anterior to all human legislation were held inapplicable to the negro family .... In almost every nation and every clime the time has come for the extinction of servitude.'[16] That advance could only lead to their liberation becoming a moral duty, and thus equal in moral value to the revolutionary grandeur of the South.

However, at this period, there is no doubt that Acton believed the American Constitution had failed in the failure of the southern confederation. An aspect of the matter which acquires significance in the light of Acton's later attitude is that this was a revolution, and that Acton thought it a legitimate extension of the principles of the original War of Independence. He wrote in 1864, 'The act of the Southern States would have appeared to him [Hamilton], not a constitutional measure, but a legitimate revolution, crowning that great enterprise in which he bore a part.'[17]

Gladstone originally shared this view, and it was his admiration of Acton's article on America that began their long friendship. He invited Acton to breakfast in May 1861. But Gladstone suffered a characteristically rapid conversion from his early sympathy for the South after Lincoln's Gettysburg address. His influence worked therefore to modify Acton's over-hasty burial of American federalism. Another factor which helped to make American politics more acceptable to Acton was the behaviour of the North American bishops at the Vatican Council. Archbishop Peter Kenrick of St Louis and Bishop Connolly of Halifax were among the most reliable anti-Infallibilists, and Acton's admiration for Chéverus, the first Catholic bishop of

Boston, dated from the respect in which he had been held by Döllinger's circle at Munich. Acton reported from the Council, 'One of the American bishops lately said, "Nobody should be elected Pope who has not lived three years in the United States, and thus learnt to comprehend what is possible at this day in a freely governed Commonwealth."'[18]

We shall have to deal with Acton's treatment of America under two heads, for it is quite plain that his views did not develop with equal rapidity and force. It was only with the review of Bryce's *American Commonwealth* in 1889, that both the revolutionary and constitutional logic of the American example were shown as springing from the same doctrine of conscience. We shall analyse how Acton thought of the American Revolution as representing the first conscious activity of scientific liberalism, and then turn to the development of Acton's views about the mechanics of the American Constitution.

Acton's view of America formed 1877–82

But first it is necessary to attempt to substantiate the claim that the five years after the Bridgnorth lectures in 1877 were when his views on the centrality of America crystallised. In 1866 the American example was dangerous to other states because it was seductive, it offered attractions that could not be sustained. In 1889 it was dangerous because it was *right*; it had become a universalist quasi-religious moral proposition. The turning point came around 1878 – when the great multi-volume History of Liberty was still a practical possibility.

For the three years between 1877 and 1880 there are a considerable number of notebooks, essays, and notes which can be dated. This is particularly fortunate if it is in this period that the critical shift of emphasis took place. In spite of this comparative richness, such an interpretation depends for its full weight on three documents of which it can only be said that there is a high probability that they were written in 1877–8. In order of importance, these are Add. MS 5602 (a notebook), Add. MS 4895 (a box labelled *America*), and Add. MS 5392 (a box labelled *Christianity*).

It is probable that Add. MS 5602 was written in the winter and spring of 1877. It contains a reference to Creighton's *Montfort*, which was published in 1876, and which we know Acton read after October of that year.[19] On the other hand, it contains no reference to the Quakers. After 1878 Acton normally substituted the Quakers for the Independents in his picture of what he came to say with increasing emphasis was – for him – the central theme of history. While this cannot be conclusive evidence, there is so much parallelism with the ideas expressed and with the phraseology used in work which is known to be of this time that we may at least use this dating for our hypothesis.

Add. MS 4895 is a box of cards, and presents the perennial problem of how far Acton's boxes were composed of cards written or transcribed at the same time. Several cards exist in this box which are dated 1877, and they are written on the same type of card and adjacent to those which we wish to use. One of these cards runs, 'America 1821. Here I ought to stop, but – It grew richer, stronger, more educated. Freed its slaves .... But lost ground as to liberty. N.B. Republic not so enduring as Monarchy. So come over to Europe, trying to get permanence by monarchy.' This is clearly in preparation for a lecture, and probably lies behind the conclusion of his Bridgnorth lecture of May 1877. Other cards rephrase passages from these lectures and the Erskine May review. However, where this box is of most importance is in the question of Bancroft's influence.

Pennsylvania the crisis of world history

George Bancroft was one of the first Americans to travel and be educated in Europe after the Revolution. He studied in Germany in the 1820s under Eichorn and Schleiermacher and, on his return to New England, became a Jacksonian Democrat and an ardent disciple of the eclectic transcendentalism of the French philosopher Victor Cousin. Acton once described Cousin's Eclecticism as analogous to 'Catholic development'.[20] Schlesinger describes Bancroft as 'carrying out the same revolt against the dead hand of John Locke in politics, which the transcendentalists were carrying on in religion',[21] and quotes him as saying, 'The cause of democracy is the cause of true religion not less than of justice; it is the cause of practical Christianity.' The resemblance to Acton's 'Whig church' standpoint is clear. It is interesting to note that Bancroft's contemporary, Orestes A. Brownson, with whom he shared his admiration for Cousin, was visited by Acton on his American journey in 1853, and that they subsequently corresponded with each other as fellow editors of Catholic periodicals.[22]

Bancroft's unusual enthusiasm for the influence of the Quakers is generally recognised. It appears from a letter to Emerson that, even in 1836, Bancroft was seeing Penn's liberalism as the true antithesis to that of Locke. This distinction was taken over by Acton and identified with the liberalism of 'conscience' and of 'property' respectively.[23] Schlesinger says, 'In his brilliant chapter on the Quakers ... Bancroft set forth in luminous prose his conception of the relations between the liberation of the soul of man and his body.' A characteristic passage from this chapter runs: 'The rise of the people called Quakers is one of the memorable events in the history of man. It marks the moment when intellectual freedom was claimed unconditionally by the people as an inalienable birthright. To the masses of that age all reflection on politics and morals presented itself under a theological form. The Quaker doctrine is philosophy summoned from the cloister, the college and the saloon, and planted among the most despised of the people.'[24] In his review of Erskine May in January 1878 Acton wrote, 'it was through Franklin and the Quaker State that America influenced political opinion in Europe, and that the fanaticism of one revolutionary epoch (i.e. the 17th century) was converted into the rationalism of another'.[25] This is the first mention of the Quakers by Acton known to me. After this time, the references are continuous and central.

There are two equally important books of Bancroft's in the Acton Library. The *History of the American Revolution* (1852) is marked by clippings from the *Times* of 1878, and the *History of the United States* (London, 1849)[26] is marked by clippings from *The Times* of August 1887, where the chapter entitled 'The People Called Quakers' is almost continuously marked and lined. Many of these lined passages are transcribed in Add. MS 4895, with Acton's comments upon them. And there is a continuous thread of argument through the box in which these comments find a natural, and apparently seminal, position.

There are therefore two alternatives. Either Acton read and transcribed this chapter in 1878, and then inserted fresh markers in 1887, or he read it first in 1887, when he had already been led to ascribe a special importance to the Quakers through other sources. It is known for instance that the Quakers entered Acton's discussion with George Eliot about a scientific morality. The first alternative depends upon the assumptions that Add. MS 4895 forms a sequence of cards from a limited time period[27]; that the first references to the Quakers in the Erskine May essay are inspired by Bancroft; and that Acton could not have derived the specifically historical emphasis of his treatment of the Quakers in that essay from conversations of the type he had with George Eliot.[28] If we adopt it, it produces an alignment of Acton's development which is circumstancially convincing and throws Acton's thought in these three years into a dramatic pattern.

We have suggested that Acton placed the Quaker contribution to political science which he derived directly from Bancroft at the turning-point of what he termed his 'central theme'. What was this process, this 'theme'? He said in in his Inaugural Lecture in 1895, 'It became a boast that religion was the mother of freedom, that freedom was the lawful offspring of religion .... Beginning with the strongest religious movement and the most refined despotism ever known, it has led to the superiority of politics over divinity in the life of nations, and terminates in the equal claim of every man to be unhindered by man in the fulfilment of duty to God[29] – a doctrine laden with storm and havoc, which is the secret essence of the Rights of Man, and the indestructible soul of Revolution.'[30]

Acton saw the Quakers of Pennsylvania as the 'elect' group which revealed the true nature of Christianity as it developed its own implications and became the philosophy of a Liberal State. Drawing their energy from the Protestant Reformation, which Acton had been trained to consider tyranny, they provided the soil in which the doctrines of the American Revolution took root. Conscience was the crux of their contribution. Bancroft had been concerned to show that Pennsylvania was a direct product of the Quaker notion of conscience, that the idea of conscience is the key to democracy and progress, and that it was the Quakers who first made political rights universal to men as men. He asked whether Penn would follow Locke in making his constitution. 'To Locke, "Conscience is nothing else than our own opinion of our own actions", to Penn it is the image of God, and his oracle in the soul .... And now that the men who had gone about to turn the world upside down, were possessed of a province, what system of politics would they adopt? ... 1677, fundamental laws of W. New Jersey.'[31] Acton transcribed this, commenting, 'they made a constitution for it on the basis of the will of equal people. No privilege, no oppression, no slavery, no intolerance.'[32] And again from Bancroft, which is lined by Acton, 'To take away the great charter of freedom of conscience is to prevent the progress of society; or rather, as the beneficent course of Providence cannot be checked, it is in men of the present generation but knotting a whipcord to lash their own posterity.'[33] And on their universality, again lined by Acton, 'The Quaker is no materialist; truth and conscience are not one thing at Rome, and another at Athens: they cannot be abrogated by senate or people.'[34] On this, Acton made the following comments, reinforcing them with 'NB' in the margin, 'Believed in an infallible light within. This gave a new force to the rights of man. The light being within, there can be no external control, for there is no external test or guide.'[35]

Bancroft proclaimed, 'Democracy has given to conscience absolute liberty.'[36] He meant that the act of conscience was purer in a larger group. He did not mean that democracy is wilful atomism. He was a thorough German Idealist, and it was precisely from this point of view that he was first drawn to admire the Quaker political organisation, the general meeting and its corollary in State government, the single chamber.[37] For the Quakers believed that the final 'sense of the meeting' was a far truer indication of the real nature of each man's Inner Light than his own first individual inkling of it. Penn had compared the emergence of the Holy Spirit in the community of the Quaker Meeting as like oil coming to the surface of water. Similarly, free debate enabled the citizen to find out what he really thought. The results of a successful debate were rationally and absolutely valid, and resistance to them could hardly claim to be on the grounds of a mature conscience. This conception of conscience is vital to a true understanding of Acton's interpretation of the American Revolution, and of Liberalism generally.

Expressed in this way, it is clear that Acton could never have derived these principles from the Quakers as the common historiographical picture has painted them. There, the apostles of Pennsylvania as a luminous idyll had for the most part been 18th-century French *philosophes*. Immediately before 1789, the abbé Raynal had painted a vivid picture of the primitive bliss and genial good order which reigned in Pennsylvania.[38] Voltaire spoke of it, as Acton often remarked, as the 'best government'. But, although Acton showed a perhaps undue awareness of the importance of this influence on the outbreak of the French Revolution in his Cambridge lectures,[39] it is not from these sources that he could have derived a connection with Idealist democracy. It is significant that his copy of Raynal's *Établissements des Deux Indes*, the *locus classicus*, is unmarked.

What is at first sight puzzling in Acton's attitude to the Quakers is the way in which Fox is completely subordinated to Penn. Acton bracketed Penn with Plato, St Augustine, and Hegel,[40] and claimed that he was a 'deeper divine' than St John Fisher,[41] for Fisher could see no remedy 'for religious error but fire and steel'.[42] It is clear that Acton considered Penn one of those few men, the 'greatest and best', who practise the highest sort of conscience and know how to 'rise above the pressure of time and race and circumstance, to choose the star that guides [their] course, to correct and test and assay [their] convictions by the light within, and with a resolute conscience and ideal courage, to remodel and reconstitute the character which birth and education gave [them]'.[43] Acton phrased a criticism of Döllinger by saying that we 'cannot understand ... Penn by studies made in the parish'.[44]

It is precisely because Penn applied Quaker doctrines to politics, that he was forced to do so in setting up his 'Holy Experiment', that Acton saw in him the significant represent- ative of his sect. He broke through the passive obedience of the Protestant tradition almost by accident, or more properly in Acton's eyes, by providence. It was no special novelty that he should see that theoretical Christianity required Toleration, Equality and Freedom. It was above all by his action in a necessarily political sphere that in one of the 'critical moments when the struggle seemed for ever desperate',[45] Penn made his colony enjoy 'the most democratic constitution in the world, and held up to the admiration of the eighteenth century an almost solitary example of freedom.'[46]

Acton identified Pennsylvania with 'undeveloped Christianity'.[47] It embodied the two basic principles of Christian- ity, conscience and the separation of Church and State. Yet there was a sense in which it was 'pre-adolescent', for it lacked both a true doctrine of the Church and a theory of political resistance. Acton wrote, in the box 'Christianity', 'The greatest instance of Christianity and Liberty is Penn – the religion in which there is least of Christianity – and hard to say how Penn was superior to Epictetus'[48] and 'Liberty and Christianity. The progress of one not identical with the other. Decided value of error and unbelief. Quakers – without sacraments or faith in Christ.'[49] This attribu- tion of value to error marks a crucial step in the putting together of Acton's 'central theme'.

It was a major change. In 1861 Acton had written to Simpson, 'The word *Religion* is too indefinite – only truths come true: and only true religion corresponds to the truth in politics.'[50] By the summer of 1882[51] he had become so overwhelmed with horror at what he had discovered in his archival researches about ultramontane involvement in 'lies and murder' that he saw dogma and morality in 'different heavens'. The key question was about the conscience-lessness of reputed saints. The lives of erring heretics such as Penn and Bayle were exemplary by comparison with their orthodox contemporaries who plotted the Revocation of the Edict of Nantes.[52]

Even the pacifism of the Quakers could appear providentially liberated from its normal impotence. In Europe it was 'The theory of virtuous and religious men. That, and no more, was enjoined by the N.T. ... It renounced the examples by which Christian society had been transformed. They preferred the example of Christians in pagan times, to their example in Christian times.'[53] But America gave the chance of an exodus-route out of the dilemma: 'But the Quakers would not employ force for reforms. So they could effect nothing in Europe. America gave a field for such liberals as did not choose to employ violence.'[54] It was because America provided such a refuge from the armies and establishments of Europe, a kind of laboratory where a collection of emigrant sectarians was forced by circumstances to become a state, that Acton spoke of Columbus as inaugurating the 'reign of the future'.[55]

Acton believed, therefore, that Pennsylvania was peculiarly significant in the discovery that certain 'Liberal' political ideas were of the essence of Christianity. It was, in the strictest sense, the beginning of a new age.[56] Bancroft, on this assumption, was quite right to juxtapose Christ's nativity with the outbreak of the American Revolution, for that revolution was only the practical manifestation on a larger scene of what had been accomplished by the Christian apostolate of Penn. Acton lined the conclusion of Bancroft's *History of the American Revolution* which stresses the complete impotency of the contemporary Old World, and echoes the Miltonic picture of wars everywhere ceasing at Christ's incarnation: 'This decay of the old forms of liberty was the symptom of the fore-runner of a new creation .... Kings sat still in awe, and nations turned to watch the issue.' Modern historians of Bancroft regard this passage and his chapter on the Quakers as enshrining his special contribution.

This perception of the decisiveness of Penn's Quaker State remained a central topic of Acton's subsequent reflexion. 'C'est des forêts non pas de la Germanie mais de la Pennsylvanie qu'elle (i.e., la liberté) nous vient .... Ce qui sépare les deux époques et creuse un gouffre entre les "old and new Whigs", c'est le développement, presque le découverte de la Conscience. Cette notion a poussé lentement, et n'a pas pris son grand essor qu'à la fin du XVII siecle et pendant tout le XVIII .... C'est venu lorsque le Christianisme s'est trouvé reduit à sa plus simple expression, sans église, sans sacrement, sans clergé, sans rituel, et qu'il est arrivé au point de se confondre avec la morale universelle. Dans cette forme-là le Christianisme a fondé un état et crée une constitution, où il n'y avait guère autre chose de sauvegarde que l'individualisme. Et par la suite des choses, la sauvegarde de l'individu, c'est-à-dire la Conscience, a pris la place de bien des dogmes, et a notablement grandi. Si la conscience humaine est véritablement ce qui Butler et Kant affirment, elle est suprême .... Ce qui rend la vie politique si digne, si intraitable, c'est l'élément qui nous vient d'Amérique, c'est le raisonnement qui a forcé la Revolution.'[57] In his notes in preparation for the *Lectures on Modern History*, Acton wrote, 'Conscience, understood in this way, supplied a new basis for freedom. It carried further than the reign of Whiggism. The deeper Quakers perceived the consequences. Penn drew the consequences in the constitution of Pennsylvania. It was the standard of a new Party and a new World.'[58]

Acton believed profoundly that the Rights of Man were Christian, in spite of the undoubted opposition of the churches to their proclamation. This was the paradox he faced in beginning to write his history of liberty, and which this understanding of the Pennsylvania Quakers was able to resolve. The cards show this, e.g., 'Liberty flourished chiefly when the force of religious convictions decayed. It was promoted chiefly by sects that retained least of its dogma. And it served often as an enemy.'[59]

The scientific revolution in 1775

Numerous passages show that Döllinger viewed the history of Protestantism as the history of the exhaustion of error. Acton's interpretation of the political revolution which arose out of the Pennsylvanian religious experiment is a subtly different variation on such a belief. Error is transmuted and made available by providence for purposes which could not easily be served by other instruments: 'Rights of Man, in Quakers, a product of the Christian religion. So it was handed over to Deism and Scepticism, an inheritance of the religious ages, and the latest, ripest product of the Reformation movement. – From the Protestant movement in its greatest intensity',[60] and 'the last growth of the Protestant principle – Develop the Rights of Man on the grounds of Conscience',[61] and 'How Religion produced Liberty, in reference to Conscience and Slavery'.[62]

This last is clearly a reference to the 1696 resolution of the
Philadelphia yearly meeting that slavery is 'contrary to the first
principles of Christ'.[63] These ideas are very characteristic of
Acton's pattern as a historian: the perception of a linear
development that is blocked and resumes its course by an *umweg*
or diversion, and the attribution of significance to obscure men
and provincial events. When Acton in 1895 spoke of a 'heart of his
subject' he was referring to the growth from Aquinas to the
Quakers of Pennsylvania and the idea of the Rights of Man and
to its expression in the Revolution.

For such a belief to be held by a historian who dealt in more
than mere climates of opinion, it was necessary that there should
be mediating links. Acton found these in Paine and Franklin. He
quoted Conway on Paine: he is 'explicable only by the intensity
of his Quakerism, consuming its own traditions as once the
church's ceremonies and sacraments.'[64] Franklin, in Acton's
lectures on the French Revolution, stands for the doctrine that
'The judgment of a whole people ... is looked upon to be
infallible.'[65] The characteristic features of Acton's history of the
American Revolution are to be derived from his conviction that
it was an act of conscience on the part of a whole people, and that
that act of conscience can only be understood in the light of the
attributes of infallibility, rationality, and community which the
Quaker 'Inner Light' possessed. Divorced from its religious roots
in the persons of Paine and Franklin, Acton believed that such a
conception of conscience had become available to political science,
that is to say, to all men everywhere.

It would be a mistake, when dealing with a mind of Acton's
richness and complexity, to imagine that he thought the relation
of Quaker principles to the American Revolution was causal. The
very hinge-quality which he gave the date 1775 meant that it was
to be considered in the light of the whole process of world history.
Acton believed profoundly in a teleological God, and within
careful limits even in Progress. He was educated in Germany,
where the philosophers saw history as the revelation of God's
purpose in the unfolding of his nature.

The part, therefore, which he allotted to the Quakers in
preparing the organisational and ideological roots on which the
first 'scientific' political revolution could be nourished must be
seen in perspective. Acton wrote, 'French Revolution – pathology,
American, normal development of ideas'.[66] It exemplified what he
meant when he said, 'The history of ideas rescues continuity.
Nothing is more deeply seated in the chain of history than the

Revolution which is the breach of it. For it is a break in externals – it is founded on the thought of previous generations. That is the link of Past and Present.'[67] To see the Americans as Acton saw them, it is necessary to make a short excursus to the English Civil War.

Acton thought of the 17th century as the crisis in the history of conscience; it was marked by a too simple and complete triumph of such notions in England under the Commonwealth and then destroyed by Hobbes. The 1688 Whigs had – according to Acton – to collect the pieces and construct a more balanced doctrine. Acton saw the same pattern in the history of liberty. In 1889 he asserted, 'Yet it is in political science only that America occupies the first rank.'[68] It is clear from this that Acton is speaking of the liberty which had been perfected in the tradition of the Whig Revolution as the organisational shape of a constitution. But in this aspect, too, Acton's starting-point was really 1642. It is a measure of the change in Acton's basic historiographical pattern that he came to share the English historian Goldwin Smith's view of Cromwell, that 'his statue should be at Washington, not Westminster.'[69]

Acton believed that there was one process at work, whether it was between the generation of Pym and Selden and that of Magna Carta, or of Paine and Franklin. He had established the line of his thought on this connection by 1877.[70] The Roundheads had taken, in Acton's view, three steps which were the *sine qua non* of the American Revolution. They had evolved a theory of conscience, they had rejected the authority of tradition, and had got used to the practice of 'abstract ideas'.[71] 'Habit of abstract ideas – Rhode I[sland], Pennsylvania – via Religion and Puritan struggle – so went beyond conservation of natural rights – the Rights of Man grew out of English toleration – the link between toleration and abstraction.'[72] 'It was liberty of conscience, the root from which the theory of liberty grew. The motive of the enthusiasm, the impelling force within .... It was the cause of a religious party before it became the faith of a political party. Stripped of its religious elements, dissociated – released – from the religious interests – from the confinement of sectarian interests and antagonisms – made universal. To Selden or Pym – the legal view was national – the other was sectarian. The union of both made it universal.'[73] The American Revolution was the practical effect and symbol of this universalisation. Its actual working out took place in England.

A number of notebooks which are dated 1878[74] show Acton to have been particularly concerned in that year with the 'whig' opposition to Charles II in the 1660s, and it seems clear that he came to consider this dissociation of Roundhead politics from religion as having been achieved by that generation. 'What they wanted was the wisdom without the narrowness, the politics apart from the religion and the national law. To dissociate what was permanent in all these ideas from what was temporary and local and transient. How this was done in the Whig doctrine between 1670 and 1690. Halifax, Temple, Somers, – (*et al.*).'[75] In the Cambridge lectures, he said, 'The Liberal ideas bred in sectarian circles here and in America did not become the common property of mankind until they were detached from their theological root and became the creed of a party. That is the transition which occupies the reign of Charles II.'[76] These ideas had to wait for a century for their application as a governing force to politics, but it is clear that here is the working out of a secular politics of duty which Acton dubbed his central theme. He wrote, 'History of Liberty is the history of 140 years .... In 1683 there was none. In 1823, when the const[itution] of Mass[achusetts] was revised, it was complete. Not prosperity or material progress, not happiness or civilisation, not science or religion, not democracy or nationality. All these things have been its tributaries and servants, but they have, in turn, been rivals and obstacles.'[77]

Penn and Locke both came from of this *milieu*. Following Bancroft, Acton saw the liberalism of Penn as the true form, for it was based on conscience. Locke's was only based on man's property. He dismissed the 'whigs' of the Walpolean era as 'diluted', 'pedestrian', and above all 'insincere'. Paradoxically therefore, it was against the 'whig' constitution of the Hanoverians that, in the course of time, true liberalism had to fight. Acton added the note, 'NB. This distinction begins now', to a card quoting Burke as saying in 1776, '[Whigs] will oppose parliament if parliament becomes an instrument of oppression.'[78]

Acton painted the crisis of 1775 in as dramatic terms as Bancroft. He saw no hope in the 'enlightened despotism' of the continent,[79] and in his reflexion in 1878 on America and Liberty went so far as to claim: 'The American war saved English liberty .... If the American war had not discredited the king, and awakened republican ideas, the constitution would have been crushed.'[80] So Burke and the Americans at one and the same time saved the English constitution, American liberty, and the future of political science. This is not the place to study the important question of Acton's relationship to Burke,[81] but it seems clear that as Acton grew older it was Burke's American writings that became sympathetic. It is a measure of Acton's commitment to writing history as the history of ideas that the American crisis is given its key place in his history as much for the opportunities it afforded the Rockingham Whigs as for the birth of the new American nation. He wrote of them that '[they] became philosophers after being politicians. Their temporary expedients were transformed into a system for the world. The ideas of one generation were found available for all time. The man who accomplished this change was Burke'[82] and, in the Cambridge lectures, that it was 'through him [Burke] and through American influence upon him, [that] the sordid policy of the Walpolean Whigs became a philosophy, and combination of expedients was changed into a system of general principles'.[83]

The outbreak of the American Revolution, therefore, led back in Acton's mind to the English Puritans in two ways. On the one hand was the Whig tradition of English political life, in which the 'general principles' set out in the Civil War could be used by Burke[84] in a secular dress; on the other hand were the colonies themselves, which were the direct successors of Parliamentarian/ Puritan migrations. Acton considered them in some sense more 'pure' than England because free of history, and therefore more able to appreciate abstract political liberalism. There is ample evidence that he was persuaded by Rousseau's romantic notion of the 'original freedom' of unsocialised individual man. 'American colonisation removed the repressing forces. Then it appeared natural to the Englishman to govern himself like a free man. Undo the work of history, remove the civilising influence of centuries, and you found – a free man – the remainder, the residue.'[85]

America offered a context where, in the absence of the familiar obstacles, it was possible for a free society to be not only 'natural' in the Rousseau-ist sense, but also, in the practice of the Quaker 'inner light', to inherit a generally accessible form of the Puritan life of grace. 'Europe incapable. America – virgin soil – Escaping from tradition, authority. There the Quakers and Independents – between episcopalian and presbyterian – were able to work out their ideas .... Their inward light resisted external influences. In a country without fear of neighbours, no court, no established church, no aristocracy, no army, no poverty, no fear of neighbours.'[86] Such a society had the unique possibility of choosing to be non-violent and conservative in becoming free.

The American Revolution was the turning point of world

history for Acton. It is consequently foolish to understand its significance for him in any but the largest categories. He was not a Byron, romantically identifying himself with a small oppressed nation. If his emotions were freely lavished on the interpretation of that decade, as Kochan claims, it was for a thoroughly intellectual reason; in the same way that any Christian theologian must be something more than a spectator in discerning the growth of the primitive church. In both cases, it seems natural to introduce providence to explain the way in which such significant events could happen in a remote part of the civilised world. It is particularly remarkable how strongly Acton asserts the coming together of the strands of liberal opinion in the 1770s. He often noted the conjunction of circumstances by which, in the same year, the Declaration of Independence was drawn up and both Adam Smith and Turgot published.[87] Acton believed that systems of achieved liberty could be enjoyed in the world (and not only in America) only after the revolutionaries had won their case.

G. M. Trevelyan recalled a conversation with Acton in which he said history began to be interesting with Luther, for that was the first true revolution – 'a revolution being defined as a political change carried out as the consequence of an idea'. A card echoing Bishop Berkeley (and Bancroft) runs: '[Liberty] from nation to nation, moving westward .... Influence of political theory, of theory apart from interests, which we call Revolution. More and more.'[88] He applied a phrase like 'divine right' to the 'rights of man'. It is here, rather than in 1688, that we can discover the heart of what can fairly be called Acton's system.

Several writers on Acton have made the mistake of seeing him as, above all, a 1688 Whig.[89] In the Cambridge lectures, however, Acton makes an explicit comparison of 1688 and 1775, and dismisses the earlier 'whigs' as 'a combination of men rather than a doctrine, and the idea of fidelity to comrades was often stronger among them than the idea of fidelity to truths.'[90]

It is clear from the notes at Cambridge that Acton used the opportunity, when addressing himself to preparing a History of Liberty in the 1870s, to sketch a system in the full German sense. He began with basic postulates and rethought his whole historical and theological position. The duty to revolt to establish a liberal political order became an absolute which was worked out in parallel with his absolute condemnation of every persecutor as a murderer. It becomes apparent that it was both of these absolutes, and not merely the latter, which led to the estrangement from Döllinger after 1879. The following card, 'Largest possible induction. What is the way of Providence? Towards Liberty, its security, conception, enjoyment. Conscience ever fuller, deeper. Secured immunity. For me and others, only good and unselfish motives'[91] illuminates the connection of these absolutes. The American Revolution served as Acton's guarantee that the process of history pointed toward a world where persecution could no longer take place.

Acton was deeply influenced by Burke in 1877–8 when he was working out his view of the revolution, and he saw in him a congenial abstractness. He said in 1877 at Bridgnorth, 'From the elements of that crisis [1775], Burke built up the noblest political philosophy in the world. "I do not know the method", said he, "of drawing up an indictment against a whole people. The natural rights of mankind are indeed sacred things."'[92] In a later card he wrote, 'Deliverance of the Whig mind by America – Otis, Gadsden, S. Adams, J. Adams, Chatham, Camden ... (et al.). But especially seen in Burke. Whiggism becomes a science.'[93] It was entirely characteristic of Acton that he should seek to establish in Otis's speech of 16 December 1773 the precise moment at which this watershed of world history was crossed. He declared, 'The case was fought out on the ground of the Law of Nature, more properly speaking, of Divine Right. On that evening ... it became for the first time the reigning force in History',[94] and 'When science invaded government: with political economy, with the Rights of Man, with Burke.'[95]

However it is clear in the cards that Acton was aware of Burke's equivocal value as a support for his own revolutionary 'Whiggism'. Acton saw Burke as stretched on the rack of financial embarrassment on the one hand, and a too clear vision of the connection between coercion of 'unrepresented America' and his native Ireland on the other.[96] He ascribed the impoverished liberalism of the post-1782 Burke to these facts.[97] In a card written after Döllinger's death, Acton distinguished his own attitude from the one prevalent at Munich, where the interest was in the Burke who had opposed French Jacobism. He wrote, 'A genuine student of Burke would see in him more than was seen by Gentz, Niebuhr, Stahl, etc. – also the master of Webster and Macaulay. Ready for the year of Revolutions, for the proc[lamation] of universal rights, for the parliament of theorists. He takes a broader view than many of his friends.'[98] Acton believed Burke was a profoundly important representative of the generation which first began to think about Liberal politics in a 'scientific' way.

The question arises of how Acton would define 'scientific' in such a context. It is illuminated by the following succinct account in the Cambridge lectures: 'A hundred years passed before Whiggism assumed the universal and scientific character. In the American speeches of Chatham and Camden, in Burke's writings from 1778 to 1783, in the *Wealth of Nations*, and the tracts of Sir William Jones there is an immense development. The national bounds are overcome. The principles are sacred irrespective of interests. The charter of Rhode Island is worth more than the British Constitution and Whig statesmen ... rejoice that America has resisted.'[99] 'The progress is entirely consistent.'[100]

Conscience and the rights of man

Especially after 1878 the notes suggest Acton compared the British with the American constitutions to the disadvantage of the former, on the grounds that the British was evolutionary and unformulated while the American was theoretical and rational. In 1880 he wrote, 'English constitution not universal .... They have surely modified the idea. have found new things – and what is constant is solid – America, Paris 1789, Spain'[101] and 'absence of first principles in our [English] debates. English History not so instructive.'[102]

Acton connected this new ability to think in terms of abstractly correct principles of constitutional law with the contemporary sciences. In astronomy and economics, and above all in law, the Enlightenment had contrasted knowledge which was 'scientific' with confused local traditions and prejudices. It had turned from tradition to a view of socio-political institutions based on a principle of conscience; there followed automatically a wide and coherent range of 'liberal' ideas, e.g. free trade, emancipation, and prison reform: 'Camden on Taxation and Representation. Jefferson. No retrospective punishments. Sieyès. Beccaria. S. Thomas. Above history – authority supreme – abstract. Divine right applied to Rights of Man.'[103]

Acton believed the Americans' greatness lay in a similar search for abstract principles in the field of politics. He wrote, 'In the same age, men saw that all was bad, in fact, at the same time the human mind was beginning a new epoch of discovery. Sublime truths of astronomy .... It seemed within the powers of the new force thus revealed to make laws, a code, a constitution. America had just done it. Got rid of prejudice like astrology, alchemy, magic.'[104] Acton saw the connection between Puritanism and America, therefore, in this way: whereas the Reformed Protestants had rebelled in order to establish the presbyterian form of church-government as abstractly obligatory on the ground of Scripture, the irreconcilable element in the American rebellion had been its vision of a form of government based on the natural – and therefore abstract – rights of man as man.

Whether the actual historical events of 1775 can bear such an interpretation is at this point immaterial.[105] From 1877 onward, Acton laid such special stress on this aspect of the American Revolution that its central place in his scheme of general history is indisputable. Unfortunately, however, he spent more time in showing how his interpretation of the Revolution might affect general history than in how his interpretation was related to the historical information.

To discuss the question of how Acton saw the role of conscience in the American revolt, we must first stress the non-religious character of this conscience. 'Religious element in Revolution: – Savanarola, Bauernkrieg, Ligue, Netherlands, Roundheads, Anabaptists, Whigs. It is not science until it is independent of religion',[106] and (in 1879) 'Whigs – Politics could not stand on religious or philosophic postulates. For they would then change everywhere, and not last. They could have only a moral basis, for that is of all ages. The very point was that it should not be dependent on particular churches, but do for all.'[107]

'Doing for all' was part of Acton's general perception of science. There were strong currents of opinion in contemporary Britain working towards the usage of 'science' in political discussion, and it is worth noting how the direction of development of public [private] school ethos in these years was from the comprehensive but essentially religious protestantism characterised by Thomas Arnold at Rugby to the religiously inclusive but secularised moralism of games-field and imperial service at the turn of the century.[108] Acton admired the moral quality of those Americans who sacrificed their lives for the sake of political duty and with no thought of heavenly reward, whether it was in 1775 or in the Civil War: he wrote of '[the war's] historic grandeur ... very much due to four or five men, most of whom took arms under compulsion of an imperative law, in obedience to duty in its least attractive form.'[109] He regarded this as clearly akin to George Eliot's secular system of ethics. His material on her repeatedly emphasised the painful and harsh rewards that can be expected from doing one's duty: 'Duty as the basis of the revolutionary theory. Duty to God implying rights against man. Therefore Socialism is no part of the theory. It does not complete it. The height of the theory is, when revolution is least provoked. That is in America.'[110]

Basic to Acton's whole emphasis on revolution, therefore, is his particular theory of conscience. In each man's conscience can be discovered abstract knowledge of what constitutes a true political system, and a continuous moral pressure to realise such a system. It was this latter 'duty' which Acton believed the Americans as a political community were first courageous enough to exemplify.

He drew from this premise the conclusion that it was only self examination, or – as he more commonly said – 'sincerity', which was needed to make both the objective and the duty to secure it plain to all men's 'inner light'. The Americans had been the heralds of such 'scientific' politics; 'It was their honesty – not their talent or their wisdom – and gave us the best form of government that was ever made.'[111] Indeed, Acton was never impressed with the personalities of the founders of American independence. 'The breach was not accomplished by men of heroic inventiveness. They were, generally, men of the second rank, without originality or intellectual grandeur .... The situation, without speculative force, wrought out the result.'[112] 'The Americans resorted to generalities because their actual case was not decisive.'[113] Their success was the *dénouement* of a drama which was abstract, and rooted in the whole historical process.

Acton saw this process going back to Aquinas[114] and thence to the political 'forms' of the Greeks. These ideas, he said in 1877, 'long locked in the breast of solitary thinkers, and hidden among Latin folios [as natural law][115] – burst forth like a conqueror upon the world they were destined to transform, under the title of the Rights of Man'.[116] Acton repeatedly quotes Hamilton's famous saying that the principles of political justice are 'written on the conscience of mankind by the finger of God'. In the American Revolution, Acton believed, the national sense of justice had expressed what was universal natural law.

The Americans had shown that democracy could be an effective technique for ascertaining morality.[117] The Quakers had led directly to 'scientific' and then to 'universal' politics. The Americans 'acted also on the principle, which was not new, which came down indeed from medieval divines, but which was newly invested with universal authority, that the law is not the will of the sovereign who commands but of the nation that obeys.'[118] '[The] arguments of Otis, Franklin, Jefferson, Hamilton, incorporated in the Declaration of Independence. Set up a new theory of government. The governed have to decide on grounds universally applicable. This is not grown on English pastures. It is the mere theory of Revolution. It is Rousseau and Tom Paine. It is the absolute condemnation of European politics.'[119]

In the critical period of Acton's formulation of these ideas, in 1878–9, this was a principle consciously expressed in terms congruent with Penn's teaching of synteresis: 'Do to others as you would be done by. And Kant's formula. This is the leading precept of politics – Put yourself in his place. Invert the position.'[120] and 'Greatest happiness principle identical with the principle to do to others what we wish them to do to us .... Liberty founded on doubt is not liberty at all, for it is liberty without security.'[121] From this manner of thinking, it followed logically that, if, as Acton declared, politics were 'the ethics of public life',[122] a body-corporate (e.g. a national or religious community) capable of moral identity had the same right to moral (and therefore political) self-determination as an individual personality. The perpetual wardship of an empire or an autocracy must in such cases be immoral.

It is at this point that it becomes clear why Acton should have elaborated his abstract doctrine of revolution at the same time as he became more rigidly convinced that persecution is a corrosive and absolute evil. In both cases, it was a question of moral autonomy. He wrote, 'Every religion may be sincerely held, but the man who deprives another of his legitimate freedom cannot be sincere. Hence, violence of passions in the strife between liberty and power.'[123] Every thinking person has the capacity to discover fundamental moral truths. The famous correspondence with Creighton about the historian as 'hanging judge' took place only two years before Acton's equally intransigent review of Bryce. The two issues – Inquisition and America – were two faces of the same coin.

The one side of Acton's thinking, his absolute condemnation of all who lend their consent to church killings 'in the public interest', has received too much attention. Its complement, a rigid political intolerance of any form of government that permits them, has not been given its proper place. If only one system of politics is 'scientific' and that system is presumed to press itself upon the conscience of every natural man, opposition to it must be criminal, and *carte blanche* is given to its imposition (which can be termed a 'liberation') by violent revolution. 'Liberty is conscience – ergo, morality. Disregard one, disregard the other.

No basis for an opponent of liberalism to avoid crime. [For him] end justifies the means.' Acton's attitude to Dupanloup and then to Disraeli makes it plain that he was almost pathologically implacable in this kind of logic.[124]

As a consequence of orientating his political thought to the necessity of preventing persecution, Acton eventually adopted the hypothesis that there existed a set of God-given political norms which had been enshrined in the American Constitution. In so doing, however, he only transposed the dilemma, for on this assumption freedom could only be the choice of one type of liberalism, in exactly the same way that, for the Inquisition, true knowledge of God could only follow the choice of orthodox Catholic faith.[125] It is not necessarily untrue that there are human rights or that there is one normative form of political freedom, any more than that there is but one way to the knowledge of God. Acton's form of the proposition, however, is at least presented by him as dependent upon the cognitive function of conscience. This should be empirically verifiable, but there is scant evidence to support it.

Thus, the politics of revolution became a dogmatic affair for Acton. The slightest divergence from the correct pattern of liberal politics should compel conscientious men to rise in revolt. It was the very slightness of the American grievances which made their action so important: it marked the 'delicacy' and 'sensitiveness' of their consciences.[126] It was this too which divided him from Döllinger, whom Acton never considered a Liberal in spite of his leadership of the German liberals in 1848 and 1870. In a notebook labelled 'Döllinger' he wrote, 'Men objected to the Bulgarian or Armenian horrors without being Whigs. A Whig was one to whom the horrors made no difference, constituted no additional argument in an absolute government. He condemns, not Nero ... but Charles V. He fights ... not to resist the intolerable reality of oppression, but the remote possibility of wrong of diminished freedom.'[127]

In what admittedly is the most volcanic expression of this position, Acton wrote, 'The story of the revolted colonies impresses us first and most distinctly as the supreme manifestation of the Law of resistance, as the abstract revolution in its purest and most perfect shape. No people was so free as the insurgents; no government less oppressive than the government which they overthrew .... Their example presents a thorn, not a cushion, and threatens all existing political forms, with the doubtful exception of the federal constitution of 1874.[128] It teaches that men ought to be in arms even against a remote and constructive danger to their freedom; that even if the cloud is no bigger than a man's hand, it is their right and duty to stake the national existence, to sacrifice lives and fortunes, and to cover the country with a lake of blood .... Here or nowhere we have the broken chain .... Ideas rooted in the future, reason cutting as clean as Atropos.'[129] In this review of Bryce's *American Commonwealth*, Acton was exposing 'the boundless innovation, the unfathomed gulf'[130] produced by American independence.

This is a consistently held viewpoint going back to 1878: 'When this theory arose, it threatened the whole existing basis of society. For in the conflict between what is and what ought to be, the issue is not doubtful. It was, being general, not a political or human contrivance, but a moral obligation .... Europe passed from the shelter of tradition and authority into the Sea of Revolution .... If inherent rights, then personal liberty, free command over his person, his conscience and his property, is such a right. And if so, a government that does not recognize it is no government and has no right to allegiance – but stands condemned. It denies the rightfulness of absolute states.'[131] Another card probably of the same year says, 'America – First established the idea that absolutism is wrong. Till then, it has been inconvenient .... But liberty was an acquired privilege, not a universal right .... In the M[iddle] A[ges] the idea that the heterodox are equal, that rights belong to individuals apart from their land, their faith, their colour – was not known .... It arose in America. It arose after Rationalism had made way.'[132]

That it was the rigid pursuit of the professedly ecumenical principles of historical 'science' which led him to such conclusions, where he had left his old master Döllinger behind and was 'absolutely alone', is ironic.

The constitution as limit and guarantee

It followed naturally from the views which made Acton a voracious revolutionary elsewhere that, when his *America felix* had been established, subsequent change should become a matter of caution, if not always regret.[133] He identified himself with the 'Liberal Conservatism' of the 'Seven Champions of Leman'.[134] 'The Seven Champions of Liberal Conservatism came from the banks of the Lake of Geneva – in one generation. Mme de Staël, B. Constant, Dumont, Sismondi, Rossi, Vinet, Cherbuliez. Their doctrine – distilled essence ... in the oracle of the Left Centre in the Third Republic. Laboulaye.'[135] It was within this Liberal Conservative pattern of thinking that he admired Hamilton so profoundly, for he saw him as determined after the revolution to replace the gap left by the removal of King George III's powers with self-imposed constitutional checks. Acton described his perception of the mechanical problems involved as 'true conservatism, apart from interests'[136] and as demonstrating once again the 'scientific' approach of the Americans to politics.

The best-known of Acton's insights, that power corrupts, was not a particularly original one in his generation,[137] but it was one to which his theory of conscience gave particular force. Acton viewed reason and conscience as opposed primarily to pride – to greed, self-centredness, lack of imagination. Liberty, the 'reign of Conscience', required that these appetites should be disciplined and opened to others. He therefore devoted anxious attention to the various ways in which individuals and groups, and especially whole peoples or 'democracies', could mutually check each other's capacity to indulge their lust for power. He wrote, 'The great secret of constitutional government is the division of power. In the democracy and in absolute monarchy, united .... People and monarch, something not the people, should combine and check each other always. This must run through the whole system.'[138] and 'difference between Democracy and Liberty: one looks to the way government is composed, the other to the way it is controlled'[139] and 'Never destroy a force. When it is not dominant, it may serve to check dominion.'[140] Only when this balance has been achieved could the whole community enter into a fully rational debate with the pure intention of seeking the dictate of the 'inward voice' of conscience.

Acton did not believe such a rational debate would occur naturally in a democracy. He was acutely aware of the dangers of government by the people. It was primarily because America had to face these dangers in an intense form that Acton was concerned to analyse so carefully the various dykes she had erected against them. In the period between 1875 and 1880 Acton appears to have seen the principle of federalism collapsing, not only in Europe, but in America too. It is possible that this may have been due partly to the Prussian writers Holst and Knapp, who decried the effects of federal politics in America in order to encourage an enthusiasm for the new German empire.[141] As a result of this feeling, Acton still saw the heyday of America as in the past. It was not until the 1880s that Acton became convinced that America offered the only effective balance against democracy. In 1886 he ascribed this to her division of sovereignty and predicted that in twenty years she would be twice as rich as England.[142] The Americans were altogether more secure than the English, e.g.: 'American checks on Democracy. The Senate. The Supreme Court. None of these exist in England.'[143]

When, too, he pursued his frequent comparisons of the French and American Revolutions, Acton wrote that the French 'Failed by rejecting the American example. The refusal is not surprising, and demands no aid from the mystery of nationality. 1. There was nobody to be parties to a contract. 2. Federation. 3. The Court of Revision was not developed. 4. Religious liberty was not in the Constitution.'[144] These are useful pointers to which dykes Acton, in the last twenty years of his life, considered effective. It was only after 1880 that Acton saw the Supreme Court and the various churches as effective power centres in the battle against unitary democracy.

But from his very early years Acton had been a convinced federalist. At first his hopes rested on the Habsburg empire, and his principal interest was in its capacity to hold together by such means very different levels of civilisation.[145] He believed it was a specially Catholic form of government.[146] At the end of his life he closed his Cambridge lectures with the ringing claim that it was by reason of its federal structure that America had 'produced a community more powerful, more prosperous, more intelligent and more free than any other which the world has seen.'[147]

The manner in which Acton believed such potent effects were obtained was two-fold. First, it provided contracting parties to the constitution: 'written constitution – a compact between Americans. Therefore not changeable, setting a limit to own power.'[148] Second, it spread power among conflicting organisations: 'How self-government and rep[resentative] government contradict each other. In Democracy. Two distinct principles. One is a check on the other'[149] and 'Federalism .... Greatest check on central power .... Prevents centralization – a local government which has to resign so many powers to a central power, cannot tyrannize.'[150] In both situations, however, the object was the same. Federalism, he wrote, was the 'supreme guarantee' because 'it was the shape in which the dogma survived that the nation cannot do what it likes.'[151]

The Supreme Court was similarly valuable. In a state where the national tradition was peculiarly universalist and revolutionary, the Supreme Court became the guardian of right reason and a developmental progress in monitoring the national law. 'To this axiom [democracy] ... the Federalist Judiciary opposed what amounted to a flat negative. Chief Justice Marshall and his colleagues meant to interpret the Constitution as seemed to them right, and they admitted no appeal from their decision.'[152] There, most immediately powerful of all, was the check against a momentary 'general will' destroying the high insights of the Revolution.

Acton believed conscience itself could furnish powerful forces in the search for a political balance. Rather curiously (in the light of his non-religious interpretation of the Revolution), he laid special emphasis on the power of the religious, and especially of the Catholic, conscience. He associated the constitutional fruits of this with the total separation of Church and State in America. The intense loyalties of denominational Christianity would never be canalised and brought together by the American state; neither could they, while the churches remained strong, ever be absorbed in a totalitarian democracy. They therefore worked as the most fundamental check of all. Acton saw the Middle Ages, in contrast to this, as a time when the power of religious conscience could not, on the whole, be used to resist authority, and therefore a time when there was no freedom.[153]

Acton believed that the Catholic church – or to a lesser degree Christianity (and the other denominations) – impinged upon Whig politics at two levels. More than any other society within the state it required the negative liberty of complete separation so that the individual religious conscience might mature unseduced by political privilege. At the same time, in so far as the church preached the moral truths of 'natural law', it could only be satisfied with one form of state and must act politically to preserve it. There was there an inescapable tension with which the 20th-century church has become very familiar; 'Dist[inction] of Ch[urch] and St[ate] imperfect in OT, only in the New. Church outside parties – Yet, if all pol[itics] morality – she should go in.'[154] Perhaps rather forlornly, it is at this point that Acton's Whiggism and Catholicism come together; there in America, at least, he could be confident that the Catholic church would always operate to buttress a Liberal Constitution and be kept pure in the process. It was to its corporate interest to do so.

The idea of conscience was enmeshed in Acton's whole picture of American history. From the time in 1878 when he distinguished between Locke and Penn, between the liberty of property and conscience, and decided that the latter was the true liberty, he continually spoke of conscience as the political absolute[155] and of

America as its home. It was the root and 'basis' of liberty, and, at the same time, its guardian: the 'theory of conscience – the main protector against absolutism – the one protection against democracy'.[156] The fullness of human freedom, he wrote for his *History of Liberty* on a card marked emphatically with crosses top and bottom, is 'The right of determining and doing his duty. 1775 gave means of curbing democracy. Its limit must be something independent of legislation, common to all men. The rights of conscience. If that is so, the old parties stood condemned .... The sympathy for the Whigs of 1688 was qualified by the fact that they did not respect the Rights of Man.'[157]

Acton was consistent in this. To define liberty as the political 'reign of conscience' necessitated a late date for its 'birth'. It had to be a secured and in principle a universal system. To illustrate and pinpoint his interpretation it was plausible to choose America. It may be objected that in doing so, he not only idealised the historical raw material in a selective way, but brought to light the incompatibilities in his own thinking which debilitated the magic concept of 'science'. Nonetheless, if we look back to the passage in his *Inaugural Lecture*[158] with which this chapter began, where Acton sets out the 'heart' of all modern history, our interpretation is confirmed. He says there of the Puritans that what 'had been done by authority and outward discipline and organized violence' they attempted to do 'by division of power, and committed to the intellect and conscience of free men. Thus was exchanged the dominion of will over will for the dominion of reason over reason'. That is clearly America and clearly Pennsylvania.

6
Acton's Universal History: the Prologue

So Acton believed the drama of the conception and birth of distinctively modern history to be the events leading from Aquinas and his contemporaries to the foundation of the United States of America. The drama was not without preparation and it took place against a lively backcloth. This and the following chapter set out Acton's over-view of general history, the context of this 'salvation-story'.

Having spent so much of his life compressing his thoughts on to thousands of pithy and often ambiguous cards, it is hardly surprising that even his connected writings should display an epigrammatic style. In general, Acton's history of the past is like the view from a mountain on a misty morning. Rising from the apparent sea of cloud are other hills and plateaus whose detail is clearly delineated in the sun, but which have no evident interconnection. In fact, however, there were few topics of historiography up until his time with which he was not acquainted, and upon which he did not have a considered opinion; and it would be a mistake to suppose that the peaks so characteristically visible in Acton's historical landscape are not located on his mind's map in relation to wide plains and valleys that are hidden.[1] Acton began his history of the coming of the reign of conscience in the ancient world.

Conscience in pre-Christian philosophy

Acton read a great deal of classical Greek philosophy and through his friends he had access to the best information of his generation on the societies which lay outside the European humanist tradition. It is clear from his notes that the existence of conscience among these peoples was of serious concern to him.[2] If it did not exist there at all, or varied – as it seemed to do – with neighbouring tribes on such important aspects of the moral law as stealing and lying, it was not easy to maintain that a conscience (or at least a conscience equipped with the axioms of the natural law) is the possession of a man *qua* man.

Although he occasionally spoke of the ethical achievements of a few eastern thinkers,[3] Acton attempted to solve this difficulty by requiring civilisation before anticipating conscience. Perhaps Acton was never sure whether he stood with Rousseau in seeing liberty in opposition to all culture or found it impractical to anticipate liberty until a particular culture had been established. He several times spoke of liberty 'pregnant with culture'. But, as the civilisation to which he referred in this connection was always Graeco-Roman civilisation, this argument is flimsy. It is curious in this respect that the contemporary 'enemies of conscience', whom he frequently listed (such as the Stephenses, Mill, and Darwin), normally criticised conscience on this precise ground of its merely social origin. Acton tried to ride two horses at the same time. He claimed in his own time that the moral content of conscience was universal and valid against society. But the whole drift of his historical work on America was to assert conscience to be the peculiar and distinguishing product of that society, and one thread of the tradition which went back to the classical period of Greece.

Acton, like Jeremy Taylor, supposed God to be a gardener. A gardener has to prepare seed-beds for his chosen plants, and, occasionally, to allow weeds and unnecessary plants to grow with them and draw them up. But the object of the gardener is that eventually the garden should contain only those plants which he chooses to grow. Acton was a child of the Christian scriptures. He believed in the divinity of the Mosaic old covenant and its transcendence by a higher revelation, which, taking advantage of the *praeparatio evangelica*, should ultimately work itself out and spread and fill the world. His teleological world-picture is perhaps best shown in the record of his instruction of his son, Richard, in church history. This is dated 1890 at Tegernsee.[4] It begins as follows: 'We are to believe in a continued belief in God existing among an ever-increasing few from the beginning of all things. This ever-increasing few were the Jews, the chosen people. — Amongst the Jews there was a gradual growth and development of religion, of the Religion which was to become Christianity. The exponents of religion were not the Priests, nor the official leaders of the people, but an unofficial set of men inspired and appointed by God, the Prophets. It was by their action, under God's influence, that a system of religion was gradually formed. — At this time, there were two distinct processes at work, one among the Pagans, one among the Jews. The pagans, by their philosophical and ethical development were

108

being ripened for the arrival of the Christian era. The Jews, by the action of their prophets, were themselves moulding a religion which contained the truths of Christianity. — At the moment when the civilized world had become unified, when a monarchy was established, that is to say at the moment when the exquisitely Christian idea of Unity was established, Christ was born. One great operation set at work by Christ is the Preparation of the Nations. But it works very slowly, for, until 1492, America heard nothing of Christianity, and it is not satisfactory, for millions of Chinese of today know nothing of Christ or of Xty. — What are we to think of those who live pure and good lives but are without reach of Christianity? are they lost? We cannot judge.' It is notable how large a part prophetic inspiration (or 'conscience') and unity (or 'science') play in this picture.

In such a case, it is not surprising that what are, in due time, to be the characteristics of salvation for all men should at an early period only be visible in germ among a very limited number of men. Although this interpretation could claim on Christian premises to be reasonable, it is quite patently not scientific, as Acton would claim. It is hard to reconcile the allowances for 'preparation' which Acton made for the cruelties of Columbus and of the Teutonic barbarians, with the complete lack of such allowance for the medieval church.

Acton's early history of conscience concentrates, therefore, on the Greeks and the Jews. Among the Greeks, Acton took Socrates as the vehicle of the initial appearance of conscience as a factor in human consciousness. Two cards writtien on the same day run: 'Conscience comes into play in Sophocles, Euripides, Socrates at the turning of Greek life, at the break-down of mythology and the rise of Democracy'[5] and (on Greece and conscience), 'First, instead of sacred tradition, present authority of general consent. This led to the extreme of democracy. Reaction against this, in the third stage, Conscience, or the appeal to personal autonomy – Socrates.'[6] Acton compared Socrates to the 18th-century rationalists[7] who, similarly, sought to find in reason an alternative political absolute to Hobbesian voluntarism, after the collapse of the authority of national tradition. In 1878 he laid a good deal of stress on the way this Socratic teaching about conscience tended to democracy (in the modern constitutional sense). It taught men 'to judge of right and wrong, not by the will or sentiment of others, but by the light which God has set in each man's reason and conscience.'[8] This phrase about the 'light of conscience' is redolent of William Penn, who always claimed his descent from Plato.

Here Acton appears to assume a conscience mature enough to carry out the 'higher law' even in the Greek population of that time. In 1877, he spoke of the Hebrew prophets appealing 'to the healing forces that slept in the uncorrupted consciences of the masses.'[9] Acton was generous. If both the Hebrew and Greek peoples were equipped with perfectly adequate consciences at this time, the one without civilisation, the other without the Law of Moses, all men everywhere might claim to be endowed with this knowledge and apparatus. Consequently, Acton's subsequent riders about training conscience and filling it 'with the notion of the Holy Spirit' are counsels of perfection, and any cannibal, and *a fortiori* any Parsee, might in logic expect to receive from a historian the full penalty of conscious murder. He says as much: 'Idea of liberty, as sacred as life and property. Not new. Ancient world, classical world, full of it. Therefore, we make no great allowance for times.'[10]

The drawbacks for Acton of the Socratic theory – and of the Christian gospels – were that they provided no sanction for political resistance. It was questionable how far Socrates could speak to non-Greeks. This extension was achieved by the Stoics. He exclaims: 'How much philosophy advanced from Parmenides to Epictetus — From Socrates and his school to the early Empire – to the conception of the rights of man, fraternity, unity, and charity.'[11]

The other kind of conscience of which the classical Greeks spoke had to do with guilt and was that typified by the story of Orestes and the Furies. Acton was accustomed to speak of this in connection with George Eliot. He thought her system very similar. But he denied that this 'negative', 'warning', 'pathological' analysis of conscience was what he meant by the word.[12]

With regard to the Jews, Acton never produced a clear picture. He compiled a list of occasions when 'heart' was used in the sense of conscience and he notes Luther's claim to have detected the idea in the Old Testament, but he found most significance in the way in which the history of the Jews showed the evolution of the spirit from the letter.[13] 'Judaism did not connect the individual with God, but the nation. So that the conscience had no real protection. Christianity revealed the individual conscience. Man, by himself, in relation to God. This is the new element, apart from the institution.'[14] He did note, however, how powerful the concept of resistance was in Jewish history, and how valuable was the example they provided of a nation under divine law, to which all political authority was answerable.[15] 'The doctrine of resistance flourished among the Jews. They thought of meeting the Romans as they met the Syrians. The modern attitude is much nearer that of those Jews, which the apostles so vehemently condemned, than that of the early Christians who refused to be involved in the same issue.'[16]

It is surprising that Acton did not lay more stress on the roots which conscience in his sense could legitimately claim in Jewish thinking. It is an ancient Jewish tradition that 'original sin' is balanced by 'original righteousness'. Verses of Jeremiah express exactly this concept of God's law in the individual heart as an aspect of the coming of the messiah: 'But this is the covenant which I will make with Israel after those days, says the Lord: I will set my law within them and write it on their hearts; I will become their God and they shall become my people.'[17] Ezekiel and Isaiah, as well as other verses of Jeremiah, support interior-isation as a sign of the future time of salvation. It was to this tradition that Christ appealed – the New Covenant – when abrogating Moses' allowance of divorce on account of the hardness of the Jews' hearts. And Jewish religious thought held that whatever was outside the detailed prescription of the Law was 'left to the conscience and right feeling of the individual'.[18]

Part of the explanation for this must be sought in the direction of contemporary biblical scholarship. Schweitzer wrote in *My Life and Thought* that in 1911 he had to establish that, 'the attempt, then universally regarded as promising success, to trace back to Greek ideas the Apostle's mystical teaching about redemption – could not be carried through, and that there could be no question of any explanation other than one provided by eschatology'.[19] The work of Bohlig on St Paul's theory of conscience, which showed it to be Jewish in its basic conception, and not – as had been supposed – Stoic, appeared in 1914. Since that time, it has been impossible to see Paul as fundamentally Greek in his contri-bution to Christian thinking. But Acton lived at the height of the German theologians' attempt to set up an antithesis between Pauline and Synoptic theology on the basis of Greek and Jewish traditions. The Christian contribution to the history of conscience would now appear to have been more to do with the Hebrew 'Wisdom' than the Stoic 'particle of divinity'.

111

The coming of Christianity

Acton's thinking about the life of Christ is dominated by his interpretation of 'Render unto Caesar'. In his account of church history for his son, the resurrexion is not mentioned at all, neither are any miracles. Although Acton was not on the whole sympathetic to the notion, he does speak of 'the miraculous Presence' of Christ which ascended into heaven, and he frequently refers to his deep trust in heaven and its angels. Christ's ethical teaching, he says, was collected from his contemporaries. The religion Christ preached was the Jewish religion: 'Christ – up to the time of his death, taught nothing new. – Up to the time of his death, Christ preached the Jewish religion and addressed himself exclusively to the Jews.'[20] What was new and important was the foundation of the Christian – specifically the Roman Catholic church. 'After his death, Christ founded a corporation, a church, on the principles of Unity, Authority and Primacy. *"et tibi dabo claves regni coelorum."* A catholic should live and die with those words ringing in his ears. – Since the ascension, the Church has always existed. – We must look upon the Church, not as we look at an ancient MS as the silent testimony of a long dead hand, but we must look on it as a vessel carrying Christ in person.'[21] It was this – so Acton argued – which gave more than human energy and continuity to a body which could serve everywhere as the focus of a duty to God which contrasts so clearly with any duty to the state.

The conclusion of Acton's *History of Freedom in Antiquity* explains very clearly what significance he saw in the church's foundation. The classical world knew everything, but was able to accomplish nothing. The problem was largely political. Until 'a new power came forth from Galilee, giving what was wanting to the efficacy of human knowledge to redeem societies as well as men,'[22] the ancient world had had no experience of a government limited by a 'co-equal force within it, which could represent the 'metaphysical barrier'. 'To maintain the necessary immunity in one supreme sphere, to reduce all political authority within defined limits, ceased to be an aspiration of patient reasoners, and was made the perpetual charge and care of the most energetic institution and the most universal association in the world.'[23] Civil obedience and civil resistance were together put 'under the protection of conscience'. Perhaps it was Ranke who had pointed Acton in this direction: 'In this separation of the Church from the State consists perhaps the greatest, the most pervading and influential, peculiarity of all Christian times.'[24] Acton therefore did not look primarily to theology and dogmatics for the distinctive character of Christianity.

Acton wrote to Creighton that 'Christianity is (not) a mere system of metaphysics which borrowed some ethics from elsewhere. It is rather a system of ethics which borrowed its metaphysics elsewhere.'[25] On this assumption, it was difficult to see any theoretical peculiarity in Christianity at all: its special grace rested only on the promise of the Holy Spirit to the church which it set up.

In his view of the relation of Christianity to the pagan world, it is clear that Acton was much influenced by Lasaulx, who was an important figure in his life at Munich. He left Acton his library, and Lady Blennerhasset said Acton remembered him 'with special regard'.[26] Lasaulx's tendency was 'to see Plato, Epictetus, Aristotle, where we attribute the merit to Christianity. Opposed to persecution and slavery – Yet Christianity suppressed neither. So there came to appear a superiority in paganism over Christianity. Socrates and Christ typical of the whole.'[27]

As early as 1865, possibly under the influence of Lasaulx, Acton set himself the task of gauging the 'approach of heathen speculation to the threshold of Christianity', [28] and in 1877, he wrote to Gladstone that 'it would be very difficult indeed to show that the interval between the Ethics of Seneca and the Ethics of S. Ambrose could never have been bridged over by the progress and combination of Stoic, Alexandrian and Chinese morality as they stood, apart from the Gospel.'[29]

This was not Döllinger's position: 'In contrast to Lasaulx and Baur, whose object was to give depth and seriousness and significance to paganism, – as a great step in the approach to truth – D. showed not how much they had, but what they wanted.'[30] Acton was influenced by the notion of 'primitive revelation', which became current in Liberal Catholicism through Lamennais, and it is interesting that Bishop Butler could also be a source of such thinking.[31] Acton himself early admired Victor Cousin's exposition of an 'eclectic' philosophy. 'A new theory, the only safe one – *sens commun* – unity of all religions. Developed into Christianity, which only completes them. The essential revelation is the primitive one. Christianity is only a development.'[32]

Cards of the late 1870s indicate that Acton was thinking a good deal about the nature of the Christian revelation in itself, at the same time as he was brooding about the wickedness of the

Inquisition and the Quaker creation of Pennsylvania. He collected the 'political knowledge of the ancients before Christianity'[33] and lists every item of his liberal dogma except the separation of church and state. He noted that 'the law of nature was not codified before. Christianity was less innovation than collection and sorting out of truths, and new energy imparted to them.'[34]

In a centrally significant card headed 'Fulness of Time', he wrote: 'A doctrine to save souls existed already. Time not wanted for that. Time was chosen for a doctrine that could shape society. The social role of Christianity needed a particular condition of the world. The kingdom of God – not the salvation of souls – a doctrine that could spread and win men.'[35] While it would be unwise to place too much emphasis upon this, it is a remarkable version of what became the normal pattern of his thought. Here he is proclaiming the political structures of rational liberalism as the purpose and essence of the Gospel; that conscience and reason could achieve individual salvation, but that the existence of a Church enjoying its proper 'liberty' was necessary if the political balance was to be achieved which could lead to the 'reign of conscience', to right reason and the kingdom of God.

A mass of material in the Acton manuscripts shows how closely – and unflatteringly – Acton drew the inheritance of Christian ethics from Stoic and Essene sources. He noted that Christianity was to be understood by studying them, in the same way that Luther was to be interpreted in the light of Erasmus.[36]

Acton found the Essene tradition a focus for discussion with George Eliot,[37] and it is interesting to see that he connects their supposed reliance on conscience with their 'conception of society' and the fact that their example afforded 'the strongest condemnation of their contemporaries'.[38] As the Essenes were then thought to have no connection with Christianity,[39] Acton gives evidence here of his thesis that Christianity was not necessary to individual salvation. The Essenes freed their slaves.

It was with the Stoics, however, that Acton was chiefly concerned. Zeno (in the list of the '100 Best Books') 'led men up to the Gate of Christianity'.[40] If 'we possessed Zeno, Chrysippus etc, we should understand better how the world was made ready for the faith; and how many of the Christian ideas were familiar to the early converts.'[41] 'The Stoics were as "profound" as the Christians.'[42] It was they who in fact 'formed the notion of conscience. Yet believing in no God and no immortal soul.'[43] In the Bridgnorth Lectures and the review of Erskine May which express Acton's thinking in 1877, the Stoics are given as high a place as Penn's Quakers in the story of liberty: 'By that law, which is superior to religious traditions and national authorities, and which every man can learn from a guardian angel who neither sleeps nor errs, all are governed alike, all are equal — one community and children of the same God. – In every collision between authority and conscience they preferred the inner to the outer guide; and in the words of Epictetus, regarded the laws of the Gods, not the wretched laws of the dead.'[44]

It is interesting to compare a note Acton copied from Epictetus: 'As children we are watched by a nurse, as men by an innate conscience. – with S. Paul. In *Gal.* 3: 24–5, he speaks of the law being a *paidagogos* [a kind of private tutor] to take us to Christ. But "now that faith has come", we are no longer under him.'[45] In the Bridgnorth lectures Acton interpreted Cicero, Seneca, and Philo as saying, 'The true guide of our conduct is no outward authority, but the voice of God[46] who comes down to dwell in our souls, who knows all our thoughts, to whom are owing all the truth we know, and all the good we do; for vice is voluntary, and virtue comes from the grace of the heavenly spirit within. Therefore, we must treat others as we wish to be treated by them.'[47] Virtue, according to Epictetus, depended on complete knowledge. It was a process of aligning the will with the rational nature of things. It is incorrect for Acton to use such words as 'grace' and 'heavenly spirit' in this context. If vice is 'voluntary', the mind has natural knowledge of virtue. These propositions are the essence of Pelagius' position against St Augustine.

The Stoic atmosphere had so much in common with the late 18th-century rationalists in Europe and was so completely satisfactory to Acton that he felt compelled to defend its supersession by Christianity on the grounds of the incapacity of Stoicism to propagate itself: 'Christianity introduced no new virtue unknown to Stoics — But stronger motives. — So, impute to unbelief less a want of enumeration than a want of energy' and 'High as the ideas were, paganism had lost the means of realizing them. Religion was dying. Philosophy could not move the masses of mankind. It has no institutions.'[48] This was especially a problem in the context of the coming barbarian invasions: 'Stoicism useless for the Teutonic races. It could never have civilized them.'[49]

The moral ideas of antiquity were absorbed by Christianity. 'Why do we hear nothing of antagonism to Christianity by the Stoics or the Essenes? They merged without resistance and vanished.'[50] They were reissued under the guise of Christian liberty. Liberty was in the 'spirit of Christianity', it was 'that which is aroused by the contemplation of the life and death of Christ.'[51] 'Absolute power is condemned by no text. Yet it contradicts the entire scheme of Christianity. It is not expressly forbidden. In reality, it is more adverse than anything actually forbidden. Definite commandments may be interpreted. This cannot be qualified or modified.'[52] Christianity 'introduced the principle of liberty. By the notion of the Church distinct from the State – and the supremacy of the soul – of immortal soul. Was not this Stoic?'[53]

Acton collected the texts and passages of the New Testament which in this way founded liberty.[54] He quotes Hegel as saying that Christianity was 'quite revolutionary' and 'disregarded actual conditions'.[55] He himself wrote in a notebook of 1878, 'Christianity. Revolutionary element. It overthrew very ancient authorities. It taught men to enquire, not of their country but of themselves. It required them to believe that they had lived and prospered for thousands of years under an imposture — that all their prayers, their sacrifices, their heroic deeds, had been offered up to an unclean spirit.'[56]

Yet, however much Acton asserted that he had found the rational liberal revolution in the Gospels, he also admitted the unsatisfactory evidence on which he had to build his case. He repeatedly goes back to the 'spirit' of Christianity for his interpretation. He denies that Christianity is universal, because it requires settled and not nomadic or pastoral societies.[57] He finds considerable ground for dissatisfaction with the Jesus of history in a card of the late 1870s: 'How any one can find fault with Christ except Jews. He did so little for society and public life. All the moral ideas he adopted; not all social. There is no better ancient morality; but there are better politics. Might he not have said something to shorten suffering? Yet his whole teaching was for the benefit of the poor. But not definite.'[58]

The early church

Acton is not strikingly more enthusiastic about the church of the first four centuries. Against the infallibilists of his own day and against St Augustine, he wished to maintain with St Vincent of Lérins the authority of universal tradition as the norm of Christian doctrine. Against the Lutherans, the descendants of the Non-Jurors, the adherents of the Temporal Power, he wished to stress the prerogative authority of Liberalism in the development of doctrine. To run at the same time with Bossuet and Newman led, foreseeably, to considerable difficulties when it came to work on the Church Fathers. Acton was certainly influenced by Möhler, whom he quoted from the *Symbolik*, 'L'esprit de Dieu qui gouverne et vivifie l'église, enfante dans l'homme, en s'unissant à lui, un instinct, un tact éminemment chrétien, qui le conduit a toute vraie doctrine. Ce sentiment commun, cette *conscience* de l'église, est la tradition dans le sens subjectif du mot.'[59] This puts doctrinal authority in the Church into the hands of the consensus of the faithful, but in a way which can change with the passage of time. Acton aligned himself with what he claimed was the 17th-century English Catholic view, 'placing the authority, executively, only in general Councils confirmed by the Pope, but fundamentally and radically in the Church, upon whose approbation all depends.'[60]

There were, according to Acton, two conflicting tendencies in the early church, 'on one side to be submissive, indifferent, apathetic, averse from politics, never resisting, careless of the morrow, maintain slavery. On the other: to raise up the poor, to limit state power, to raise up conscience, to abolish punishment for sin, to work for livelihood.'[61] It was the second of these of which Acton spoke when he referred to the Fathers as interpreting Christianity in the same way as the New interpreted the Old Testament.[62] The distinction between sin and crime was a characteristic Actonian theme; it was between private vice and public wrong-doing. Only the latter he believed was a matter for punishment by the law.

Acton asserted in 1880 that liberty and, with it, conscience were discovered by the church at an early stage. 'Liberty comes first in Pseudo-Clementine books – towards 160 – not in ap[ostolic] Fathers or Justin. Strong, then in Irenaeus, and so on to Augustine. The two Greek words. Yet it made Liberty a sacred word – though not applied straight – sacredness of conscience.'[63] In a card of the same period he wrote: 'The words of Christ – Instituted a Church. Very slow influence on politics. Reasons why. But on many points, their collective wisdom anticipates ideas and doctrines which were to triumph – to constitute the pride and glory of our age. Political Economy. Communism. Charity. Emancipation. Doctrine of Progress. Equality. Individualism. Self-government. Separation of Church and State. Toleration. Conscience. Poverty of Church. Truth blushes only [to be concealed]. Involved all liberties but one.'[64] 'Liberty', he said, 'was in the early Church', and cited the names of Lactantius, Tertullian,[65] and Athanasius.[66]

But the Fathers were by no means clear in their vision of the requirements of liberty. Acton admitted in the Bridgnorth lectures that 'Down almost to the time of Chrysostom, they shrank from contemplating the obligation to emancipate the slaves. Although the doctrine of self-reliance and self-denial, which is the foundation of political economy, was written as legibly in the New Testament as in the Wealth of Nations, it was not recognized until our age,'[67] and he drew attention to a number of political illiberalisms of which the greatest Fathers had been guilty.[68] It was 'So long before they wrote Ethics. Only S. Ambrose. There were books on Paradise etc. before they took to this. – So they are not authorities on politics. They long wished Christianity to keep aloof from it.'[69]

Acton places special stress on St John Chrysostom in the evolution of this ethical thinking.[70] He noted that Chrysostom invoked 'conscience most often among the Fathers'[71]: that he spoke of it as 'the incorruptible judge' and a 'sufficient guide to virtue'.[72] An important card, which begins, 'Chrysostom, the only Father who deals much with conscience, takes his departure more from Cicero than the Bible',[73] goes on to give an extract from his commentary on Genesis.[74] From another card, it appears that Chrysostom's thinking about this natural knowledge of the moral law sprang very largely from his consideration of the Old Testament.[75] Even before Moses, the Scriptures did not picture the patriarchs as ignorant of the moral law, for they had conscience to teach them.

It is significant that St Jerome, with whose works Acton was familiar, was also notorious for the vision in which an angel appeared telling him, 'Thou art more a Ciceronian than a Christian.' The stream of thought which Acton considered as representing the real spirit of the Gospel owed its cohesion largely to undue Stoic influence. However, the question does arise whether in fact – in some form – conscience *was* in the spirit of the Gospel.

There is a notebook, probably dating from the 1880s, in which Acton set out a history of England from 1494 to 1642 for his younger children. In it he writes of the heart of Christianity in a way which illustrates again his constant concern for the poor and the uneducated – not the normal Stoic constituency: 'Our Lord sent out twelve poor fishermen and workmen to teach all nations, not twelve kings. If governments could decide what the people may or may not believe, the apostles would have had no chance. It would have been necessary for Christ to begin by converting the men who were in power over the nations, in order that they might order their subjects to become Christians. Instead of that, he began with the poor.'[76] (One might add, if so, that 'he began' in a style very different from the later Germanic folk-conversions.)

The preaching of Christianity, Acton said to Gladstone in a letter of 1888, demanded 'a time when monotheism had made some way. Also a time in which ethical science had been thought out.'[77] At its initial propagation, Christianity was an appeal, under the conditions of a supra-national civilisation, to the moral nature of ordinary men.

In a real sense, later scholarship has tended to show that the supersession of the law by the conscience was indeed a centrally significant part of the preaching of both Christ and St Paul.[78] Amos Wilder writes that the discarding of the code of clean and unclean is 'latent and prepared in Jesus' words, but only took effect in the time of the early church,' and that when Jesus claims the authority to 'rule freely upon ethical issues, the fulfilment of the law [passes] over logically into transcendence of it'. Thornton-Duesbury, citing *I Pet.* 2: 19, asserts that the 'final authority of conscience rests upon God's will'. He, too, agrees that it is the Wisdom Literature which 'brings us to the threshold of the NT and the distinctively Christian use of the word'. The logos becomes identified with the whole principle of creation in its development through time.

St Paul takes this transcendence of the law further, but it is transcendence by grace. It is significant that Hodges finds the kernel of the doctrine of justifying faith in the verse of St Paul's *Letter to the Romans* 14: 23, which Acton used to build his history of conscience. Hodges writes, 'The kind of action S. Paul has in mind here is the breaking of a tabu, and to do it "from faith" is to take to oneself the freedom of a Christian man ... because one believes that this is God's guidance to one in Christ. Without this motive, S. Paul says, the action cannot be guiltless. Here is the doctrine of justifying faith in a nutshell .... faith is ... a motive which issues in action, and ... it is this motive ... which justifies the act and the agent.'[79] Acton was therefore right to stress the germinal importance of this aspect of Paul's argument, but was eccentric in setting it in a context of rational integrity rather than grace and will. The Stoic and Christian conscience are so far apart, when they are put in their own contexts, that it is not

surprising that their divergence should have led to the battles of
the Pelagian heresy, the deepest and longest rumbling in the
history of Christian doctrine. Acton tended to look at the
Christian conscience in the early Church more through the eyes
of Chrysostom than St Paul.

St Augustine

It is in the period dominated by St Augustine when the church
has already inherited political power that it is clear Acton has
become an engaged spectator. This is the point in the history of
liberty at which Acton argues that the true Christian idea of
conscience was deliberately perverted, in order to serve the
purposes of a dogmatic controversy. At Munich Acton was
educated to distrust Augustine. Lasaulx, Möhler, and Döllinger[80]
– through their desire both to confound Luther and to do justice
to the smaller men and the losing causes of history – were eager
to reassess the contribution which Augustine's many opponents
might make to the development of Christian thought. Döllinger,
indeed, professed to see in Augustinianism the denial of the
whole idea of God's justice and mercy.[81]

Acton shared and developed this position from the special angle
afforded by his conception of the conscience. He saw, as we have
seen, the gradual appropriation of the ideas of 'liberty' among the
early Fathers: free will and the natural law were gaining wide
acceptance. Ambrose, Jerome, and Chrysostom all believed
strongly in the connexion between the Roman Empire's acceptance of Christianity under Constantine and a progress and
happiness that might stretch indefinitely into the future.[82]
Augustine denied their biblical credentials. The controversies he
waged, against the Donatists, the Manichees, and the Pelagians,
were all concerned from one aspect or another in maintaining the
transcendent character of Christianity, and – in spite of his deep
debt to Cicero – in recovering from the Scriptures the elements
which were foreign to lay Stoic thought.[83]

Acton believed Augustine had gone too far, in nearly all of
these controversies. For instance, there is much evidence that
Acton had some sympathy with the Donatist attitude. At one
time he doubted the validity of Ultramontane sacraments. The
most explicit occasion, in 1879, was at a time of great stress and
should not be taken too seriously,[84] but it lends point to other
more specifically historical references.[85] He makes much of the
difficulties encountered by the early Church as a result of the

'flood of pagan proselytes', or of the fact that Christians were no longer 'picked men'; but the serious damage is done by Augustine's systematic and theoretical exposition of the nature of free will. He wrote, around 1880, 'Augustine. The man who chooses evil is not free. He had gone wrong under compulsion of his depraved nature, compelled by original sin. So that liberty does not consist in the power of choosing, but in the certainty of choice. What we have to protect is not the power of doing what we like, but the impossibility of doing evil.'[86] Also, 'S. Augustine on liberty. In one sense all men are free to play the piano. But there is no identity between the liberty to play enjoyed by one who knows how to play, and the one who is not trained. A man is free, not in proportion as his choice is open, but as it is certain.'[87] In this way, Acton concluded at this time, Augustine 'changed' early Christian liberty into the propositions that 'The will is not free when captive to sin. Therefore compulsion is deliverance. Persecution is charity. Restraint is freedom.'[88] Thus he 'made non-liberty a theory'.[89] He 'had no notion of natural law', and what 'was good for a soul was right'.[90] Augustinianism was 'an impediment to the idea of conscience'.[91] It was 'the philosophy of persecution'.[92]

In the box labelled 'Conscience', there is a card which reveals how consciously Acton was prepared to come down on the Pelagian side of the fence. It runs, 'Conscience. Fathers describe it as sufficient and unerring. But then differences of opinion cannot be conscientious, at least not in things requiring salvation. So there is no respect due to the dissentient, to error. Pelagius appeals to conscience – Augustine goes against him. To affirm that guide seemed to deny original sin. Augustine removed the criterion from within to outside. An external authority alone safe. For the inner man is corrupted by Original Sin, does not distinguish good from evil, and does not resist evil.'[93]

If he was to retain his conviction that the means of salvation were open to all, irrespective of Christianity, Acton was obliged to oppose Augustine from two points of view. He believed Augustine both exaggerated the position of the church and was ethically unscientific. 'S. Augustine. Church the only road to heaven. So it would not be wrong to compel entrance. — This makes Church everything – enlarges its sphere indefinitely. And reduces the state to a necessary evil – an unnecessary evil. State power superfluous. Church power good for everything.'[94] and, 'He positively admired slavery. It was beneficial. So far was he from the notion of human freedom. The use of authority seemed to him more efficient than the use of liberty. One was given by God – not the other. God instituted definite authorities for the salvation of mankind.'[95] Thus, by virtue of putting salvific authority in the church rather than in the individual conscience, Acton believed Augustine to have laid the foundation of the medieval theocracy and its inquisition.

Acton also believed this confidence in state-imposed religion was in practice ill judged, even if one were to grant that it might be in the service of true religion. 'That no persecutor can be sincere – That the denial of sincerity must accompany persecution. Accordingly that theory followed on the other. NB. S Augustine.'[96] Practising Kantian ethical science involves being able to put oneself into another's thought world. How could someone do this, and be so convinced afterwards by the absolute rightness of his own opinions that he was able to persecute? Acton argued that those who promoted persecution from a Christian standpoint were not only 'unscientific' but the agents of conscious perversion. To repress heresy as crime was such a perversion. In 1879 Acton was preoccupied with William Penn's golden rule of 'do as you would be done by' both because its rejection had created the tradition of Christians killing for heresy and because its acceptance had created Pennsylvania. He had a characteristically dramatic conception of the birth of Christian persecution. It sprang 'fully-armed' from 'the brain of one man', who was himself made to suffer as an early victim of the process he inaugurated. This man was Priscillian (*d.* 385), a Spanish bishop and theologian, accused of practices similar to those of the later Cathari.[97]

Although persecution was not Augustine's invention, a philosophic basis for it remained one of his major legacies to Christian thought in the West. Acton believed it could only be arrived at by an intolerable misreading of *Romans* 14: 23.[98] It was also ludicrously ill adapted to the situation of any church life since the collapse of the Roman Empire. 'S. Augustine. The objection which seems so obvious and conclusive, that if states may exterminate religions, Christianity has no chance against paganism – and the majority will prevail – did not apply. They did not expect to spread among the barbarian nations. The cross should follow the eagles. Long before it should conquer the world beyond, the prophecies would be fulfilled, and anti-Christ would appear.'[99]

But almost the principal objection to persecution was that it marked a decisive innovation in the life of the Christian church

– 'Yet it was a new morality and a new system.'[100] It was St Ambrose who saw clearer into the future. He refused to be in communion with the bishops who had executed Priscillian for his dogmatic belief, and, 'seeing that the empire was falling, and the Church must stand by itself', cried, 'Convince and cure, not conquer'.[101]

Acton and Pelagianism

It is difficult to avoid discussing how far Acton diverged from the orthodox Christian conception of the nature of original sin – the point at issue between Augustine and Pelagius. Original sin cannot be part of 'scientific' ethics. In his introduction to Augustine's manifesto against the Pelagians, Prof. Burnaby speaks of Pelagius feeling himself called upon to 'stop the rot' of contemporary morality: 'The religion of Pelagius was firmly based upon two axioms: that God is just, and that man is responsible – which means free. –- A just God can give an unfair start to no-one. And he can command nothing which any man is unable to perform: the existence of a divine command necessarily implies ability in all to whom it is given to obey it. All men *can* keep the commandments of God if they will. — It is open to all Christians without exception to set themselves, by a life in accordance with the Gospel ideal of poverty, chastity and well-doing, to earn the supreme rewards which only such a life can win. And if it is open to all, it is incumbent upon all.'[102] A state of grace was possible for the man who put himself in the position to achieve it. The work of Christ on this account is essentially the superhumanly difficult new law of the Sermon on the Mount, rather than the 'good news' of a saving faith. It was an interpretation of Christianity much current in German theological circles at the end of the 19th century. 'The theology of Pelagius', Burnaby concludes, 'was the theology of Deism: his ethics were the ethics of naturalism'.[103]

It is clear that in this sense Acton was completely Pelagian. His widespread condemnation of figures of the historical past was based on the proposition that they knew better, and that, as he repeated so many times, men were to be judged by their lowest level. This is a quite extraordinary and unchristian criterion. It is particularly hard on those who swing like Belloc's little girl from being 'very very good' to being 'horrid'. A careful consideration of Acton's notes shows that he was brought up several times against the question of how far he was a heretic;

most notably in his conversations with George Eliot. In general he was, as he said, unprepared to 'work things out', and therefore continued to hold universalist and immanentist ideas which, logically, were incompatible with traditional orthodox Christianity.

As usual, it is useful to turn to the Munich background. Acton repeatedly says how much Döllinger admired Butler and Fénelon.[104] Both these figures were extreme minimisers of the Fall. Butler was notorious for his semi-Pelagianism. He spoke of religion having to be acquired not accepted, of the world being converted merely by the 'exemplification' of Christianity 'in the lives of the Christian nations', and of original sin as existing only in the 'repetition of irregularities' which produce the 'habits' of depravity.[105] Döllinger was 'surrounded by 18th-century influences. Rationalist, sceptic, deist, abounded.'[106] He maintained a continual war against Luther's moral teaching, because it stressed the doctrine of imputation, 'which is incompatible with any system of moral theology'.[107] They both wished to establish that moral effort is necessary for progress on earth and salvation in heaven.[108] It was for this reason that Acton was baffled, as well as distressed, when Döllinger refused in 1879 to share his 'ethical position' and 'found no end of excuses'.[109]

The kernel of this ethical position was expressed in the card, 'One must apply principles that cut either way, in politics. If you are guided by any object, then that object must be the highest. Men may then say, the highest object is religion. Therefore persecution is the right thing. To counter this, you must have some object higher even than religion. That is, either politics are [an] affair of morality, or the purposes of religion transcend it. If politics transcend religion, that is, if you are Liberal, it is because the ethical purpose is supreme.'[110] There is an ideological side to Acton which carries this attribution of sovereign value to political liberalism to the point where it is hard to see what (in the absence of religious dogma) could stand in its way should constitutional governments think it necessary for their own survival to persecute, e.g. fascists. At a gentler level he seems to be saying with S. T. Coleridge, 'He who loves Christianity better than Truth, will love his sect or church better than Christianity, and end by loving himself best of all.'

Liberal politics have become the essence of morality, and morality is the object of the divine purpose. The authority of the church is therefore in moral, not in ecclesiastical, politics. Acton looked upon the *Politiques* in 16th-century France as a great step forward, because, between conflicting churches, they brought forward an independent notion of political morality.[111] Acton wrote, 'Conscience. Authority that speaks through the conscience is divine. That which is perceived through the senses is human. Therefore Locke denied divine right.'[112] In a series of important cards, Acton was forced to the conclusion that if, as we have seen he did, he accepted political morality as the absolute of history, and conscience as the sovereign arbiter of political morality, he had very largely placed himself in a camp dominated by 18th-century Deists and unbelievers. He came to recognise this as his 'Whig Church'.

In two cards headed 'Influence of Unbelief' in the George Eliot box, written on succeeding days, he wrote, 'Now it is precisely in those things peculiar to Deism that the progress took place. Torture, Criminal Law, Toleration, Slavery, Education, Political Economy, International Law' and 'By what dogmas? – Rejection of original sin. Denial of divine authority leaves all society to Contract. Desire not to punish vice or crimes against religion made them mitigate the severity of criminal law.'[113] And in the 'Conscience' boxes he wrote, '18th century conscience. Rationalism taught that Reason suffices without dogma. It followed that they encouraged the inner light also in ethics. The guide to truth is in the mind, not outside,'[114] and 'Conscience the great resource of unbelief. They have done most to develop the notion. Fully prepared by Butler. Then Rousseau, Kant, Fichte, denying original sin. It came to the front about 1700',[115] and 'Rousseau develops conscience so that he concludes from it that man is originally good and is only corrupted by outward influences. The inward influence which is the man himself is right and good.'[116]

Acton was clearly aware of the unorthodox doctrinal position to which his 'ethical science' might lead, removed from the typically Catholic context of revelation and the authority of the church. There is a certain amount of evidence to show that he believed he had guarded himself against that danger. In his list of the '100 Best Books', he says Pelagius gave 'religious form to the most powerful of errors'.[117] A number of cards stress how no historian 'thinks well of human nature'.[118] Others draw from the proposition that 'conscience starts from sin', the supposition that 'denial of Fall is denial of conscience'.[119]

Can these be a defence of his orthodoxy? The conscience which 'starts from sin' is not the conscience of which Acton usually speaks. He deceives himself by using the same word. That kind of conscience is the moral pain of which George Eliot and

Sophocles spoke, not the moral knowledge which the Stoics and Pelagius had in mind, and which the Scholastics spoke of as *synteresis*. If Acton's absolute of liberty was in fact, as he often repeated, the 'reign of conscience', it could not be the empire of moral pain. It would be a meaningless concept. It must mean a rational conscience.

It is when Acton deems that men – especially great men – are sinners and criminals, when they come under historical scrutiny, that he seems to be more secure doctrinally. This is at the heart of Acton's consciously developed system. But the very force of Acton's judicial vocation, which had the crude power to shock the historical minds of Döllinger and Creighton, sprang from his contention that knowledge should be sufficient for good action. He condemned Wolsey and the medieval popes because they knew the Apostles' Creed. He condemned the Greeks because they knew as much as the Essenes. Perhaps indeed these people did enjoy this ethical 'knowledge'. But St Paul addressed the 'good news' of Christianity precisely to those weighed down by failure to do the good they 'knew'.

There are a few cards, such as 'The doctrines of morality can be taught apart from religion, but not observed. The force that repents, that returns, comes from religion. Without religion, nothing supplies them',[120] which stress exactly this point, that the Old World knew the good, but required Christianity to achieve it. Sometimes, in a platonic way, Acton writes of the 'passions' as the normal obstacle to salvation.[121] Yet Acton's argument for the discovery of liberty at the American Revolution is that the Christian world knew liberty (which for Acton was a large part of morality), but required Deists to achieve it. It remains an astonishing fact that Acton made this the central dynamic thread of his history.

It might be argued that in all these passages Acton is speaking as a historian, eager to maintain a moral standard, but not to judge the final value of characters before God: that he described crime, rather than predicted damnation. Yet against this, there is the passage we quoted, which speaks of the means of 'salvation' existing for the individual before Christ. Salvation is a theological term. We are talking about union with God.

It is always valuable in studying Acton to compare his position with that of the Quakers and of Leibnitz. The Quakers would not impute to mankind any kind of guilt from original sin.[122] Leibnitz too came at the end of a century in which, as in Jeremy Taylor, the account of the Fall had been mythologised. He wrote his

Theodicy with the intention of opposing St Augustine's plan of providence.[123] Austin Farrer has written of Leibnitz that the Christian scheme of redemption 'hardly looks like being for him a crucial deliverance from perdition .... God's benevolence is known by pure reason and apart from Christian revelation.'[124] This is surely where Acton stood. His was not a 'born again' Christianity.

Like St Vincent of Lérins, Acton wished to allow human free will far more than Augustine. He was prepared to resist the contemporary church in doing so. And like St Vincent, his argument against Augustine was tradition. Cardinal Manning denied this argument: 'The appeal to antiquity is both a treason and a heresy. It is a treason because it rejects the divine voice of the Church at this hour, and a heresy because it denies that voice to be divine.'[125]

It is ironic that Acton too should have spoken so readily of a direct Cartesian 'divine voice', but as the property of individuals. Manning claimed that the pope personally enjoys a quality of communication with God in his conscience beside which any other experience of conscience loses its authority.[126] Faced with this extreme view, Acton wrote, 'S. Vincent tells us what to do to ascertain orthodoxy. It required research. It became a question of information. Thus rather reduces the importance of authority.'[127] Vincent's criterion for tradition depended on consensus.[128] Acton seems to have been much impressed by Newman's argument in the *Rambler* that it was not the bishops, and not the previous Fathers, but the Christian people as a whole, who determined that Arianism was heresy.[129] In that case, tradition could change, provided it did so on a broad front and became development.

Therefore, Acton was very far from Bossuet in his appeal to the early church's tradition. He proposed the historian instead of the church as the authority for what were the beliefs of that tradition,[130] and he proposed that that tradition was not static, but could be modified by the consensus of subsequent reasonable opinion. Nevertheless, Acton's rational predispositions made him interpret the early church in a radically misleading light. He so consistently maximised the Stoic elements in its history that, though he would not call himself a Pelagian, he naturalised Christianity in a comparable way. Like the Quakers, he was quite unprepared to identify salvation with church membership.[131] He tended to equate the essence of the Gospel with its political consequences, which became his own interpretation of Liberalism.

The foundation of Teutonic Christianity

Nevertheless, it was Augustine who put his stamp on the Middle Ages. The year 500 was of peculiar importance to Acton. Two processes were set on foot which were to determine the Reformation struggle of the 16th century. By virtue of one, the hierarchy of the church began to establish ideas of its temporal authority on the basis of various forged 'donations', and so began the introduction of what Acton called the 'pagan' element into the church.[132] Until 1100, however, the institution was not powerful enough to make the new ideas effective, and the gospel tradition was largely preserved.

The other process was to be considered as the root of liberty, and of sufficient value to balance the human misery and the destruction of civilisation at the break-up of Rome. It justified the hypothesis of providence. Christianity required German ideas of society for it to be able to 'work out its thoughts'.[133] The separation of powers, the essence of the New Testament in Acton's view, stretched the habitual mind-set of Mediterranean Christians beyond their capacity.[134]

Acton wrote in a card preparatory to the Bridgnorth lectures that 'Early Christianity knew everything except resistance. Rome preached Christianity. Our Lord paid tribute to the Emperor. It has a special sacredness. The passages were applied to it. Afterwards, the Germans brought in other ideas. Their state did not absorb all authority. Their magistrates did not represent the united voice of all. Their allegiance was conditional. Their laws too important to impose themselves on all men. To men accustomed to the science, philosophy, profound jurisprudence of Rome, the new states were not very imposing. The clergy approached them as strangers.'[135] Also, at the same time, and with interesting relevance to the experience of Pennsylvania, 'It [the church] was so long under persecution, when retirement was the best plan – that it could not realize how it would govern a state. It became free without any notions of using freedom. The monastic *weltflucht* was a survival. Then, faith becoming reliance on authority, became external. Authority was carried so far that any authority would do. The Scholastic idea of conscience confused, because, what was the mistaken conscience to do? Salvianus.'[136]

Acton took a special interest in Salvianus (A.D. 390–470). In the same box he wrote, 'Salvianus, *De Avaritia*, the first attempt to remodel society on Christian principles. He was one of the few who saw that a new day was dawning.'[137] In the *Dictionnaire de*

Théologie Catholique, G Bardy relates Salvianus to Rousseau in his comparison of the virtuous barbarian with the vicious product of Roman civilisation. Salvianus was one of the Lérins circle of monastics. He declared that if the Germans had been led astray into Arianism, the reason for their heresy was to be sought in the bad behaviour of the orthodox they knew: a position with which Acton, in his contemporary situation, had some sympathy.[138]

A few cards even indicate that Acton derived the politics of identifying natural law with conscience from German tribal law. In both the 'Conscience' boxes there occurs the thought, 'Conscience – The German nation introduces the higher law, vaguely, not thought out. It is ascertained how? By an oracle? Or from within? See the history of Individualism. It is known not from outside, but from within. Not will, but law. That is the solution. Not what each man chooses – But what all believe, is law.'[139]

It certainly appears that Acton had been educated under the impression common among contemporary German writers that, even if there might not be liberty in all primitive peoples,[140] there was something peculiarly open to liberty in barbaric German peoples.[141] The belief at Munich was that liberty was the product of Christianity acting upon German institutions.[142] In 1859, Acton painted the condition of Western Europe between 500 and Hildebrand as a Golden Age. '[Then] were laid the foundations of all the happiness that has since been enjoyed, and of all the greatness that has been achieved, by man. — It was not an age of conspicuous saints, but sanctity was at no time so general. — In such a state of the world, the Christian ideas were able to become incarnate, so to speak, in durable forms, and succeeded in animating the political institutions, as well as the social life, of the nations. — But the Teutonic race received the Catholic ideas wholly and without reserve. There was no region into which they failed to penetrate. The nation was collectively Catholic, as well as individually.'[143] Even the early medieval church, he says, was a 'model of constitutional polity'.[144]

In the same kind of way and at the same time that Acton conceived Pennsylvania to have been the result of a Christian society having to make its political arrangements, he conceived of these medieval Germanic kingdoms creating the idea of a Christendom within political boundaries. Inside these boundaries, the completely secular could have no place. Caesar did not therefore exist, and the Gospel injunctions to obey him had to lapse. Their Christian kings were crowned by the church, and drew their inspiration from King David. So politics became a matter of rational, Christian discussion, sanctioned by rebellion. In no other way, he said (*c.* 1850), could resistance have been made a part of Christian politics. 'As the command to obey rulers was unqualified, how did the Christians get over it? In Rome, never. The authority remained unassailed by them. But when they specially sanctioned monarchy by crowning, etc., they also rejected such as they did not sanction. But how did it begin? The idea of the superiority of the church over state was the only road by which they could overcome the strict precepts of the NT.'[145] Acton accepted the bloody war of American Independence and the oppression of the American Indians by Columbus for the sake of the ultimate end of the realised liberal state. What however is extraordinary, given his discipleship of Vinet and his devotion to St Paul's text in *Romans* 14: 23, is his allowance of the use of force to convert the German tribes. They had a subordinate, but essential, part to play in the central history of mankind.[146]

Believing that the barbarian invasions were an indispensable stage in the evolution of rational liberalism, Acton was prepared to let that justify the misery and bloodshed that was the other side of that 'Golden Age'. Perhaps nowhere is the transposition of values in Acton's mind clearer. The protest Acton makes at the use of bad means for ostensibly good ends against Machiavelli and the medieval popes could logically be made against Charlemagne and even the American revolutionaries. But he wrote: 'The question was, should the laws be based on pagan or on Christian notions. The breach was infinite. Barbarous customs had to be changed into civilized Christianity. This required great force; men had to be compelled to give up customs founded on paganism. The civilizing states necessarily assumed the right of abridging religious liberty in the interest of Christian civilization.'[147] Liberty, the achievement of certain specific Liberal maxims, is, he held, a good of such eventual sovereign worth that involuntary as well as self-sacrificial suffering is to be welcomed in its realisation.

He was quite conscious why it was dangerous for a religion on its own to be entitled to claim such privilege: 'If the Church is the only way to heaven, the kingdom of God on earth, it is better to fight for its extension than for any other cause. If there is no salvation outside it, it is no hardship to be forced into it. If we may fight to extend territory, to impose trade, why not to extend the Church, and impose salvation?'[148]

By the time of the full conversion of the barbarian tribes – the bearers of 'Teutonic' feudal liberty – into a recognisable constellation of Christian kingdoms at the end of the first Christian millennium, the elements of a happy balance had been lost. The two 'churches' were in tension. The reformed Hilde-brandine papacy had the poison of forgery in its bloodstream for which that non-historical age could have no cure. 'Nothing speculative in Hildebrand. Mere adoption of feudal notions. Then came ideas of Roman law, then, emanation of all power. See especially the letters of Dionysius Ar[eopagiticus]. Written at Alexandria end of Vth century. Time of Proclus [an ardent pagan and neo-Platonist], and under his influence. So this was a distinctly pagan element in the Church, foreign, false, crimin-al.'[149]

The dynamic of the consequent interaction was, according to Acton, to be the substance of modern history.

7
Acton's Universal History: the Drama of Modern History

The Scholastic origins of the Liberal conscience

The first of Acton's *Lectures on Modern History* discusses the birth in the 13th century of that Liberal conscience which in the last of them he describes as having issued in the American achievement of a Liberal state. Especially in the last years of his life he became insistent that the idea of revolution, which was the key to that liberal achievement, was a product of medieval thought. In the box Add. MS 4960, preparatory to the Cambridge lectures, are these cards: 'Revolution comes from the Middle Ages. Hildebrand. Salisbury. Aquinas. Franciscans. Bracton.[1] Constance[2]' and 'The great constant influence of the Middle Ages on Modern was not in institutions or customs, but in ideas. It was done by books, and by individual writers of books, many of whom found no audience in their time. Against the outer world, the product, modern times rebelled. The nether world of thought subsisted, and contributed to the building up of a new world. It is the Revolution. The idea of what ought to be — of combating history by design, the Past. Progress, rights of the individual conscience, self-government.'[3] All this required the notion of Christendom to have been established, in which power could balance power.

Acton, believing as he did that the separation of powers was central to the Christian Gospel, did not hold that Christendom implied a church-state after the old Graeco-Roman pattern. He saw the fact that there was no experience of duality of power at Rome under the old regime of the Temporal Power as a major factor in the problems of Pio Nono's curia.[4] The elements in the Middle Ages which were hierocratic and neoplatonic, and which gave rise to the principles of the Inquisition, were, he thought, essentially foreign to Christianity. Some had come in by the various forgeries, especially through Pseudo-Dionysius (whose works, interestingly enough, had been edited by Darboy – the archbishop of Paris who was Acton's close friend at the Council

– in 1845). Others had arisen from the necessities of existence in an immature society, where the church had to act for a time as the schoolmaster of all civilisation. Acton believed these outmoded and foreign elements were sloughed off intellectually by a few thinkers in the 13th century, and more practically and on a larger scale after the Reformation. They still needed to be rooted out.

A discussion of Acton's interpretation of this aspect of history must begin with the famous and hitherto ambiguous passage in his introduction to the Cambridge course of lectures on Modern History. After pointing out the general sense of decay current in the Middle Ages, he said, 'Yet the most profound and penetrating of the causes that have transformed society is a medieval inheritance. It was late in the thirteenth century that the psychology of Conscience was closely studied for the first time, and men began to speak of it as the audible voice of God, that never misleads or fails, and that ought to be obeyed always, whether enlightened or darkened, right or wrong. The notion was restrained, on its appearance, by the practice of regarding opposition to Church power as equivalent to specific heresy, which depressed the secret monitor below the public and visible authority. With the decline of Coercion, the claim of Conscience rose, and the ground abandoned by the Inquisitor was gained by the individual .... When it had been defined and recognised as something divine in human nature, its action was to limit power by causing the sovereign voice within to be heard above the expressed will and settled custom of surrounding men. By that hypothesis, the soul became more sacred than the state, because it receives light from above, as well as because its concerns are eternal, and out of all proportion with the common interests of government.'[5] In searching for this 'discovery', we have therefore to look for some theory of conscience which talks in terms of a divine 'voice within' or 'light from above', but which is unwilling to allow that this individual perception can operate against the corporate voice of the church.

Although the interpretation of conscience in this way was for Acton something of a corporate achievement by the 13th-century Scholastics, there can be no doubt that he saw St Thomas Aquinas as the fundamental innovator, and therefore as the true Moses of the pilgrimage to the American Constitution. Acton spoke of the Thomist conscience as possessing those qualities of revolution and natural reason which were the practical contribution of the Americans. He wrote, 'Denial of History. Not XVIII

133

century but XIII. Not Sieyès but Aquinas'[6] and 'Idea of Conscience after XIII Century. Found S. Thomas on that. It arose in full tide of persecution. It gradually undermined it.'[7] and 'Romans XIV.23 – How S. Thomas made it the basis of a theory of conscience. Was it known before him or was that his discovery? If so, it was a great step in the ways of freedom. Point out how S. Augustine misinterpreted it.'[8] This centrality of St Thomas in the development of conscience is discernible among the notes of all periods.

It is probable that Acton was led into a study of medieval ideas of conscience by the doctoral thesis of Jahnel (a pupil of Trendelenburg),[9] *De Conscientia Notione*, which was published at Berlin in 1862. Acton's copy is profusely lined, and it is notable that Jahnel's picture of the history of conscience starts with Socrates and the Stoics, as opposed to Sophocles and the Orestes tradition, and goes on to place the essence of conscience among the Scholastics, and especially on those of them, Saints Bernard, Bonaventure, and Thomas, who played a like role in Acton's world-picture.

Before elaborating those particular points which Acton and Jahnel saw in Aquinas, it must be admitted that Acton's emphasis on the Thomist contribution to the idea of conscience is justifiable.[10] Acton's peculiar contribution was to put this development of the notion of the prerogative power of conscience in the context of political liberalism. The rational conscience had pre-eminently political implications for Acton, and it is uncertain whether Aquinas would have welcomed the stress Acton puts on one part of his elaborately inter-related synthesis. Granted, however, that the teleological approach to history is an acceptable one, there is no reason why Acton's selective hindsight should, of itself, make his interpretation invalid.

Acton put Aquinas into the sequence of thought which led forward to Penn and the liberal state when, for instance, he wrote, 'Conscience. Importance of S. Thomas' use of the term. Why then did he not apply it to religion? Because he denied that religious error is conscientious. So long there was no liberty. If the state excludes all that, it does what it likes. Extend the domain of conscience to religious error, and then only is liberty possible',[11] and 'S. Thomas. As to penal laws, he went with his generation. For half a century, when he wrote, not a voice had been raised for toleration. — But in respect of conscience he innovated. He went further than all his time in proclaiming its authority. This was peculiarly his own idea – set out by him, and gifted with power – in time – to overcome the other.'[12] This is not a capricious interpretation of the nature of European history. He is being more fanciful, however, when he wrote of St Thomas, 'Taught by the Church, by the laws of Rome, by the philosophy of Greece, extorted Aristotle from the Arabians – and so enabled to develop ideas and institutions which in the gristle were visible on the Elbe'.[13] Acton's transposition of religious language to politics follows his belief that the liberal propositions were innately present to the sincere conscience of the natural man in the same way that Aquinas claimed orthodox theological propositions were apparent to the Christian man.

Acton's other major emphasis regarding Aquinas is on the commentary which he gave to St Paul's verse, 'And he that doubteth is damned if he eat [pagan meats], because he eateth not of faith: for whatsoever is not of faith is sin' (*Romans* XIV.23). He saw in this the 'basis of a theory of conscience'. It is typical of Acton that in putting such stress on the *Commentary to the Romans* he chose one of the very small number of Aquinas's works which had not been translated into English.[14] In it Aquinas argues that the clause, 'for whatever is not of faith is sin', is to be understood in two senses. In the one, 'fides' is to be taken as 'virtus'; in the other, as 'conscientia'. An act of conscience is an instance in space and time of a universal obligation, and therefore the situation may well arise where what is in general a meritorious act is the opposite of meritorious for a historical person. An individual requires faith to make his action meritorious – 'it is impossible to please God without faith'. If, in the case of Aquinas, 'fides' has a sub-meaning of 'conscientia', St Paul's assertion can be compared with Abelard's famous tag, 'it is not a sin unless it is against the conscience'.[15] It is at any rate clear from this comment of Aquinas that forced conversions lead to damnation. Only by a presupposition that, as Aquinas declared, there is an instinctive recognition of orthodoxy can the heretic be excluded.

In the box which contains cards preparing for the *Lectures in Modern History*, there are extracts which illuminate the particular aspect of Aquinas which Acton chose as in fact being the first 'close study of conscience'. In these Aquinas speaks of the divine law of grace not denying the natural law of human reason, and cites the testimony given by conscience to good and evil as evidence for the law being written upon 'the heart of man' as prophesied in *Jeremiah* 31.33.[16]

To prove that Aquinas was the founder of the 'conscience'

spoken of in the *Lectures*, his work had to contain three statements about conscience: that it was innate in every man, received 'light from above', and was not to be believed against the voice of the church. He satisfies these requirements.[17] It is clear however that Acton, though he gave the primacy to Aquinas, thought of the 13th-century discovery of conscience as a much wider movement, which included Simon de Montfort, St Francis and St Bonaventure.

There is a typical polarity of dramatic light and darkness in Acton's view of the situation in that particular generation. With God and Devil both on stage, it is for Acton a moment of significance for universal history: 'Conscience. It arose at the time when persecution was at its height. Inquisition instituted, organized towards 1230. Conscience begins in Alexander of Hales, St Thomas and St Bonaventure.'[18]

Acton and Döllinger devoted much effort and research to the question, 'how did the church become Ultramontane?' It was the question that was preoccupying Acton in 1874 at the moment when the Gladstone crisis broke over his head.[19] They both came to the conclusion that the late 13th century was specially important, and that it was a kind of revolution, a revolution begun by Hildebrand and completed by the imposition on the church of the theory of the Inquisition in the 13th century. Acton wrote of the 'exquisitely complex psychological revolution that proceeded, after the year 1200, about the Gulf of Lyons and the Tyrrhene Sea.'[20] And on two other cards, marked 'NB': 'Inquisition established power of Church over State. What Gregory [VII] attempted by revolution, Innocent [III] attempted by law' and 'Thereby the Popes recovered indirectly the power they had claimed directly.'[21] (As was his habit, Acton ascribed the idea of the Inquisition to a particular man, Raymond of Pennaforte, at a particular time, 1230–51.)[22] This revolution was possible because the church had lost the apostolic tradition, and was forced to substitute for it Scholastic theories: 'In Middle Ages they required something instead of Tradition, which was lost. The living Church naturally took its place. They could not work with the Traditions they did not possess. That is how Scholasticism created the Roman theory. While history is the independent witness.'[23]

Aquinas thus had to appear, paradoxically, on the one hand as the greatest of the Schoolmen spinning out from his head an unsure basis for church authority, and on the other as the exponent of the true 'spirit of Christianity' which had been developed by contact with German folk institutions. One was innovation, the other natural evolution. By discerning the providential direction of things – a rather odd, if creative, role — History would have to be the judge.

Acton's analysis of the 13th century was never published. From the great number and significance of cards in the box preparatory to the Cambridge lectures (Add. MS 4960), it is clear that this period bulked large in his interpretation of general history. The Franciscans, for instance, who are extremely important for his history of conscience in that box, scarcely appear at all in the earlier notes.[24] It was a topic on which he was working until very late in his life. Acton was to have contributed the first chapter of the first volume of the *Cambridge Modern History* on the inheritance of the Middle Ages.

Acton described the difficulty for any medieval individualism: 'authority, discipline, control – Men in the mass. Result of endeavour to break in the barbarians. They were in groups – never standing alone,'[25] and, on an extremely important card, 'Tendency to make men dependent on others – laity on clergy, small on great. So they did not like men to have a sure guide within – But the theorists did not accept that line. They did not call the influence making for good "conscience" – the word "synteresis" begins with Alexander of Hales.'[26] It was given the status of a 'herald' or 'voice of God'[27] and made infallible by St Bonaventure. An important card for preparations for the Cambridge lectures runs: 'Franciscans began to analyse the notion of Conscience. Voice of God in the heart of man. Therefore infallible as well as universal.[28] – And when they said that it might be darkened by ignorance or perverted by sin, they insisted that it ought nevertheless to be obeyed. – So something sacred in each individual. To convince, to enlighten – but never to be forced to act against his inward guide. Constantly protesting against the existing state of guilt, of imperfect training, of imperfect light. Therefore always making for improvement, for progress.'[29]

Practically as well as philosophically, the Franciscans lived in a way that undermined the new tendencies to cesaro-papal absolutism: 'The more they grasped their idea, that poverty belongs to Christianity,[30] the more they implied that wealth excludes it. So they censured the very instrument of the power of the Church .... NB. These opposition reforms begin when the character of the Church changed; all was united until the Church turned against freedom.'[31] Interpreted in this way, it is clear how Acton came to regard the medievals as foreshadowing his own idea of conscience, and, indeed, as creating it.

Although Acton's own use of the word 'conscience' can best be understood if it is equated with the theological term 'synteresis', there can be no question that the Scholastics were quite clear that there were two distinct meanings to the two terms. Some looseness may have entered their discussion, when this was not the fundamental point at issue – and it is notable that Acton prefers to quote from the less explicit and architectural parts of Aquinas' work – but most of this springs from the flabbiness of the Latin *conscientia*, a word which Pierce has criticised for the ease with which it can be translated as 'moral common-sense'. The general Scholastic position was that each man had been endowed with a faculty which recognised good and evil for what they were. It might be overlaid and disused, but never lost. It could be argued that this was the necessary fruit of the story of Adam's fall. This faculty was called 'synteresis'.[32]

As it stands, this bears considerable resemblance to Hutcheson's 'moral sense', but it was considerably influenced in St Thomas Aquinas by its relation to the natural law and to conscience. He tended to speak of synteresis as filled with moral knowledge, rather than as a capacity for moral perception.

When the Scholastics distinguished between conscience and synteresis, they distinguished between action and knowledge. The conscience was to be understood as relative to the will and to a particular situation. One could use the analogy of a purse full of money. This purse contains the 'knowledge' of synteresis. To use that knowledge, to spend the money, is the action of conscience, which partakes of a depraved and 'fallen' human nature. Therefore, although the money is in itself good, its use, and the decision whether to use it or not, is a matter in which the will, and consequently sin, must enter. Conscience, then, according to the Schoolmen, is subject to error and is fundamentally the application of what we know to what we do. In his conscience a good man recalls his moral knowledge and puts a particular action alongside that knowledge, and in doing so develops the moral potential of the personality in an Aristotelian way.

It seems, again from the Cambridge cards of the 1890s, that Acton may have misunderstood or confused Aquinas, and also used 'natural law' as equivalent to 'synteresis': 'Conscience. According to S. Thomas, Conscience = knowledge of the natural law. Scotus distinguishes the knowledge of the law of Nature, and Conscience, which applies it practically. Two ideas – Law of

Nature, infallible conscience, and Conscience.'[33] Assuming man is endowed with infallible moral knowledge, it would be quite wrong to cite the support of St Thomas for the view that conscience and the actions of the will based on that knowledge are also infallible. It is worth noting how aware Acton was in these last years of the direction in which Duns Scotus developed his thought: 'Scotus develops the notion of the Will as that which decides ... that which is within, not that which is around him – defines and explains a man's character and conduct. The ultimate seat of freedom, in the Will. A man is most himself when he is alone with God.'[34]

As we have seen, Acton was unable to reconcile himself to the fact that that between 1250 and 1550 so many of the best men countenanced the principles of the Inquisition. He was therefore particularly pleased to be able to argue in the Cambridge lectures that the first generations of friars were aware that 'To speak in general or abstract terms of the sovereign conscience was to urge the contrast between the Roman Inquisition and the spirit of early Christianity and to promote a breach with the Catholicism of Southern Europe.'[35] If a liberal politics of conscience is part of the natural law, then it could be claimed that the leading Scholastics taught them as infallibly given to men in synteresis. An American commentator on St Thomas writes: '
S. Thomas is an outspoken and determined defender of freedom of conscience. Aristotle had taught him the autonomy of the soul, and this doctrine he found to be entirely in accord with the Christian view of the soul.'[36] Yet Thomas did not allow that heresy could be the sincere product of an erroneous conscience, and therefore did not tolerate it. He believed that 'Error is a sin when it is avoidable and when it refers to something that everybody should know.'[37]

In exactly the same way, Acton believed that the dogmas of Liberalism were something 'everybody should know'. He therefore refused to accept that Charles I and George III could have been honest or 'sincere' when they adopted 'illiberal' courses and, at the same time, claimed to be acting on the ground of 'conscience'. One of the chief obstacles in the working out of conscience as a leading idea was that massacres and absolutisms could claim to be the most conspicuous and conscious products of its historical existence. The problem recurs frequently in his notes, and could only be resolved by accusing such claims of being pathological or 'unscientific'. Acton transposed to suit 'liberal' natural law precisely those attributes of 'catholic' synteresis which he burningly criticised as leading to persecution of heretics in the Middle Ages.

Acton thus came to believe that the full-blown 'whiggism' of Aquinas was a consequence of his theory of conscience rather than an inheritance from the political thought of Aristotle. Two consecutive Cambridge cards comment on a quotation which purports to attach Wycliffe to the cause of 'no taxation without representation' e.g: 'How Wiclif came by that theory. See especially S. Thomas and S. Bonaventure'[38] Elsewhere he writes 'Middle Ages believed in institutions. arrival of Conscience – co-incides with Constitutionalism.'[39] Obedience conditional on a right order of society was therefore the principal contribution of the Middle Ages: the establishment of coronation services led to Magna Carta. Providentially discovered in Teutonic Christendom at a time when the power of church and state was in tension, it was a principle claimed as an absolute truth about the relation of conscience to constitutional politics.

The hybris of the Inquisition

Acton, like many recent historians, was inclined to see the 16th century as the *dénouement* of the Middle Ages rather than as the beginning of a period which could be called 'modern'. His thought about this century changed and altered its emphasis during his life more perhaps than any other. It was never a century with which he seems to have felt kinship: it was, after all, the century of Machiavelli. But it had an Armageddon-like quality for a good Catholic like Acton. As he came, at the end of his life, to flesh out his 'theodicy', he saw the Reformation as terrible in its demonstration of the energy of the evil which inevitably flowed from the perversion of the church in the 13th century. The confusion of the temporal and spiritual orders, above all Raymond of Pennaforte's institution of the Inquisition which symbolised it: these were the causes of the tragedy of a broken Christendom and of the hellenistic monarchies which arose on its ruins.[40]

Acton developed this notion in a way radically different from the position he had held in 1861, when he wrote: 'The Reformation was a great movement against the freedom of conscience – an effort to subject it to a new authority, the arbitrary initiative of a prince who might differ in religion from all his subjects.'[41] In 1877 he said, 'How did the 16th century husband the treasure which the Middle Ages had stored up? ...

decline of religion .... It appeared to [Machiavelli] that the most vexatious obstacle to intellect is conscience .... The way was paved for absolute monarchy to triumph over the spirit and institutions of a better age ... by a studied philosophy of crime.'[42] It appears that Acton discovered the Reformation as a step on the road to liberty *c.* 1880, and in a post-1890 notebook he wrote, 'Sap Scholasticism, you sap the system Luther was provoked to attack, and demolish the argument against him. It is justified by authority ... if it is wrong there is no divine protectorate [of the visible Church].'[43]

Necessary to Luther's salutary purgation of past error – if there was still to be a God of salvation-history – were the small groups of a quasi-biblical 'Remnant'. The tradition of thought which the evil direction of affairs had never been able to suppress came into its own. Ineffectual and scattered sources of light, they prepared the 'great period' of conscience in the 17th century, when the political systems of conscience and absolutism were laid bare as the alternatives which Penn and Hobbes were respectively to represent.

Acton went back into the 15th century to interpret Luther. The church had failed; it was 'not a practically elevating force'.[44] In that century 'They had not a clear idea of conscience. They had to insist on silencing it, for very good reasons. The scaffolding of forgeries was breaking down. It brought down with it the tradition in literature. For those men had depended on these forgeries. If the Canon Law fell. If men followed scientific convictions, what would happen?'[45] Acton had much sympathy with the Conciliar movement. The names of Zabarella,[46] Gerson, and Cusa appear frequently among the ancestors of liberty, and Acton's picture of the 15th century is strongly marked by their defeat. The Papacy issued 'from the struggle with the Councils' and from defeating the reforming movement there, with 'its spirit weakened, and its energy ... exhausted'.[47] It was immediately captured by the Renaissance Humanists who, 'introduced the note of indifference to sin – disregard for the turpitude of society', and thus produced the 'sacrifice of seriousness'[48] which provoked the appearance of Luther.

Acton saw another stream outside the church hierarchy. This was characterised by intense moral earnestness and mysticism. The chief figure was St Thomas of Kempen, whom Acton saw as the apogee of the Catholic spirit, as 'touching the largest number of Christian souls'.[49] He represented best of all the spirit of prayer and self-examination which characterised Acton's own 'inner direction' and which he largely identified with conscience (again from the Cambridge notes): 'Conscience. The Mystics, the Brethren, above all, the Imitation [of Christ] – dwelt less on institutions and authorities than on self-examination, introspection, the perpetual searchlight cast upon the dark recesses of the soul. – That is to say, formation of character.'[50]

In her obituary of Acton, Lady Blennerhasset wrote that the following quotation from Rothe's *Ethik* rendered 'the Englishman's' innermost thought. 'My critical direction in science leads me to a continual criticism of my own ideas, and not those of others.'[51] Acton had cited this passage as a note (n. 22) to his Inaugural Lecture when he was speaking of someone who could properly be called a Great Man, who would have the ability 'to choose the star that guides his course, to correct, and test, and assay his convictions by the light within'. The reference by Lady Blennerhasset, who knew him so well, makes it clear that Acton put the conception of self-conscious development of the moral personality at the centre of his understanding of conscience. In a note on George Eliot he used a striking simile for the process: 'To form the character as a man trains his ear for music. Not her view.'

Acton attributed a great deal in the development of this tradition of prayerful self-improvement to the influence of Seneca, who was 'more read after the 12th century than any other Latin prose writer'.[52] He described the Renaissance man, to whom 'Seneca was an oracle. For he is the classic of mental discipline, vigilant self-study, and the examination of conscience. It is under these influences that the modern type of individual man took shape. The action of religion, by reason of the divided Church and the hierarchy *in partibus* was at a low point: and no age had been so corrupt, so barbarous, in the midst of culture.'[53] The 15th century was thus a time of the development of individual conscience based on Stoic influences. The Bohemian Brethren[54] and associations of mystics played a critical part.[55] Altogether there was a process of 'separation from the outer church'[56] that was a kind of 'liberty', and in which sects were important.[57]

Lady Blennerhassett chose Erasmus to compare with Acton.[58] Acton's notes show that he was a sympathetic figure, and on several occasions he expressed the opinion that there was a moment in 1512 when all might have been saved, if the church had followed Erasmus. Such development was turned back and the tragedy of the Reformation finally unleashed by the disobedient action of a pope.[59]

The defeat of Conciliar reform in the 15th century was of great importance for Acton: it forced providence to make a gigantic tangled detour through a progressively less dogmatic Protestantism. 'After Servetus, Protestantism was not a reform. Things had got worse. [Had been] one church that did not persecute. Now there were two that did. Only by *umweg*, indirectly, by decomposition, could it return.'[60] Acton devotes much attention, not only to Erasmus, but to Aegidio di Viterbo and Cardinal Contarini. In a card dated 1897, he writes, 'The germs that were to ripen. — Constance, Cusa, Renaissance, who were the men? the tendency to toleration. the idea of Conscience. Erasmus, Sadolet, Contarini, Aegidius, Postel, Bovillus, Zorzo, Condemnation of existing evil. How this movement was stunted. Unity – Leading up to America.'[61] Acton admired the universality of Erasmus, his scepticism about the magical. It was 'reform through learning',[62] and Acton believed this must naturally lead to the theory and practice of conscience: 'Deliverance from their time and country. Citizens of the world. Erasmus the great example. More, thinking away from home — in the Commonwealth of Nowhere. They could look at their own surroundings from outside. Preliminary to hearing the voice within – Kempis, Thamer. NB.'[63]

Acton laid great stress on the classical contribution to Erasmus's thought; he 'had his free-will from Cicero and the Greek Fathers',[64] and it is primarily Erasmus whom Acton had as an example when in a number of the Cambridge cards he asserted that, 'The lines of thought most vigorously followed were those on which Christian and classic independently converge – that is, the existence of Conscience, and of a Natural Law. Seneca. S. Thomas. S Bonaventure.'[65] On the other hand, Acton saw the emergence of Luther as a re-enactment of the stifling of conscience in the early church by St Augustine.[66] He heralded a century in which there was to be little room for ethical science between theological Grace and national Power. Hope was to lie with the tradition of classical learning and with the sectaries of the radical reformation: 'Stoicism the philosophy of the Renaissance ... implied Conscience .... Importance of Seneca. That was resisted by Luther – promoted by Frank, Denk, the Sectaries of the Reformation.'[67]

Döllinger had made it his business to show Luther at the bottom of all evil, and Acton may himself have drawn the beginnings of his 'scientific' ethics from horror of 'imputed merit'. Acton soon came to an independent estimate of Luther's place in the history of conscience, which was more positive than Döllinger's. It is a comment, however, on Acton's intellectual approach to history that he never gave Luther his full importance, for he seems to have been unable to see him outside Erasmus's shadow. His ideas, so long as they are good ideas, were Erasmus's: 'Erasmus more radical than Luther. Doubts Bible miracles. Dogma human, not divine, directly. Dist[inguishes] gospel teaching from apostolic. Luther was shocked at any such criticism. Erasmus claimed an amount of liberty that Lutheranism denied.'[68] The humanists had broken the notion of Christendom before Luther.[69] It was his existential decision to revolt against Rome, inconsistent with his later life and based on no clear knowledge, which alone – Acton thought – gave him the right to a place in significant history.

Acton and Döllinger[70] believed that it was the Anabaptists whom Luther had slaughtered who were more important in this history of freedom. At one point, Acton thought these Anabaptists had taken the step which remained to be taken after Aquinas, and had allowed that religious error too could be conscientious.[71] They were a 'liberal force',[72] who, though they themselves did not survive, fed the Socinians and Independents. It was of them tha Acton wrote in 1893, 'Weakness of all medieval Liberalism. Not spiritual. Rights and interests, not duties. Reformation introduced that other motive. Religion produced Liberalism.'[73]

Acton took some time to work out in an acceptable way the dilemma that rooted Liberalism in the sects. In a notebook of the 1870s, he wrote, 'Conflict of the Reformation ... quite infernal .... Out of this arose the opinion that right and wrong are independent of religious truth, that laws and justice are known apart from Revelation ... Politiques .... This is the origin of Grotius and the Law of Nature. All this was not to further liberty.'[74] Another notebook, of 1881, has him working at his nagging problem: how could the natural law be articulated and made politically effective after the disappearance of the medieval church? 'Reformation made nations independent .... First, this produced absolutism. Especially in Catholic countries. In Protestant countries it ended by healing itself. How Dualism failed. Objective order ... the disinterested, the faithful exponent of a higher law ... in 1517, to the divisions of power within the state. No exponent of a higher law left .... They depend on their own resources. Individualism comes forward – How slowly! Centuries before the new force works .... Use of religion to liberty obvious. First unbelief [for liberty] – Hobbes absolutistic. Yet later on it became liberal. How was that?'[75] Acton really depended on his interpretation of the English Civil War – a running together of the ideas of religious duty and natural law – to demonstrate the validity of his hypothesis about the preceding period.

The crisis of conscience

In his 'advice' to Creighton in 1887, Acton wrote, 'The moral code in its main lines is not new, it has long been known .... But the notion and analysis of conscience is scarcely older than 1700.'[76] The development of conscience into a self-conscious system was a process which Acton believed could be discerned as the work of a remarkable generation in suddenly favourable conditions: 'It [liberty] depends on Toleration and the theory of Conscience, on International Law, on the predominance of Science, on the notion of Progress, on the refuge beyond the sea. All this is the work of that generation which begins with Galileo Bacon Grotius Descartes Pascal. From 1610 to 1665.'[77] The 17th century is of high importance in Acton's history of conscience. Acton's apostolic generation goes from Descartes through Sarasa and Fénelon to William Penn. Typically it includes some surprising names.

A card from the History of Liberty boxes shows how Acton interpreted the meaning of the Reformation and the English Civil War in the light of conscience. 'The new principle, which the Reformation had started in vain, was efficiently put forward in England. Here the theory of conscience was avowed. By English Sects, powerful in the State. Middle of the 17th century. Just then, too, the theory was seriously studied. Not much work in early Protestants. Nor Casuists. What they tried. Conscience was a check to outward, established authority. Theory of erring conscience. Then, of infallible conscience. Sarasa[78] little read. Butler, a great classic. Early theorists not favourable to liberty. Sanderson.'[79]

The problem for whose solution Acton was searching among 17th-century thinkers was that which he had identified in the thought of Aquinas earlier. This was the question of whether heretics were to be tolerated in the error which they claimed to be conscientious and divinely inspired. While they were not so tolerated, it could not be said that liberty existed. Yet how could it be argued that the heretic was sincere, when he claimed a knowledge of God which diverged from that taught by the church? The church, after all, claimed to be constituted by the revelation which it had both received and was licensed to interpret. As we have seen, Acton was inclined at one time to think the Anabaptists of the 1530s were prepared to allow the conscientiousness of religious error, but later this full toleration became for him the achievement of the Quakers.[80] It was necessarily based, however, on a change in the nature of true knowledge. This change arose from Descartes' theory of perception. The starting point of knowledge, on the Cartesian system, could never be a church conceived as anything more than the sum of its individuals. There was therefore no ground on which the church's knowledge of God could be said to differ in kind from that of the heretic, unless the church was seen as conserving exclusive memories of true encounters with God through times of his absence. Hence, to deny heretics toleration was epistemologically absurd.

Consequently Acton, especially later in his life, placed considerable emphasis on the contribution made by Descartes' 'doctrine of clearness' to liberty, and to the notion of an 'infallible conscience'. In one of the notebooks which Acton used immediately after 1890 to prepare the biography he was to have written of Döllinger, there are two especially illuminating passages. However naive in their description of the experience of conscience, they are the central affirmations of the life and work of his mature years. The first runs: 'Definition [of Liberty]: It is reason controlled by reason instead of will controlled by will; it is duty to God unhindered by man; it is the security of minorities; it is the reign of Conscience. It took new proportions with the growth of conscience. Descartes carried it out of the cloister into the world. clearness, certitude, divine veracity – If he [God] cannot mislead our reason, still less our conscience. He is more surely true in morals than in all philosophy. Universality, sufficiency, infallibility, permanence of Conscience. How all this grew from the conflict with the Casuists. Basis of religion, because Christianity is founded on repentance of sin.'[81] The second is even more emphatic: 'Most important – Descartes' theory of clearness is at the bottom of modern Conscience. God cannot deceive: ergo, conscience, which is His voice, is infallible. So that Cartesianism inaugurated the supreme theory of Conscience – introducing it under new conditions.'[82] These ideas are so widespread in the cards[83] that there can be no doubt that the advent of Cartesianism played an important role in Acton's drama of the emergence of liberty.

But Descartes was only one of several 'scientific' contributors to the preparation of 17th-century liberty: 'All those preliminary discoveries paved the way for political freedom – Bacon Descartes Galileo Grotius Sarasa. Science. International Law. Toleration. Conscience. Progress. Emancipation. Clearness. They were in the air, influencing man here and there, and uniting them. It went to make the Whig party. Derived from Bacon – Experiment. Descartes: Independence. Sarasa: Conscience. Grotius: International Law. Refuge: Wm. Penn.'[84] In the same generation, by their separate discoveries, they prepared the intellectual back-cloth for the struggle 'for political freedom' in the English Civil War. At that war's outbreak, it was not unusual to describe conscience by such phrases as the 'deputy divinity'.[85]

In 1640 in England, the situation was thus prepared for a constitutional conflict in which the principles of conscience and natural law could come together. Acton wrote of the Parliamentary leaders testing 'the Constitution by principles anterior and superior to all positive law'.[86] This was an aspect of the work of Grotius[87] which could coalesce with Descartes' ideas of moral certitude to make a systematic and 'liberal' political critique of tradition. A History of Liberty card dated in the critical year 1877 expresses the classical Actonian hypothesis succinctly: 'Religion striving to be free. That is, the tendency is to change the religious issue into a political one. That is what the English revolution did.'[88]

Acton believed the Independents were the occasion of this transition. They were the first exponents of the principles of politics which, through the mediation of the Quakers, were to become manifestly 'scientific' in the generation of 1775. Acton saw these Puritans not as descendants of the Reformation, but as reacting against it.[89] Indeed, they had much in common with the contemporary generations of Catholics.[90] By claiming liberty of conscience and the right to execute their king, they introduced the Revolution to practical politics.[91] And all this stemmed from their high doctrine of conscience. 'Independents. They did not depend on any outer authority or tradition. They were guided by the light within. The firm basis of that inner guide was their conscience. It was the supreme guide, the final authority. Consequently, it must be free to exercise that authority. Liberty of conscience was a direct object and condition of religion.'[92] This liberty sprang directly from the sovereignty of religious duty. In his Cambridge lectures he spoke of complete toleration as being in the 'logic of the system', although it was a position reached by only some of the Independents.[93]

The Civil War may have been the *locus classicus* in the practical application of the doctrines of liberty and conscience, but it was only the first step. The process which it inaugurated was a dialectic one. Acton viewed the Restoration as an anti-thesis against the doctrines of conscience which had multiplied under the Commonwealth.[94]

Acton was convinced that the first duty of a controversialist was to express his adversary's position in its highest form before expounding his own. He interpreted the high period of conscience in the last thirty years of the 17th century as the response to Hobbes, the ablest advocate of the prosecution case against conscience, who had said, 'Another doctrine repugnant to civil society is that whatsoever a man does against his conscience is sin.'[95] The theorists of conscience had to work out a scheme of comparable weight: 'Adam Smith ... says that the notion of conscience was first analysed in reply to Hobbes, who founded morality on human laws.'[96]

In the latter part of the century, there were two separate but intimately connected processes at work.[97] In France and Flanders it was necessarily a theoretical movement, because they were dominated by the tyranny of Louis XIV: in England, the movement found its political outlet in the revolution of 1688, which Acton put on a par with Marathon in its significance for the future of the world.[98]

To deal with the mainland Europe first: Acton centred his interpretation of the history of conscience in this generation on Sarasa and Terillus, then on Fénelon and La Placette, and, as a link between the parallel developments in England and on the Continent, Pope Innocent XI. All these figures, with the exception of Sarasa, were also centrally important for Döllinger.[99]

Acton saw La Placette[100] as applying Cartesian philosophy to the questions of conscience and discovering, in doing so, the full significance of Descartes for moral philosophy. Two cards of the 1890s have quotations from La Placette's *Traité de la Conscience*. The most important runs, 'Ils soutiennent qu'accuser la conscience de se tromper, c'est dire que Dieu nous trompe, c'est ruiner la foi et la religion, parce que c'est détruire absolument la certitude.' Acton adds notes of his own which place La Placette among Nicole, Fénelon, Malebranche, and Mabillon as members of a Cartesian 'school': 'The infallibility of Conscience founded on Descartes. Just so, Mabillon and the critics against Scepticism in history.'[101] Both the historian publicly and the individual conscience privately need a working hypothesis of certainty if they are to have the authority to judge.

It is however the shadowy figure of Sarasa who first formulated the infallibility of conscience.[102] The second part of his *Ars Semper Gaudendi*, which is the part which specifically deals with conscience, was written in 1666, a year before Sarasa's death. In three cards for the Cambridge lectures which are transcripts from it,[103] conscience is described as the Vicar of God, and to be followed implicitly. The moral quality of my action is said to be what my conscience deems it to be. Seneca and Epictetus are quoted liberally. Acton wrote to Gladstone that it was from Sarasa's system that Butler had borrowed his doctrine of conscience.[104] He also (very significantly from the point of view of his own project) traced the specifically historical aspect of Leibnitz's *Theodicy* to Sarasa, and claimed that Sarasa was the first to connect 'conscience and Progress'.[105]

These are claims which have not appeared elsewhere. It is entirely characteristic of Acton that his history of liberty should have such obscure figures as Sarasa and Vinet as lynch-pins. He delighted to give significance at the turning-points of history to men scarcely even of the second rank. But it is his interpretation of conscience, rather than his history of it, which can be challenged. By accepting Vinet's conception of conscience as an internal conversation with God or a mystical ecstasy, as the normative definition to which the history of conscience had been leading, it became reasonable to give an unconventional shape to that history.

Fénelon's importance in any history of conscience is indisputable. He was a major object of interest and admiration from Acton's student days at Munich onward. It is easy to see why, for in opening his lectures on the French Revolution, Acton said: 'The revolt of conscience began with him before the glory of the monarchy was clouded over .... He learnt to refer the problem of government, like the conduct of private life, to the mere standard of morals, and extended further than anyone the plain but hazardous practice of deciding all things by the exclusive precepts of enlightened virtue.'[106] Fénelon was a good liberal: he was for toleration, and against aggressive wars, and, as Acton confessed, came very near to abandoning the concept of original sin. Acton thought the whole French 17th century was a specially significant epoch. He wrote of it in the language of 'unfolding': 'Catholicism only got into full bloom in France in the 17th century. It had a philosophy, a history, a criticism, became conscious of itself.'[107]

The crux of Fénelon's role in this is in his description of the soul's relation with God in the conscience. 'Notre faible raison est à tout moment redressée au dedans de nous par une autre raison supérieure que nous consultons et qui nous corrige, que nous ne pouvons changer, parce que nous en avons besoin. C'est un soleil dont la lumière éclaire les esprits, comme le soleil éclaire les corps. Cette raison suprême ... où nous puisons tous, est le Dieu que nous cherchons.'[108] This is a view of conscience, immanentist and yet exploratory, which has much in common with the Stoics and the Quakers, and with the tradition of Sarasa and Vinet. It is because his liberal political thinking springs from this kind of philosophical premise that Fénelon is so important for Acton. It was from him and from St Thomas of Kempen that Acton manufactured his picture of what was the essence of the Catholic spirit.

If it were indeed so, Acton could maintain that the broad lines of his intepretation of the history and nature of conscience were Catholic. It is also possible to claim that a direct representative of that wing of late 17th-century Catholic theology was Robert Barclay, who studied in Paris and became a Quaker. It was in his theology, pre-eminently, that the nature of the conscience was analysed in this way, and given, in consequence, the central place in religious experience. It is clear Acton judged the theoretical development of conscience reached its climax with Quakerism. He wrote in the box of 'conscience' cards: 'Conscience connected with Quakerism as Penn understood it. Ritschl. Mysticism. Pietism. an epoch when the Church had less authority. Fénelon's idea of God – Corneille – not a Christ, an incipient Deism tells the same way. All this gives a new support and background to Liberalism.'[109] And, his stuttering overcome: 'The theory of Conscience was full grown. It had assumed, in one of the Sects, a very peculiar shape. The doctrine of the inner light. Quakers not originally liberal – But the inner light struggled vigorously for freedom. In the very days in which the theory of Conscience reached its extreme term: W. Penn proclaimed liberty of Conscience as the teaching of his Sect. And so it became the basis of Pennsylvania – Voltaire's best government.'[110] This was of course also the time of Locke's version of liberalism, founded on property. But like Bancroft, Acton judged American liberalism to be better than that.[111] There is a perceptive reference to Quakers and Stoics in a notebook of 1881: 'Speaking of least Christian theology = highest politics, such as Quakers, observe that the highest Greek ethics, the Stoical, were founded on the lowest theology.'[112]

It was, nonetheless, from a background in the liberalism of Locke and of the Glorious Revolution that Acton began his *History of Liberty*. When he arrived as a student at Munich he was an enthusiatic admirer of Macaulay, and he never wholly lost either his respect for Macaulay or the conviction that 1688 was the central event in history.[113] The series of notes which are labelled 'History of Liberty' cover with special detail the latter half of the 17th century in England. 1679 is referred to as 'the birth of the Whig party'.[114] In 1689, 'politics passed into the sea of revolution'.[115] Before this time, there was 'little ethical science. Protestants poor; Catholics grievously astray'.[116] And in the Cambridge lectures, '[1688] was not restitution but inversion. Passive obedience had been the law of England. Conditional obedience and the right of resistance became the law. Authority was regulated and controlled. The Whig theory of government was substituted for the Tory theory on the fundamental points of political science.'[117]

There were three particular strands in that Whig settlement which Acton selected. First, it was a movement in which the papacy had allied itself with the 'ascending cause of freedom'.[118] Second, it was the work of men who had come to think in terms of secular natural law; men like Shaftesbury, Sidney, and Halifax, 'rescued Whiggism from the sectarian grasp. It became national. If not universal.'[119] Third, it was a revolution which saw clearly into the mechanical realities of government, and therefore halted itself at the point where it had established a balance of forces in the constitution.

Analysing 1688 in these categories, it is clear how Acton was able to view it as a substantial foreshadowing of the more perfect, because more 'scientific', American Revolution. All these theoretical elements were developed in the latter, and drawn together by a conscious founding of them on a doctrine of universal (in the first instance 'generally Christian') conscience and natural law. Acton here anticipates the judgment that the late 17th century was the 'crisis of consciousness' in European history. As Acton understood it, the 18th century was largely occupied in integrating into a new culture the various political, ethical, and scientific conceptions of the Newtonian generation. As regards politics, this meant the marriage of the constitutional guarantees of 1688 with the living religious zeal of the Quakers.[120]

The century of conscience

Five men dominate Acton's 'golden age of conscience': Butler, Rousseau, Kant, Fichte, and Vinet.[121] They brought the notion to its full deveopment, and made it the centre of their system. It came, in their hands, to be considered as a process whose conclusions had an unconditional validity, which Acton described as 'infallible'. Another word which Acton applied to their achievement was 'scientific', for he found great significance in the fact that 'all parties met, from different regions, to accept conscience. Sarasa, Butler, Rousseau, Kant, Fichte, Vinet.'[122] It might therefore be plausible to argue that the 'Church of the Future' would be built on the basis of conscience.

That these men all maintained that everyone was naturally endowed with the mechanism to discover such moral imperatives was important to Acton from another aspect. It made 'liberalism' also scientifically discernible. For, if there existed an objective order of moral values, whether rational or divine, which could be directly apprehended by the individual, and which could be equated with the old Law of Nature,[123] it was reasonable to suppose that this order included political values which could also be supposed to be 'natural' and 'scientific'. What resulted from abstract reason working with the criterion of 'do as you would be done by' were Liberal propositions. Acton regarded Free Trade and a reformed Penal Code, for example, as both scientific and moral. They were not scientific because they produced more wealth, or fewer criminals, but because every man in possession of his faculties could see clearly that he would not wish his wares to be discriminated against or his own person tortured. And he would see this whether he was Catholic, Protestant, or Atheist. Acton had established this position by 1878.[124] Anyone who did not see this must be 'insincere': 'Every religion must be sincerely held, but the man who deprives another of his legitimate freedom cannot be sincere.'[125]

The end result of this reasoning was that the propositions of Liberalism were to be regarded as normatively 'natural'. No man acting on other premises could claim ignorance, or even avoid the penal consequences of 'crime': 'Lib[erty] is conscience – ergo, morality. Disregard one, disregard the other. No basis for an opponent of lib[erty] to avoid crime. End justifies means.'[126]

It was because Vinet made these connections and arrived at this conclusion about the political implications of conscience that he was so significant to Acton. 'The whole modern theory of Conscience culminates in Vinet. Something of it in the English sects. But in their time the notion of conscience was imperfectly analysed. Perkins and Ames. Butler blooms out in Vinet.'[127] And Vinet applied conscience to political thought: 'Theory of Concience – did not secure entire liberality in its teachers – Butler, Rousseau, Kant, Fichte were not Liberals. It is Vinet who wrought that alliance and drew that consequence. Immense authority of this tradition. Above everything – both for the influence of names, and its generality and breadth.'[128] So far, this view of Vinet as being of quite capital importance remains peculiar to Acton.

Acton was introduced to Vinet's work at Munich. In 1863 he lends Simpson eight of his books and describes Vinet as a 'portent in the history of Calvinism'. In 1864 Acton and Döllinger study him together. In 1866, Döllinger writes to Lady Blennerhassett in praise of Vinet – his 'catholicism' – and they are all reading his *Études sur Blaise Pascal*. In 1889, at the death of Vinet's biographer Schérer, Acton remarks that he had spent time with him each year either at Paris or Geneva. It is reasonable to conclude that Acton's own beliefs on the nature and politial requirements of conscience reflected Vinet's. Acton's '100 Best Books' concludes with Vinet's work, which is summed up as, 'Conscience and Liberty a law in Church and State'.[129]

Vinet drew the political conclusions of Liberalism from a particular description of conscience. What was that description? 'Conscience is not ourselves: it is against us, therefore it is something other than ourselves. But if it is other than ourselves, what can it be but God? And if it be God, we must give it the honour due to God: we cannot reverence the sovereign less than the ambassador.'[130] This definition of Vinet's is transcribed in several of the manuscript notes, and is the 'deification of conscience' in a far more explicit form than Butler's, which had originally earned the description. It is for this reason Acton said 'Butler blooms out in Vinet.'

If Acton identified himself with this position (and nowhere did he criticise Vinet), it must follow that Acton used the word 'conscience' primarily to denote communication with God. This makes sense of Acton's saying that the idea of conscience is 'full of the Holy Spirit' to the Christian. It also explains Acton's special interest in and admiration for the Quakers and Stoics. Like S. T. Coleridge,[131] he found that their doctrines of the Inner Light and of the immanence of a 'spark of divinity' within the soul were comparable.

Vinet preferred many of the same authors as Acton. He has

153

been called a Christian Rousseau. He particularly admired St Thomas of Kempen, St Francis de Sales, Bourdaloue, Pascal, and, above all, Kant.[132] His absolute opposition to established churches led him to an admiration for the American Constitution which had much in common with Acton's. There, 'le sentiment religieux est en état de se créer à soi-même sa forme et ses moyens.'[133] Perhaps it was his familiarity with Vinet's writings, and the high value which he and Döllinger put on them, that provided the background for the peculiarly central role of America in Acton's universal history.

The organic connection in Acton's system between conscience and natural law has a parallel in the way Vinet drew that connection. Vinet was concerned to establish two propositions: that experience of conscience included something 'wholly other', and that it led to coherence. Actions based on the purest sense of duty and conscience would tend of their nature to produce concord and subordination, rather than faction and disintegration.[134] The parallel with Quakerism is striking. The opposite judgment, the obvious criticism of any system which elevates conscience so high, had been Hobbes's chief plank.

By saying that conscience is God-in-us,[135] Vinet was able to posit that, there being but one God, all duties that are discovered in the conscience are from the same source and of the same kind. A phrase of Vinet's, 'Frappées d'un certain côté, les âmes rendent le même son',[136] is very reminiscent of Hutcheson, whose 'moral sense' theory of conscience is perhaps one of the most satisfactory explanations that have been put forward.[137] It appears that Acton was too dominated by Kantian rationalism to explore this approach to conscience further. Vinet saw the Fall as the factor which has fractured the perceptions of conscience so that it has become the power behind apparently antithetic objectives.[138]

Vinet was, however, not entirely Unitarian or deist. God (the 'logos', or 'word', or 'wisdom') has always been available to the conscience of man certainly, but his incarnation and the gospel which was its result were necessary to the animation of that conscience. Thus Vinet attempted quite properly to define the essence of the coming of Christianity in terms of the New Covenant, and to make the human conscience – the Old Testament prophets' 'law of God in the heart' – the bridge between Grace and Nature. He describes their relation: 'Ceux à qui la grace de Dieu en donnera la volonté [will find God in their conscience]; en sorte que l'adoption du christianisme est à la fois une chose naturelle, puisque c'est la conscience immédiatement qui reconnait et accepte la vérité, et une chose surnaturelle, puisque c'est Dieu qui nous donne de descendre jusqu'au fond de notre conscience et de prêter l'oreille à sa plus secrète voix.'[139]

A true understanding of Christianity as New Covenant therefore makes it the 'religion of conscience'.[140] For this reason Acton was not prepared to put the 18th-century rationalists and sceptics outside the course of Christian history. 'The ethical ideas of Christianity have partly been drawn out by philosophy. Ethical science really only began with Kant and the Rationalists',[141] and 'when the 18th century insisted on the claims of the poor and the duties of the rich, they followed S. Ambrose and S. Chrysostom. When they spoke of the right of revolution, they applied S. Thomas.'[142] As Acton turned his mind to the History of Liberty, he saw the great anti-clerical revolutions of the 18th century, not as essentially anti-Christian, but as the fruit of the New Covenant: 'The people who ... had tortured witches suddenly appeard infamous, brutal, idiotic.'[143] This was a step toward true Christianity. There is a liberalism implicit in the Gospels which every Christian should fight to establish. 'Liberalism ultimately grounded on idea of conscience, a man must live by the light within. Prefer God's voice to man's.'[144]

It is clear that the generation of Burke and Rousseau was the beginning, and not the end, of normative Christendom for Acton. As with any liberalism it was individualistic: 'Towards the end of last century, Conscience was developed as a substitute for religion. Vicaire Savoyard. At the same time scientific methods came in. This developed individualism. Force of public opinion, corrective of Individualism.'[145] But the particular glory of that crisis generation was the Americans who had not only turned 'to obey the light within'[146] but for the first time had made it possible for a properly 'national' and 'constitutional' conscience to emerge. So that their liberalism became also corporate: 'In the 18th century [conscience] became not only judge, but law-giver. Nations less bound by their own habit – and more by the opinion of the day. The conscience of a people as well as that of individuals can at last become law.'[147]

Acton had spoken of 'ethical science' beginning with Kant and the Rationalists. This is obviously important for him. There is however, for this kind of question, very little material in the Acton Collection and he never wrote an article which bore on this subject.

Acton drew a genealogical tree back from Vinet through Kant to Butler, to Leibnitz, and then to Sarasa.[148] He wrote to

Gladstone in 1892, 'Butler is very little remembered or read in Germany, because of Kant. They do not know it, but Kant is the macrocosm of Butler. His main argument, founded on the deification of conscience, came to him from the *Analogy* and the *Sermons*.[149] I do not mean to say that Butler was the innovator and discoverer in ethical science that people (like Martineau) say he was. It is not impossible, I maintain, to show where he got that theory of conscience which has so much influenced political as well as religious thought. But it is pretty certain that Kant, who was no great reader, took it from him, and dug no deeper into 17th-century literature.'[150]

As with Vinet's, Acton saw the force of Kant's doctrine of the conscience primarily in its relation to politics. He saw Kant firmly set in the transition from a politics based on property to a politics based on conscience. In the '100 Best Books', Kant stands for 'infallible reign of conscience substituted for God'.[151] This, as we have seen, is the transition from Locke that Acton associated with the name of Penn. He appears to have thought of Kant as building upon the Americans of the Revolution of 1775. Acton wrote: 'Mais le système du droit naturel, des principes abstraits, du droit absolu, du droit comme forme du devoir, de la politique entendu comme science et non comme expédient – est entré — dans le monde par les juriconsultes de Boston et les théoriciens de Virginie. — Mais ils sont, pour nous, responsables du nouveau principe, au-dessus de l'histoire. Il se peut que Kant, appuyé sur Rousseau et sur les légistes Hollandais, aurait trouvé celà sans Adams et Jefferson. Mais il n'est venu qu'après eux.'[152] Kant could be understood as in some sense a synthesis: 'Locke derived all knowledge from experience – Leibnitz from intellect. The Whigs grew under the former influence. Then came Rationalism, and rejected that method, claiming to produce everything from the reason. This is the revolutionary doctrine, distinguishing 1789 from 1688. Lambert and Kant corrected and combined the two.'[153] While the Americans were achieving the political system which derived from a half-secularised but absolute doctrine of conscience, Kant was completing a philosophic system from the same premise.

The same difficulties arise in dealing with Fichte's influence on Acton, as with Kant's. He always appears in Acton's lists on the history of conscience, and – more fortunately than for Kant – there are quotations from his work in the boxes on 'Conscience' to pin-point the sense in which Acton spoke of him. But nowhere is there a specific treatment by Acton. Fichte was a figure of fundamental importance for the Munich Romantics,[154] and, as with Kant, it appears that Acton honoured him as part of his own intellectual formation rather than as an object of his historical study. He was conscious that his own education outside England had exposed him to influences which very few of his English contemporaries shared. Acton once lamented that George Eliot was born before the 'neo-Kantian revival' of the 1870s could influence her, and after the period in the 1830s when Kant had been widely studied in England.

It is from the earlier, individualist, works of Fichte that Acton quotes, where the connection between a theory of conscience and political action was drawn more intimately perhaps than in any other writer. Like Penn, he derived his political demands from the inalienable and absolute rights of the spiritual nature of the individual. Only when the society which these rights demand is everywhere achieved can revolutions be expected to cease. He believed that by the exercise of rational thought and insight 'all men must come to the same conclusion in all political matters'.[155] These are Actonian standpoints. Intellectual ingredients of Acton's liberalism which cannot find an ancestry in the English Whig tradition probably derive from the political thought of the Fichtean school in Germany. Acton transcribed this passage from Fichte: 'True atheism ... consists in this, that you indulge in subtle arguments over the consequence of your actions, that you no longer hear the voice of your conscience, till you believe you can foresee results, so that exalting your own counsel above that of God, you make yourself as God .... In a moral world-government, good can never come out of evil.'[156] Acton's identification of abstract rational political science with the particular historical exemplar of the American Constitution, however, was clearly not to be discovered in Fichte.

So Acton's 'universal history' reached the end of the Whig Church's 'Old Covenant' period of development. Butler had asserted, 'Man hath the rule of right within; what is wanting is only that he honestly attend to it'[157]; Vinet had defined conscience as God-in-us; and Fichte had declared conscience 'does not and cannot err'.[158] All that remained was for the church of the 'New Covenant' to apply it. Acton believed profoundly that it was the duty of liberal administrations such as Gladstone's to carry out to the limit the liberal principles which they held. Fichte had 'believed that if we knew what ought to be, it meant that we should act in such a way as to change what is into what ought to be.'[159] So did Acton.

157

But Acton was under no illusion as to the army of heretics and enemies which beset the completed and self-conscious faith of the Whig Church even in the latter part of the 19th century. His notes are full of lists of the contemporary rivals of liberalism, and he had no easy optimism about the direction of events in England in his time. But he held to a framework of providential teleology for God's creation, and of liberalism as a system, which demanded a general progress of some kind to be visible in this world.

8
Conclusions

A 20th-century myth of modern history

Acton's contemporaries constitute the greater part of the British contribution to the Valhalla of World Sages, whose very laundry bills are precious in the sight of publishers. To qualify to join them is not so much a question of specific achievements as of grasping the public imagination and changing its language. One thinks of Matthew Arnold, George Eliot, Dickens, Ruskin, William Morris, T. H. Huxley, Herbert Spencer, Cardinal Newman, or Gladstone himself. In an age when there were so many popes at home in Britain, it might have been judged merely distracting to quibble about infallibility at Rome.

There has not been any very clear answer to the question whether Acton can claim to be one of this 'star' class. It is a volatile market. Tennyson and John Bright are instances of names whose brilliance has dimmed. Acton has had a curiously fractured reputation. On the one hand has been the solidity that comes from the *Cambridge Modern History* and from coining 'power corrupts' – the one political adage Everyman knows (not least from 20th-century experience). On the other hand is the legend that 'he never wrote a book', that he is insubstantial and aphoristic (though that has been no handicap to the reputation of Pascal or Nietzsche). The 'science' of Providence does not at first appear to be a legitimate preoccupation of the intellectual life we have experienced in the western world since Arnold Toynbee. But there are interesting things to be said about Acton's blend of politics, history, and theology in relation to the actual problems of the last thirty years.[1]

Certainly Acton himself in his own time was not overawed by those who have graduated to become Great Victorians. His references to Newman and the photographs of him with Gladstone show that clearly enough. If Acton is in fact now the object of renewed interest, it is high time that he is given a more coherent and better resourced biographical study than any that now exists. It is too easy to underestimate him.

Acton's chosen role in the 1860s as editor of what was so

quickly becoming a highly regarded review of politics, philosophy, history, and literature would almost certainly have given him a leading public reputation in Britain. In the growing hegemony of English-speaking civilisation in the following generation, it would have become a world reputation. But he could not perform that role as a loyal Catholic, and so that future was aborted. He was to some extent a memory in his own lifetime, an Icarus figure, a Roman Catholic who had attempted the impossible task of becoming a leading Liberal; who had dared as a layman to oppose the hierarchy of his notoriously priest-ridden church, and had paid the price.

The quarter century between the First Vatican Council and Cambridge were, to the public, hidden years. But they were not idle or uncreative. He may not have been a professional academic, but in those days most scholarship other than in classics or theology was not university based. He was certainly a British Museum Library man.

There is an obvious parallel with his contemporary in that library, Karl Marx: formation in Germany, active political organisation and notoriety as a young man, long years of study for the production of a horizon-setting *magnum opus*, international fame in old age and after. It is not clear that the incomparably greater and more extensive respect in which Marx's name is held has anything to do with the quality of his academic work or writing. Admittedly *Das Kapital* was published and the *History of Liberty* was not. In many ways, however, they were both working in the shadow of the Old Testament and of mid 19th-century German Hegelianism to set out a key to understanding universal history, and therefore the future.

In his proposal for the 'Universal Modern History' to the Syndics of the Cambridge University Press in 1896 is this revealing sentence: 'Secondary states appear, in perspective, when they carry flame or fuel, not when they are isolated, irrelevant, stagnant, inarticulate, sterile, passive, when they lend nothing to the forward progress or the upward growth, and offer no aid in solving the perpetual problem of the Future.' His *History*'s 'organic unity' and the disposition of its chapters to display that unity would, he claims, provide a 'Chart and Compass for the coming Century'.[2]

Few competent academics would use Marx to understand economics. Although the world since Marx – the way in which we see it – has been almost inescapably coloured by the spectacles of Marxist categories of analysis, yet the actual succession of 'pasts' as Marx's 'future' unrolls has shown marked divergence from his predictions.

It might not be inappropriate to include Freud, the most omnipresent Victorian sage of all in our society's public discourse. It is not for the grateful millions of healed patients that Freud and his pupils are remembered. It is for establishing a language of concepts that, since the 1950s, has become the publicly acceptable framework for talking about the dynamics of the psyche and of personal relationships in the English-speaking world.[3]

In the cases of both Marx and Freud, their posthumous success has been largely due to the collapse in all but a few western societies (perhaps only excepting Ireland, Flemish Belgium, and large parts of the U.S.A.) of the licence to use their traditional Christian language in public life. Some functions of that language and its institutions have found substitutes. The language of popular Freudianism has served with greater or less adequacy to locate men and women in their sexual identity, and its new professions have provided a vicarious 'pastoral' network for the urban middle class. The language of Marxism has served at least to retranslate the tradition of biblical religions in locating western societies within 'historical process'; and it has proved an immensely attractive reductionist *lingua franca* for intellectuals. Together these scientistic 'languages' have done much to make membership of traditional churches intensely suspect to the uneducated, and faith itself a largely aesthetic private choice for those educated who (abnormally) 'need' it.

The secularisation of the European mind was happening well before Marx and Freud. Their disciples were needed to fill, however imperfectly, what was already a growing sense of loss of public meaning. In the 1870s, in middle class groups gathered round cathedral clergy, even in provincial Lincoln, E. W. Benson (later Archbishop of Canterbury) noted with a kind of strategic alarm how people now opted out, politely enough, when he presumed to talk a religious language in everyday conversation. But even in the 1980s it is still common enough, at least in Britain, for religious language to be heard in a special church building, by someone authenticated as a professional, in a particular context – in the presence of death, almost universally. It has become a phenomenon of what Peter Berger called 'alternation' – in constantly more circumscribed situations, but nonetheless where a religious language is licensed. The claims of a living religion – at least of a biblical one – require something

161

more.

Acton's status as another scientistic sage fits most properly into experience of this privatising and 'associationalising' of religious language. There is little doubt that in the 1870s he was preoccupied a good deal with the almost continuous drift he perceived as already set in toward disaffiliation from church life and towards explicit unbelief.[4] It was why he was fascinated by George Eliot, both as a person and a writer. 'If ever', he wrote, 'science or religion reigns alone over an undivided empire', her books 'might lose their central and unique importance', but they are 'the emblem of a generation distracted between the intense need of believing and the difficulty of belief'.[5]

Her combination of high moral tone (and in particular her use of the experience of conscience) and appetite for attendance at cathedral evensong (although an atheist) struck him as offering hope for a 'scientific' style of mediating the fruits of the Christian past into the new world.[6] Who is to say Acton was wrong? George Eliot was the keystone of the teaching of literary criticism by F. R. Leavis at Cambridge, and has been influential far outside that discipline. She is pervasive of recent ethical sensitivity.

At that time Acton's mind was particularly dominated by the developing hypothesis of a providential concern for political liberty.[7] He was captivated by a disciple of Feuerbach who could be like George Eliot; at the same time he was becoming more persuaded of the extraordinary possibility that, as a church shed the last vestiges of the inheritance of medieval Catholicism (and he thought particularly of the Quakers in the shape of William Penn), it was able to be used directly by God in making the 'scientific' liberal state. A secularised world might in some mysterious sense *be* the will of God. The true life of the church would in such case be something for the future to construct. There was therefore no need for the present-day church to hold on to an armoury of halberds or muskets or even of Gatlings.

Acton began to anticipate a 'modern' world of sensitive, educated, ethical persons, living under a modern liberal constitution, with a system of independent universities and a free press. Such a world would surely require the community life, the rituals, the self discipline, the motivation to service – above all, the 'given' tradition of a religious language – if it were to be humanly satisfying. Audaciously, Acton believed with increasing conviction that the Catholic church – provided it exercised ruthless self-discipline in aligning itself with its authentic nature – was equipped to out-perform all possible competition as the 'true' church for such a future. Again, it is not easy to say that he was wrong.

There was of course no obvious platform after the closure of his reviews for him to propagate these convictions. It was only in 1895, when Acton began to teach at Cambridge, that he again became a public person. The orbit of the comet that had apparently taken him away for good in 1870 brought him back for a sudden short burst of glory.

Acton was extraordinarily fortunate. He came to Cambridge both as a totally fresh face and yet as a senior and authoritative person in every sense. The development of college life (which Dr Sheldon Rothblatt has so well analysed in the *Revolution of the Dons*) had just reached its high point: a strong system of shared senior–junior loyalty rooted in college teaching, with social service opportunities opening up, political societies, team sports, and an open style of college chapel worship – all within a tight single-sex community. It was an educational *experience* – person-centred rather than discipline-centred – the opposite of the Berkeley 'knowledge-industry' multiversity of the 1960s. It was uncomplicatedly elitist. It came to flower in a period of imperial romanticism of 'responsibility' and 'service'. There was a sudden opening to graduates of prestigious careers throughout the world. Making things, or even selling them, was not highly regarded. It was aesthetics, education, mission, law, and administration that touched ambition and imagination.

Acton's lectures on modern history were profoundly influential. First and foremost they had a strong and easily perceptible structure, of the symphonic development of what we experience as 'the modern world'. This was sufficiently subtle that, while it was a 'progress', it was not a 'progress' of the kind the 1914–18 war would invalidate. It was transposed into a key of personal integrity, structures of consent, academic freedom, and abhorrence of absolutism. (Perhaps it is no accident that Cambridge has nourished more than its share of those prepared to betray their country for their beliefs.) What was presented might be used to socialise the commonwealth of nations, with or without religion, into one high-minded college. It was the Cambridge to which students had recently begun to come from all over the English-speaking world, including India and Africa.

These students who received Acton's teaching were conscious of two facts. First, they lived at a time when the states-system covering the world had been declared closed. There were no more territories on the map for Europeans to explore or lay claim to; for the first time in history the idea of 'one world', in relation to academic enquiry and to known juridical authorities, had substance. Second, it was also the time when the English-speaking peoples had every kind of excuse to see themselves as in some sense 'chosen': the name, 'British Israelites', was the sign of something far more important than an absurd contemporary sect. If they were chosen, they were in England – still their cultural centre – much less religious. The Pax Britannica was a widely accepted vocation. The universal empire of Classical Rome – however modified by loose concepts of 'spheres of influence' and 'indirect rule' – seemed a perfectly reasonable model for an age of justice, commerce, and science for all peoples, whose keystone and guardian was London, the undisputed world capital.

It would be foolish to pitch the claims for Acton at Cambridge too high. His teaching made a deep impression via a rapidly growing subject in one university at a period when both its senior and junior members numbered some of the most creative and powerful figures of the 20th century. It was his course of lectures on 'modern history' that was published and became a pervasive text book whose influence was reinforced by the university history teachers (not only at Cambridge) before and after the First World War whose imagination had been fired by personal contact with him. These disciples were not, however, dependent 'Actonians' in the way it became customary to speak of 'Leavisites', let alone of 'Marxists' or 'Freudians'.

William McNeill has hazarded the judgment that Acton was 'the first Englishman to view British, American, and Continental European history as a common whole'. His history was self-consciously 'scientific' and comprehensive and yet it did not jib at taking over the familiar English 'whig' belief that progress is essentially a question of constitutional forms of government. The mixture fused in a way that became enormously flattering to the self-esteem of the entire English-speaking world[8] and, in so far as that world has succeeded, has had a persuasive power outside it.

It is possible to remain agnostic about the extent to which Acton's contribution to the general understanding of a distinctly 'modern' history continues to be decisive, and yet to note how prominent Acton's characteristic concerns have been in it. The concepts of a world unity, of secularisation, and of personal integrity have been widely potent. Until recent years, there has been no sign of their even faltering.

At a more down-to-earth and professional level, we can

164

distinguish in his work what Acton asserted about the historian's
vocation. They follow from his 'myth' and may now seem eccentric
or, within the discipline of history itself, false. He believed with
many of his contemporaries that there is a discernible line of
'significance', a Universal History. On the other hand, neither in
his own generation or since have there been many who believed
with him that 'scientific' ideas, right ideas, can be presumed to
occur as a package,[9] predicating each other always and
everywhere across the whole range of governmental action, from
laissez-faire economics to prison reform to the electoral franchise.
This presupposition derived from men naturally having the
rational capacity to know abstract moral good (and if they are
Christian, hearing it spelled out in the Scriptures). A historian
who knew this to be so owed it to his craft, and to the future
well-being of society, to become a dentist, testing every little
corner of the psychology and actions of past 'great men' for moral
probity, and charting every instance of decay – for it will never
be the product only of ignorance or cultural variation.

These were Acton's 'hanging judge' convictions, and in his own
time and since he has been 'alone'. They have not been the ways
that historians have worked in western society. There is a
theoretician's 'purity' about Acton's world that gives his mind-set
a consistently platonising tendency. He wanted historians to be
able to examine like mathematicians and give ten out of ten. But
historians have never seen that as appropriate either for their
craft or its raw material. Yet no one was more aware of sin as a
phenomenon of the human condition than Acton.

In spite of this, it is above all to Acton that historians in the
English universities owed their acceptance of a professional
obligation to work within a world community of scholarship and
to argue from the specific case, from archives and manuscripts. It
was, too, his article 'German Schools of History' which, in
inaugurating the *English Historical Review* in 1885, laid the
foundations in Britain for the study of the presuppositions and
contextual framework of historiography itself. Acton's own work
is an example of the working out and application in historiography of an unusually comprehensive 'myth'. But in a strangely
anomalous way, his rhetoric for the *Cambridge Modern History*
project is an example of the fallacious assertion that 'myth'-free
historiography is possible at all. There were those even at the
beginning of this century who called what claimed to be so
objective, 'Lord Acton's Encyclical'.

The 'science' of Providence

Chapters 6 and 7 set out the shape of Acton's significant, or 'universal', history. The subject of 'progress' was what he called the 'Whig Church'. Like the Christian church it had its Anno Domini, and its period of obscure provincial germination, as well as its catacombs. But by breaking surface into public life in the 18th century, progress became visible, and announced 'modern history'. Acton wrote: 'By progress we mean the action of conscience. The XVIII century possessed a confused but energetic notion of conscience. It was regarded by men as far apart as Butler, Rousseau, Kant, as a perpetual and infallible force, urging mankind forward to better things.'[10] And soon after 1890, 'Progress. Then 18th century brought to light the horrible inferiority of savage races. It became impossible to attribute virtue etc. to mankind by its nature. The idea of Conscience was insufficient. It was not universal. It was developed by civilization. The fall of man preceded history. The rise of man is the work of history. This made Progress so important in those days.'[11]

'Progress' became the equivalent of what we now speak of as the obligation to develop the Third World. It involved the geographical spread and consolidation of what was already enjoyed in certain favoured leading regions. Social and economic 'human rights' had first to be secured, so that men and women could become confident enough and educated enough to work a constitution based on the rights and duties of conscience.[12]

Acton wrote of George Eliot, 'She has a place in the central chain of history, the history of Conscience.'[13] This is not an isolated statement. The universal history which we have outlined in the previous two chapters was the history that Acton in the 1870s experienced a vocation to write. It exemplifies in its subject matter, better perhaps than any other side of Acton's historical activity, what Acton meant when he contrasted the history that is a 'rope of sand' with that which is a 'continuous development – an illumination of the soul'.[14] There is a consistency about the subject, a common denominator of all the curiously diverse figures and events which contribute to it. But we are never sure whether the notion of conscience at its centre is an experience of personal identity in encounter with God or a Kantian intellectual exercise. Acton used the phrase 'rational mysticism'.[15] There was always a rather Stoic flavour about it, of a given 'particle of divinity' implanted and available in human life.[16]

If in this history there is a certain imposition of continuity upon the remarkable breadth and range of human experience being handled, there is also Acton's insistence on particularity. His history is a web of – for its time – extraordinary extent. Like the pattern in fine lace, it contains a sequence of foci.[17] These foci were often relatively obscure individuals. Acton saw in the thought as much as in the actions of people like Sarasa and Penn and Vinet the turning points of the deepest history. They did not, like the Innocent IIIs and the Napoleons, have great machines at their disposal. 'The history of progress is the history of the hard-won – dearly-bought – victories of single-handed individuals over the resistance of organized and established power ... the forces that are within over outward forces.'[18]

The working definition of conscience in Acton's Universal History is perhaps unusually rational and at the same time unusually biblical. He also has a view of history which is already prepared to accept the unique potency and significance of conscientious action by individuals: '[The History of] Conscience means also that the individual obtains a larger share of History. They resist their entourage. Increased cultivation gives them a larger area of cultivation. – That the Church is not everything, the state not supreme, the nation not the source or the limit of character, the time not decisive.'[19]

It is therefore not surprising that Acton's history should be peculiar. It is difficult to find other histories with which it can be compared, for, as Acton writes it, it is really a historically argued apologia for one interpretation of Christianity.[20] Its dogmatic character, its characteristically religious account of escape from providential crises,[21] remove it, ironically enough, fron the *genre* of 'science'. If it had been published it would have been a prodigy of scholarship and of the critical apparatus that goes with it.[22] But in the end, whether Acton's work is historically useful depends largely, as with the writers of the Old Testament, on whether there continues to be an important 'church' that believes he was right about God in History.[23]

When Acton reflected on what separated him from Döllinger, he asked, 'If you say nothing about the better cause, how can you justify God? If religious progress is nothing, what does Providence do?'[24] Progress in history was to be the proof of the existence of God. When we knew the line upon which God had so far been working, it naturally followed that we might project the end goal to which the world was oriented and the course by which during the coming years that harbour could best be approached.

As Regius Professor of Modern History at Cambridge, Acton's chief contribution was to give an extraordinary dignity and authority to the practice of history. If any man believed that his subject had inherited the medieval mantle of theology as Queen of the Sciences, it was he; and he succeeded in persuading others. The ground for this conviction is easy to isolate. Like most of his contemporaries, he believed that a general progress could be discerned in the history of civilised society.

Acton believed that the historian could know more of God than the priest. The one who has true knowledge of God can judge the utility of religious practice. The historian, rather than the pope, was the arbiter of truth. He wrote that, 'there is as much difference in the old and new notion of God before and since the discovery of the laws of history as before and since the discovery of law in Nature. And the science which describes it is the Philosophy of History.'[25] It was primarily for this reason that Acton gave so much emphasis to the period at the beginning of the 19th century which he termed that of 'Ideal Catholicism', when the Papacy 'repented' and put itself 'under the common law'. As early as 1864, he had written, 'God's handwriting exists in history independently of the Church, and no ecclesiastical exigence can alter the fact. The divine lesson has been read and it is the historian's duty to copy it faithfully without bias, and without ulterior views.'[26] This was the attitude of the Munich circles in which he was formed, and the target for Pius IX's *Syllabus Errorum.*

He spoke of the movement which resulted from this new academic integrity as 'Development', and commented, on a card in the wallet labelled 'Newman', 'Development a test of true Religion'.[27] In Acton's hands, the idea is taken beyond what Newman might have envisaged. A card dated 1894 asserts with splendid bravura: '[Development] takes away from the authority of older divines .... Makes religion a thing gradually ascertained and determined – not taught, handed down and remembered. [It used to be] better and safer the nearer the apostles – now, better and wiser and safer the further from them.'[28] Acton's Catholicism was in the end prepared to take this conclusion absolutely seriously.

If then, the high function of the historian in society was to try to discover and then be empowered to proclaim the direction in which Providence had worked in the past, it was necessary that such an activity should be 'scientific'.[29] It was so genuinely sacred and so decisive for human well-being that no passions and interests could be allowed to intrude. The historian must so far as possible project himself out of his own time and culture and survey with equal clarity the whole of human experience. He, if anyone, might glimpse the future.[30]

In the last decade of his life, Acton was particularly interested in formulating his ideas about historiography. The Döllinger materials, the various Cambridge lectures, and the projected Romanes lecture all apply and express these ideas. He often spoke of the importance of carrying forward into present consideration the whole 'baggage' of the past. 'Now, and not till now, people generally have understood that History is really a teacher, must be complete, not a master who governs, but a teacher who instructs.'[31] He referred to the high place of Ranke in modern history as due to his professional subordination of the Christian to the historian in the cause of such a passionate disinterestedness.[32]

Acton was quite sure that he himself stood in such a tradition of 'scientific history'. It provided, in conjunction with the corpus of objective moral knowledge that can be drawn from individual consciences, the basis of authority for his whole system. With such a knowledge of God, he felt able to judge the purely institutional authorities of both church and state. Such authorities had available to them the local consensus of opinion, which in special situations like revolutionary America might have the force of conscientious knowledge. Only the event could prove this to be so. So that the 'scientific' historian was the arbiter even of what had been true conscience. Acton was forced to accept that most claims for the authority of conscience had been in mistaken, barbarous, or reactionary causes. Ximenes and George III were cases in point. He had to attribute this to 'insincerity'. The paradox of building a system upon the direct authority of conscience and then allowing it no other content but Liberal morality was difficult, but not impossible, to defend. The Quakers had always claimed a consistency for the tradition that had arisen from their practice of openness to the Inner Light.

Acton believed he had discovered the object of God's providence through the course of history. It was what he repeatedly called the 'Whig Church'. A large number of passages show Acton expounding and defining this view. It was especially after 1880 that he placed this particular form of 'salvation history' at the centre. In a note for the Cambridge lectures, for instance, he wrote, 'The central line. motion that is progress. In political understanding. Promoted by the experience of each generation – by every branch of human thought. Therefore the state is the chief scene of progress and must be put in the first place[33] – and next to the state, the history of thought that takes place in politics.'[34] In the lectures themselves, he said, 'We have no thread through the enormous complexity of modern politics except the idea of progress towards more perfect and assured freedom, and the divine right of free men.'[35]

There are hints of this conclusion in the Bridgnorth lectures of 1877,[36] but it is afterwards that the typically Actonian identification of structures and constitutions with progress comes. The first systematic statement of this insight comes in 1882 when Acton wrote to Döllinger: 'There is a general unity in the history of ideas – of Conscience, of Morality, and of the means of securing it. I venture to say that the secret of the philosophy of history lies there. It is the only point of view from which one discovers a constant progress, the only one therefore which justifies the ways of God to man.'[37] If the forms of Liberal constitutions were thus the special concern of God's providence in history, Acton did not hesitate to draw the logical conclusion that a man's standing in the sight of God was to be measured by his politics, rather than by his religion. As early as 1877 he had noted, 'Christianity without Liberality will not take us far towards heaven.'[38]

The transposition of ways of thinking characteristic of the Roman Catholic Christian to apply to his 'Whig Church' was so developed by Acton that even the credal concept of the Last Things was called upon to furnish a political analogue. There was to be an end term of this providential development when what was enjoyed now in imperfect anticipation would be universal, public, and harmonious. Vinet, whom he followed so closely, had been quite explicit in suggesting that the 'Church of the Future' had been forced to await the modern constitutional democracies before it could develop its full scope and vigour. He had written, 'Jusqu'ici, le christianisme vraiment spirituel a pu atteindre quelques individus et, par certains de ceux-ci, agir occasionellement sur les masses, mais il n'a point directement façonné le corps social. Or, ce triomphe lui est promis. Une période est annoncée par l'écriture dans laquelle il y aura des peuples chrétiens selon l'intensité de ce mot.'[39]

From Acton's instruction in church history written for his son, it is clear that the unity of the Roman Church was its essential virtue, and its claim to authority. It is conspicuous how large a part unity played in Acton's thought.[40] He wrote, 'Progress has been in the direction of reconciliation. Unbelief, being never identified with a nation, does not divide mankind.'[41] It was precisely therefore the general acceptability, the secularity, of 'science' which led Acton to choose a political rather than a religious concern for divine providence.

On further investigation, Acton's plea for the separation of church and state turns out to be modified and conditioned by his overall belief that the cutting edge of God's purpose in the world is political. In the last resort this was the occasion and explanation of his growing apart from Döllinger after 1879. Acton admitted that Döllinger 'never understood that Lib[eralism] could be the rule of society, the basis of a system, the principle of a philosophy of history. The centre of all things was [for him] religion, not freedom.'[42]

The end goal of a 'Whig Church' had to be a 'Whig *Kingdom*',[43] a universal world society of the kind envisaged by Hegel and after him Marx. Acton's vision was of a society distinguished by its liberty; in the first instance its political and constitutional liberty. At bottom it would be spiritual – the reign of conscience. As in the biblical story, what began in the Eden of those wild woods in Pennsylvania would have ended with a world city, New Jerusalem, outside which nothing can exist because God is in it. There He might be found and 'enjoyed for ever' without a public Temple-precinct and without the permission of a priesthood endowed with arcane prescriptions.

This was Acton's 'myth' of secularisation. It is not so far from the thought-world of 'industrial mission' in the 1950s[44] and the saying of Cardinal Montini (later Pope Paul VI) when Archbishop of Milan, that the factory siren is called to be the temple bell of our civilisation.

The Vatican Council

The Vatican Council seems a fitting context for any conclusion, however provisional, about Acton's work. His vocation was shaped and limited by it in a complex and intensely experienced way. There is no doubt that as a young man – before the Council – he had concluded he should use his life to commend the Roman Catholic church to 'modern', 'liberal' England.[45] In 1855 he wrote to Döllinger of the difficulties historians made for the faith by trying to defend the popes too much. Catholic historians needed to win public trust. In 1869 he spoke of the embarrassment caused to intelligent Catholics by the infallibility debates: they become open to the old charge of being told what to believe: black is white if the pope says so. In 1872 he stated the main issues for Roman Catholic apologetic in England: Rome was a danger to the state and the church had been guilty of horrifying cruelties.[46] Acton's unyielding determination that a Catholic gain recognition as a 'scientific' historian who told the whole truth was fundamentally apologetic in its motivation.[47] There is a pleasant story that when Dupanloup exclaimed in astonishment at Acton's indefatigable zeal during the Council, Acton replied in all simplicity: 'C'est pour mes enfants. Je veux que la religion qu'on leur enseignera soit pure.'[48]

Though it must remain for theologians to assess, the movement of intellectual life and the choice of standing ground within the Roman Catholic church has been Acton's glorious vindication. When Pope John XXIII reconvened the Vatican Council in 1962, the door was opened for what could at the very least be called a complementing of the work of Pio Nono's Council. Whereas the First Council had only managed to vote the decree on papal infallibility before it was so precipitately adjourned, the Second Council worked patiently through a whole range of issues. The Roman Catholic church can claim that it was not transformed in any essential way, but what started as 'aggiornamento' became 'renovatio'. Its cross-cultural character and its acceptance of the disciplines of open scholarship (and particularly of biblical criticism) were clearly asserted, though they have perhaps not yet been fully demonstrated.

It would be hard to exaggerate the importance given to 'conscience' in the preparation of the Council documents. Given Acton's role in Rome in 1869–70, it is not surprising that his name was not often mentioned in the sessions a century later, but this injustice may be made good (and how appropriately Christian a treatment for the Master of the Hanging Judge!) by later historians. The name however of J. H. Newman was given great honour.

At Vatican I, and before it, Acton had identified his enemies as nourished – if he thought they had an intellectual appetite at all – by the Jesuits of the *Civiltà Cattolica*. At Vatican II the Jesuits were outstanding in their commendation of conscience. For example, Karl Rahner, who was the most substantial theologian of the Council, wrote, 'Someone who follows his own conscience, whether he thinks he should be a Christian or not, is accepted before God and by God, and can reach that eternal life we confess in our Christian faith as the goal of all.'[49] It is of obvious general interest in the context of this study of Acton that conscience played so central a role at Vatican II in the assessment of Christian faith, and of the proper vocation of the Roman Catholic church.

But what is of particular and extraordinary interest is the fact that one of the most fiercely debated documents of the Council was the Declaration on Religious Liberty, *Dignitatis Humanae*. This Declaration was very largely the fruit of the patient argument of Fr John Courtney Murray,[50] another Jesuit, formed by the American experience of the wall of separation, who as recently as 1954 had been asked by his order to stop publishing further articles on church and state. In a sense, it was the coping stone of the work of the Council, the characteristic if not the most authoritative expression of those rather heady few years. In the World Council of Churches' *Ecumenical Review* in 1966,[51] Dr Carillo de Albarnoz judged that 'The Declaration is a great document, possibly, at least in ecumenical perspective, the greatest that has emerged from the long debates of the Second Vatican Council.' 'Aggiornamento' was a cautious programme, tidying up the place, pruning out dead wood, converting the stable block into garages and offices, redecorating. There is in the Declaration a 'renovatio' that has more edge, what Acton might have called a 'repentance' or even a 'reformation'.

Fr Murray pointed out that it was in this document that the Roman Catholic church accepted the method of 'historical consciousness' or development which it had rejected in the past.[52] In the encyclical *Quanta Cura* (1864) Pope Pius IX had described the idea that 'liberty of conscience and of worship is the peculiar right of every man, which should be proclaimed by law' as a 'deliramentum' or insanity. Some principle other than 'development' is required to explain the transition in magisterium to the introductory statement of *Dignitatis Humanae*: 'This Vatican Council declares that the human person has a right to religious freedom ... no one is to be forced to act in a manner contrary to his own beliefs, whether privately or publicly, whether alone or in association with others, within due limits.'

Dignitatis Humanae is about rights to religious liberty, whether of individuals or of communities, and it is a declaration addressed from within the Roman Catholic church to the world in general. It is therefore a natural bridge to the phenomenon of abstract 'human rights', a proposition which has become that uncertain thing, a contemporary 'movement', and in western Europe even a court of law. It is a secular movement. Its scope is consciously international and comprehensive of men and women everywhere. Clearly there is a long history to the idea of 'rights of man' – and the attempt to articulate them on the basis of natural law theory has been, as Acton frequently asserted, the stuff of revolution in the history of the western world. But the present phenomenon dates from the Second World War and the enunciation by the Allies (essentially Britain and the U.S.A.) of the 'Four Freedoms' as war aims.

This rhetoric was taken over and built into the establishment of the United Nations and its associated instrumentalities at San Francisco in 1945. Its charter provides that one of its purposes should be: 'To achieve international cooperation ... in promoting and encouraging respect for human rights and for fundamental freedoms for all without distinction as to race, sex, language, or religion.' A Commission on Human Rights was established under the chairmanship of Mrs Eleanor Roosevelt and in 1948 a Universal Declaration of Human Rights was adopted. It is significant that Monsignor Roncalli – subsequently Pope John XXIII and convenor of the Second Vatican Council – was the Papal Nuncio in Paris and played an important part in drafting this Declaration.[53]

In his encyclical *Pacem in Terris* (1963) he went so far as to claim: 'In the juridical organisation of states in our time, the first requisite is that a Charter of Fundamental Human Rights be drawn up in clear and precise terms, and that it be incorporated in its entirety in the Constitution.' These conjunctions are such that – from the other side of the grave – Acton could well have said his *Nunc Dimittis*, like the aged Simeon at the presentation of the baby Jesus in the temple. His promised messianic age might at last be glimpsed; perhaps even in a sense it had begun.

The experience of the Civil Rights movement in America and elsewhere since the 1950s does indicate that the combination of legal process and a secular 'religious' language of human rights can change the mind-set and the public behaviour of whole peoples.

It would be a mistake, however, to think that Acton was ever the victim of facile optimism.[54] His historical training had above all been directed to sniffing out and displaying the discreditable vitality of what lay hidden behind the shop windows in the best and holiest exemplars of the religion he practised. He was also, as regards the field of this-worldly forces, profoundly unconvinced that what is in conscience best is best fitted to survive. In one of the most prophetic and characteristic passages of the Cambridge lectures, he commends what was to become the Welfare State almost as an act of corporate martyrdom, an act of witness to religious belief whose reward could only be anticipated in another dimension than history. He wrote: 'Progress has imposed increasing sacrifices on society, in behalf of those who can make no return, from whose welfare it derives no equivalent benefit, whose existence is a burden, an evil, eventually a peril to the community. The mean duration of life, the compendious test of improvement, is prolonged by all the chief agents of civilisation, moral and material, religious and scientific, working together, and depends on preserving, at infinite cost, which is infinite loss, the crippled child and the victim of accident, the idiot and the madman, the pauper and the culprit, the old and infirm, curable and incurable. This growing dominion of disinterested motive, this liberality towards the weak, in social life, corresponds to that respect for the minority, in political life, which is the essence of freedom. It is an application of the same principle of self-denial, and of the higher law.'[55]

Yet Acton's propositions are vehicles for hope. To recapitulate them, he asserted: (a) that the heart of Christianity is to do with conscience, the engagement of the soul with God, and that this is so in a way that can be translated, without being totally evacuated of significance, into an ultimate (because arguably eternal) value acceptable within the secular reality of plural world-religions and lack of religions; (b) that the structure of good government, its constitutional law and procedures (and particularly those which limit and separate power), is of fundamental importance to the quality of human life, and can be given abstract description; and (c) that no culturally variable absolutes – religious or political systems – should be allowed to interfere with the freedom of open enquiry, for scholarly truth is the condition of any progress at all. These are Acton's high ground. Few now deny them, at least in the west, and in public.

Notes

List of abbreviations used in the notes

Add. MS   Additional Manuscripts in the University Library, Cambridge

ASC   J. L. Altholz and D. McElrath, *The Correspondence of Lord Acton and Richard Simpson*, 3 vols., Cambridge, 1971–75

Corr.   J. N. Figgis and R. V. Laurence, *Selections from the Correspondence of the 1st Lord Acton*, vol. I, London, 1917

DB   V. Conzemius, *Ignaz v. Döllinger. Briefwechsel*, 4 vols., Munich, 1963–81

FR   J. N. Figgis and R. V. Laurence, *Lectures on the French Revolution*, London, 1910

HES   J. N. Figgis and R. V. Laurence, *Historical Essays and Studies*, London, 1908

HOF   J. N. Figgis and R. V. Laurence, *History of Freedom*, London, 1907

LMG   H. Paul, *Letters to Mary, daughter of the Rt Hon. W. E. Gladstone*, London, 1904

LMH   J. N. Figgis and R. V. Laurence, *Lectures on Modern History*, London, 1906

March-Phillips and Christian   L. March Phillips and B. Christian (eds.), *Some Hawarden Letters*, London, 1917. (Acton's list of the 'Hundred Best Books', with their descriptive epithets, is included on pp. 154 and 187.)

Quirinus   *Letters from Rome on the Council*, London, 1870

Notes to Chapter 1

1.   Acton wrote to Richard Simpson on 3 Oct. 1861: 'Francis II [King of Naples] was not strictly speaking lawful king, in the eyes of Rome, since the feudal right of the Holy See who gave the Sicilian crown has been denied. My grandfather [Sir John Acton] threw it off, by refusing the symbol, an annual white horse!' (*ASC* II, 174.)

2.   She became the first woman to be given an honorary doctorate by the University of Munich, for her work on Mme de Staël.

3.   cp. Acton to Simpson, 6 Oct. 1862: 'I believe you will find only 3 parties. 1o The old school, not warmed up by the C[ardinal] into devotion to Rome, and not intellectual or progressive …. Their strength is in the North and in the

midland counties. 2o Ourselves. 3o The zealous converts and those of the old set who are under [the] C[ardinal]'s influence, the Romanists, lovers of authority, fearing knowledge much, progress more, freedom most, and essentially unhistoric and unscientific' (*ibid.* III, 25). Acton expands 'ourselves' later in the letter (p. 26).

4. As late as 1873 he describes the dearth of English historians: Oxbridge posts are a mere vehicle for the voicing of scantily researched general observations, and there is no one competent to fill a chair (*DB* III, 109).

5. *ibid*, 257–72.

6. Noel Blakiston (ed.), *The Roman Question: Extracts from the despatches of Odo Russell from Rome 1858–70* (London 1962), p. 446. *see also* E. Campion (ed.), *Lord Acton and the First Vatican Council: a journal* (Sydney 1975).

7. '... books like those of Huber and Friedrich seem to me weapons borrowed from the enemy's arsenal' (*DB* III, 287).

8. On 15 Sept. 1871 Acton wrote to dissuade Döllinger from too close an involvement with the group that joined the Old Catholic schism: 'Sie [Friedrich *et al*] sind mit Ihnen vereint durch kein gemeinschaftliches Band positiver Überzeugung, und handelt nicht, im Grossen und Ganzen, unter der Herrschaft des Gewissens .... Sie brauchen sie alle nicht, denn der Sieg ist überhaupt für uns, und auf praktischen Weg, nicht möglich. Wir können nur den guten Samen streuen der dann, in späteren Jahren, gedeihen wird. Wir arbeiten für eine entfernte Zukunft, die nicht aus vorübergehenden öffentlichen Bewegungen, sondern aus Ihrer geistigen Arbeit ihren Profit ziehen wird' (*ibid.*, III, 33).

9. *Lord Acton. Zur Geschichte des vaticanische Concils* (Munich 1871) was put on the Index of prohibited books in September of that year.

10. Acton wrote to Simpson on 4 Nov. 1874 that he had failed to persuade Gladstone against publishing. 'I ended by saying that though not one of those attacked, I was one of those challenged, and that I should meet his challenge on my own account.' (*ASC* III, 319.) *see also* W. O. Chadwick, *Acton and Gladstone* (London 1976).

11. Acton's estimate of Newman was by this time quite low. He saw him as foxily 'decent', but as having in principle sold the pass: 'Ich rechne nicht viel darauf [*Letter to the Duke of Norfolk*, 1875] und in seinem Mund ist das Kapitel über das Gewissen halb ironisch gemeint' (28 May 1875; *DB* III, 142).

12. In a letter of 25 Nov. 1874, Acton looks forward to a 'better Pope', who might act in a way 'that would stultify these decrees as much as they stultify the decrees of Constance'. His opposition is an affair of historical, not theological, conscience, and he does not despair – especially when he sees the 'falseness and stupidity' of his opponent. (*ibid.*, 135.)

13. Simpson wrote to Acton on 9 Nov. 1874: 'Mrs Renouf protests against your letter [in that morning's *Times*]. It is, she says, as if you were waiting for an opportunity to say all the disagreeable things you could against the Vatican decrees.' (*ASC* III, 319.)

14. His daughter Annie wrote, 'He was loyal throughout his life to *the* ideal Church .... He taught his children to love truth above all else, and they were
    only called to punishment when convicted of even a childish falsehood, when his admonition to the youthful culprit would be almost tragic in its expression'. (McElrath, *Decisive Decade*, p. 48)

15. *ibid.*, p. 14.

16. 'Solidarity' is a word that occurs frequently in letters to Döllinger,

especially in 1882, where *all* Dominicans *per se* are asserted to be tarred with the crimes of Torquemada (*DB* III, 269, 290). Typical of Acton's central perception as it arose from the Borromeo case is: 'Sala, who says that Borromeo was right to get Protestants murdered, is the genuine type of Ultramontane. The same spirit produced the assassin, the Pope that canonised, and the biographer or editor who approves him.' (*ibid.*, 291)

17. McElrath, *Decisive Decade*, p. 42.
18. *DB* III, 212 (1879/80).
19. *ibid.*, 289 (1882).
20. *ibid.*, 291 (1882).
21. *ibid.*, 267, 288 (1882).
22. *ibid.*, 266 (1882).
23. *ibid.*, 271.
24. He was bowled over by her; and writes in May 1878 to Döllinger that he finds her 'die geistreichste Frau in der Welt' (*ibid.*, 200).
25. This speech by Lord Acton at a public meeting on 'The Roman Question' was reported in *The Kidderminster Shuttle* of 4 Feb. 1871. It proposed a resolution supporting the political independence of the papacy (text in McElrath, *The Decisive Decade*, pp. 240–5).
26. Letter to G. Massari, 29 April 1871, in the library of the Istituto per la Storia del Risorgimento (Busta 809/5) in Rome: 'Je crains bien que ce qu'on fera, ce n'est pas l'église libre dans l'état libre, mais le pape absolu dans l'état indifférent.' The following day, 30 April, he wrote to W. G. Ward commending the idea that the pope should no longer nominate bishops; there would then 'be no motive for any government to interfere with him, and no danger for the peace of the Church. The Italians are proceeding on the opposite principle of throwing all the spiritual power into the Pope's hands, and washing their own. By this, I think, they will make matters worse. The more the Pope is absolute, the more he is tempted to reject all conciliation. The fact is, the sheer indifference, under disguise of liberality, which the Italian Government tries to carry out, is only the mantle under which they try to smother the intense passions of the parliament. I cannot imagine the Pope permanently absent from Rome' (quoted in McElrath, *Decisive Decade*, p. 108).
27. The Munich monograph on Trent was abandoned, but Acton had agreed that he would contribute the chapter on Trent to vol. II of the *Cambridge Modern History*.
28. Told briefly by W. O. Chadwick in his review of *DB*, vol. I, in the *Journal of Ecclesiastical History* (1965), p. 114.
29. *passim* W. O. Chadwick, *The Popes and European Revolution* (Oxford 1981). In the preface Chadwick acknowledges his debt to the fact that many of the materials he used for this study had come from the particularly rich collection assembled by Acton in this area, and which is now in the Cambridge University Library. Conzemius suggests that both Acton and Lady Blennerhassett found the earlier tradition of Port Royal congenial, and indeed exemplary (*DB* IV, xxvi–xxvii).

Notes to Chapter 2

1. *HOF*, xxi (1907) and cp. Crane Brinton, 'Lord Acton's Philosophy of History', pp. 90–2, *Harvard Theological Review*, Jan. 1919, pp. 84–112.

Notes

2. *CMH* I, 2. This is also the judgment of Conzemius, in *Lord Acton oder das freie Wort in der Kirche*, p. 147.
3. *John Emerich Acton: Cattolicesimo Liberale* (Florence 1950), p. liv.
4. The detailed relation of Acton's ideas to those current in Munich when he was studying there under Döllinger in the 1850s is of great importance for Acton studies, but it falls outside the scope of this work.
5. May 1857, quoted by H. Butterfield in 'Journal of Lord Acton at Rome 1857', *Cambridge Historical Journal* (1945), p. 200. cp. this with *HOF*, 203 (1859).
6. Printed in *DB* III, 454–9 and in McElrath, *Decisive Decade*, pp. 240–5.
7. *Letters from Rome*, 'Quirinus', 832.
8. *Corr.* 42.
9. Quirinus, 442.
10. It is significant that in the *North British Review* of January 1870 he takes the opportunity of criticising the New Testament doctrine of passive obedience in a review of Lavollée's *Portalis*.
11. This is an idea which occurs frequently, from talk in 1869 of 'the permanent and incurable perversion of the moral sense wrought by a distorted piety' (*HOF*, 123) to the classical statement in his review of H. C. Lea's *History of the Inquisition* (1888).
12. Add. MS 5019.
13. Add. MS 5395/73.
14. Add. MS 4908 – cp. Vinet, 'Une religion qui n'est pas de la morale a moins de valeur qu'une morale qui n'a pas de la religion.' (Add. MS 5495)
15. Add. MS 4909, and cp. Add. MS 5392/45.
16. Add. MS 4916/233.
17. He puts into her mouth the question, 'Can you believe in science, disbelieve in the other world, develop morality, and yet not depend on discoveries, but be religious?' (Add. MS 5628, p. 35). Presumably 'not to depend on discoveries' is to be prepared to stand within a tradition.
18. e.g. Add. MS 5628, p. 70.
19. Add. MS 4966/247.
20. *HOF*, 46 (1877).
21. Add. MS 5019.
22. Add. MS 5019.
23. Add. MS 4908 (?1890–5).
24. Add. MS 5628, p. 44.
25. Add. MS 5019.
26. cp. *Taking Leave of God* (London 1980).
27. Add. MS 4909.
28. *LMH*, 6.
29. Add. MS 4960/26, and cp. also Add. MS 4960/47.
30. Add. MS 4960/33.
31. Add. MS 4960/284.
32. Miss Evelyn Underhill wrote: 'The divine nucleus, the point of contact between man's life and the divine life in which it is immersed and sustained, has been given many names in course of the development of mystical doctrines .... Sometimes it is called Synteresis.' (*Mysticism* (1930) p. 54)
33. Add. MS 5404/10.
34. Add. MS 4907.
35. Add. MS 4960/253.

36. He wrote: 'But from Jonathan Edwards to Spinoza she went over at one step. The abrupt transition may be accounted for by the probable action of Kant, who had not then become a buttress of Christianity' (*HES*, 278 (1885)); and 'Break of all contact between pleasure and virtue, virtue and reward – this is Kant's real view. – She adopts it.' (Add. MS 5019)
37. Add. MSS 4901/93, 5395/12, 5395/49 and Add. MS 4901/257.
38. Quoted in Add. MS 4947/302.
39. See the treatment of the idea of 'science' in 19th-century intellectual history in S. Collini, D. Winch, and J. Burrow, *That Noble Science of Politics* (Cambridge 1983).

Notes to Chapter 3

1. Renouf was Keeper of Oriental Antiquities at the British Museum and wrote on the religion of the Egyptians. His pamphlet on Pope Honorius and infallibility (1868) – a subject much referred to by Acton at the Council – was put on the index.
2. Add. MS 4908.
3. Vinet was professor of practical theology at Lausanne. He wrote, 'Il n'y a pas de vie ou il n'y a point de sectes: l'uniformité est le symptome de la mort.' (*Manifestation des Convictions Religieuses*, Paris 1842, 371). Along the line of thought which Adam Smith followed in the *Wealth of Nations* (Book V) and that of the Danish liberal, Bishop N. F. S. Grundtvig, also: 'La concurrence des religions — de cette diversité même il naître de bons fruits sociaux, — chacune de ses communautés ne peut s'annoncer favorablement au monde, et se raccomander a son attention, que par ses oeuvres, c'est-à-dire par des vertus sociales. Voilà, si je ne me trompe, le scandale levé.' (*Liberté des Cultes*, 30, Paris, 1826)
4. Add. MS 5467.
5. Add. MS 5416.
6. Add. MS 5607, p. 89 (1880). Here Acton lists various characteristic contributions. It can be compared with the epithet given to Fénelon in the *100 Best Books*, 'Religion dissevered from Dogma'.
7. Add. MS 4905.
8. *HOF*, 520 (1870).
9. Penn described the proposition, 'Whatsoever ye would that men should do to you, do ye so even to them', as 'that great Synteresis' (J. Stoughton, *William Penn*, p. 77).
10. Although it is dangerous to imply more than the evidence will prove on the attitude of Acton to his own church, there is – besides the whole tenor of his system – abundant evidence to show that he shared Vinet's attitude of being 'en communion d'esprit avec tous ceux qui, dans un établissement quelconque, professent et annoncent Jésus-Christ venu en chair' (Add. MS 5495). For example, in the box 'George Eliot' (Add. MS 5019): 'Did she think that my theory undermined faith? ... Perhaps my idea belongs to the Broad Church epoch, rather than to the school with which in her youth, she was most familiar. Then she would suspect that faith cannot live with such principles', and 'Men of original powers, finding that they cannot force their views on the world, adapt themselves to some one

180

current — There is some compromise and concession. Again: a man of original mind, having begun in a religion not his own choice, finds that it is not entirely his own. He assimilates part, he leaves out part, he lives in some illusion, for a time – permanently, he compromises.' Note also, this card, 'A man who gets his politics from his own state is like one who gets his religion from his own church. National forces make politics in one case. Ecclesiastical forces make religion in the other.'(Add. MS 4938/41)

11. *HOF*, 197 (1859).
12. Add. MS 5392/55.
13. Add. MS 5392/36.
14. *HES*, 443 (1887).
15. Add. MS 4906.
16. 'The church is so formed by our Lord that the real edification and piety are as great in the poorest and remotest and humblest congregations ... as in the heart and centre, which is surrounded by all the wealth and resources of the religious world. Perhaps you will be more deeply struck by the simple zeal of the poor Catholics in this Protestant country than by the splendours of St Peter's.' (London, 28 April 1865; McElrath, *Decisive Decade*, p. 61.)
17. cp. Add. MS 4915, dated 15 Jan. 1895: 'Tolerance arose naturally among Church historians. Because the Protestants were so important to them.'
18. Add. MS 5604, p. 21.
19. Add. MS 5604, p. 18.
20. Add. MS 5604 (July 1879), p. 27.
21. Add. MS 5611, p. 4: a notebook dated July 1880.
22. Add. MS 5611, p. 34.
23. Conzemius says that von Hügel was one of those few who grasped *why* Acton was so critical of his church, that it was his apologetic zeal on her behalf. He quotes this moving passage about Acton: 'Er ist wie wir alle wissen, durch Jahre qualvoller Spannung und Prüfung hindurchgegangen. Aber auf diese Prüfung konnte er nun, wie in seinen letzten Lebensjahren sagte, zurückblicken als auf einen scheusslichen Nachtmahr, von dem zu erwachen, Glanz und Frieden in die Seele brachte.' (*Lord Acton oder das freie Wort in der Kirche*, p. 155)
24. Add. MS 5401/31.
25. Add. MS 5402/18.
26. Add. MS 5608, p. 7.
27. Add. MS 5606, p. 10: a notebook dated Feb. 1878.
28. Add. MS 5605, p. 16: a notebook dated Feb. 1878.
29. Add. MS 5019.
30. Add. MS 5403/35.
31. Add. MS 5608, p. 53. The Old Man of the Mountains was leader of the fanatical sect of Assassins at the time of the first crusade, whose religious ritual required drugs, banditry, and murder.
32. Add. MS 5495.
33. Add. MS 5019.
34. Add. MS 5019.
35. Add. MS 5392/104. cp. Add. MS 5611, p. 15: 'Comprehension Tory: only Whigs ready for varieties.'
36. Add. MS 4955/282.

37. This was one of the problems for Acton about Rome in the 1860s: it did not have this proper Christian division of role. cp. 'But in Rome the clergy = the bureaucracy – which is made ludicrously apparent by giving clerical garb to secular employés. All liberty consists *in radice* in the preservation of an inner sphere exempt from state power – That reverence for conscience is the germ of all civil freedom, and the way in which Christianity served it. That is, liberty has grown out of the distinction (separation is a bad word) of Church and State. Rome, where they are not distinct, would therefore be like the Caliphate, Russia, etc. ... The security therefore is only in the objectiveness of eccles[iastical] law, and its transfer onto the state; which is precisely what asceticism overturns.' (*ASC* II, 251)

38. *HOF*, 29 (1877).

39. Add. MS 5495.

40. Add. MS 4914.

41. Add. MS 5495.

42. Add. MS 4912.

43. W. Herzberg, *Catholic, Protestant, and Jew* (New York, 1955).

44. Add. MS 4960/184.

45. Add. MS 5392/140.

46. *FR*, 10.

47. Add. MS 5416 (1710).

48. Add. MS 4960/12, cp. also Add. MS 5611, p. 36 (1880), 'The note of Christianity is its universality.'

49. Add. MS 4945/319.

50. Add. MS 4949/241.

51. Add. MS 5392/84.

52. Add. MS 5495.

53. Add. MS 4915.

54. *HOF*, 151 (1862): cp. this with *HES*, 185 (1861): 'The theory of liberty insists on the independence of the Church; the theory of liberalism insists on the omnipotence of the State as the organ of the popular will.'

55. Add. MS 4911.

56. Add. MS 4910.

57. Add. MS 4905.

58. Add. MS 4906.

59. Add. MS 4912.

60. Add. MS 4979/19. It is uncertain whether 'Gregorian' refers to Pope Gregory I or to Hildebrand, Gregory VII. cp. Add. MS 4944/161.

61. Add. MS 5019.

62. Add. MS 4979/175, a History of Liberty box. In this connexion it is interesting to note the drastic schemes of reform submitted by Bishop Strossmayer (Acton's close colleague) and by 'a Bohemian priest' to the Vatican Council (*HOF*, 494).

63. Add. MS 5019.

64. Add. MS 5611, p. 4l: notebook dated 1880.

65. Add. MS 5607, p. 77: a notebook dated March 1880.

66. Add. MS 4953/337.

67. Add. MS 5611, p. 3 (July 1880). cp. also p. 5.

68. Add. MS 5019.

69. cp. Add. MS 5628/35: '[She] wanted a religion compatible with all this – yet not an invention, beyond the reach of ordinary men. Can you believe

in science, disbelieve in the other world, develop morality, and yet not depend on discoveries, but be religious? Judaism seemed to be this. So weak in the other world. So simple in its dogma. So innocent of Christian history. Quakers equally so – why not they? No culture. Humanity of the Jews. Even to animals.'

70.　Add. MS 4979/151.
71.　Add. MS 5392/4.
72.　Add. MS 5392/54.
73.　Add. MS 4915.
74.　*ACS* II, 195.
75.　Add. MS 4955/164–5.
76.　Add. MS 5611, p. 5 (July 1880).
77.　Add. MS 5606, p. 15 (Feb. 1878).

Notes to Chapter 4

1.　Add. MS 5403 (July 1878).
2.　Add. MS 4941/332.
3.　Add. MS 4905.
4.　*The Rambler*, Jan. 1860, p. 146.
5.　*HOF*, 298 (1862).
6.　*ibid.*, 3 (1877).
7.　Add. MS 5019.
8.　Add. MS 4945/7
9.　Add. MS 4908.
10.　*The Rambler*, May 1861, pp. 48–9.
11.　Add. MS 5019.
12.　*FR*, 122.
13.　Add. MS 5500.
14.　Add. MS 4921/317.
15.　Add. MS 4945.
16.　*HOF*, 22.
17.　*HES*, 145 (1868), cp. 'the natural history of federal democracy' in 1889 (*HOF*, 577).
18.　*HOF*, 87. cp. also *FR*, 73. *see* H. Ben-Israel, *English Historians and the French Revolution* (1968)
19.　*HES*, 125 (1866).
20.　Add. MS 4965/21.
21.　Add. MS 4955/72.
22.　Add. MS 5019.
23.　Add. MS 5019.
24.　Add. MS 4960/220.
25.　Add. MS 4912.
26.　Add. MS 4908.
27.　Add. MS 4941/143.
28.　cp. 'A. Smith. He started the common idea of Liberalism. Disinterested state. No care for religion, morality, education, poor relief, health. Laissez-faire. How we have been correcting this extreme, ever since then'. (Add. MS 5486)
29.　*HOF*, 288 (1862).
30.　Add. MS 4979/83.
31.　*LMH*, 173.

32. Add. MS 4912.
33. Add. MS 4945/232–3.
34. Add. MS 4955/16.
35. Add. MS 5019.
36. *HOF*, 219.
37. *Corr.* 256.
38. Add. MS 4960/137.
39. Add. MS 4905.
40. Add. MS 4909.
41. Add. MS 5468.
42. Add. MS 4914.
43. Add. MS 4939/367.
44. Add. MS 4901/359.
45. Add. MS 4960/278.
46. Add. MS 4960/106.
47. *LMH*, 32.
48. *ibid.*, 13.
49. *ibid.*, 329, where the first note is given as from Scheidler and the second from the Danish Lutheran bishop, Martensen, whom Acton very much admired (though he was the principal figure against whom Kierkegaard reacted).
50. Add. MS 4921/325.
51. Add. MS 4949/83.
52. Add. MS 4901/98.
53. Add. MS 4960/1.
54. Add. MS 4960/188.
55. Add. MS 4960/189.
56. Add. MS 4960/295.
57. Add. MS 4960/248.
58. Add. MS 4901/358.
59. Add. MS 4912.
60. Add. MS 5486.
61. Add. MS 4939/334.
62. Add. MS 5019.
63. Add. MS 4914.
64. Add. MS 4941/111.
65. Add. MS 4942/220.
66. Add. MS 4945/89.
67. Add. MS 5395/27.
68. Add. MS 4901/254.
69. Add. MS 5495.
70. Add. MS 5495.
71. Add. MS 5607, p. 89, a notebook dated March 1880, Mentone.
72. Add. MS 4952/260.
73. Add. MS 4960/30.
74. Add. MS 4916.
75. Add. MS 4951/47.
76. *HOF*, 1 (1877).
77. Granted the special role in providential history assigned by Acton to the Quakers, note the following account of the working of the Spirit in human affairs by the Quaker leader, Isaac Penington in 1650. I am indebted to Dr W. A. Cole for this reference. 'There hath been often a naked, honest, simple, pure thing stirring in the army, which the

great ones (seeing some present use of) fell in with, and improved for
their own ends but destroyed the thing itself; so that it attained not
to the bringing forth of that righteous liberty which it seemed to aim
at (and did indeed aim in those in whom the striving did arise) but
was made use of by them to advance them in their particular interest
against their enemies, and so get them up.'

78. Add. MS 4916/11.
79. *LMH*, 13.
80. *ibid.*, 329.
81. Add. MS 4898.
82. Add. MS 4916/3.
83. Add. MS 4943/410.
84. Add. MS 5395/82.
85. Add. MS 5466.
86. Add. MS 5019.
87. cp. *HOF*, 296 (1862).
88. Add. MS 4945/184.
89. *FR*, 5.
90. Add. MS 4941/205.
91. *LMH*, 302–3.
92. Add. MS 4942/382.
93. *FR*, 13.
94. Add. MS 4960/116.
95. *HOF*, 39 (1877).
96. Add. MS 4945/213.
97. Add. MS 4979/5.
98. Add. MS 5392/95, probably a card of *c.* 1878. Acton added 'N.B.'
99. Add. MS 4945/314.
100. Add. MS 5605, p. 9.
101. Add. MS 4909.
102. See Add. MS 5392/247.
103. Add. MS 5606, p. 35.
104. Add. MS 5605, p. 26.
105. Add. MS 4908.
106. Add. MS 4942/390.
107. Add. MS 5495.
108. Add. MS 5019, though compare Add. MSS 4955/246–7 on 'Ideal Toryism'.
109. Add. MS 5006.
110. Add. MS 5468.
111. Add. MS 4955/98.
112. *FR*, 30.
113. Add. MS 4965/59.
114. *LMH*, 268.
115. Add. MS 5468.
116. Add. MS 4960/135.
117. *HES*, 123–43 (1866). Acton found the physiological metaphor congenial.
His last letter to Mary Gladstone in February 1901 (*LMG*, 203) runs,
'The country is going to pieces, as the old country gentlemen used to
say; but it is what doctors call a beautiful case, coming out normally
and regularly.'
118. For Newman, see the article 'On Consulting the Faithful in Matters of
Doctrine', which he published during his temporary editorship of the
Rambler in July 1859. For Lamennais, cp. Add. MS 4939/47.

Notes

119. Add. MS 5605, p. 35; cp. Magnus, *Gladstone* (London, 1954), pp. 164–5: '[after Lincoln's speech at Gettysburg] the whole heat and energy of Gladstone's intense nature soon closed around that concept [i.e. Democracy]. — He invested [the masses] with the quality of a spiritual tribunal before which the greatest causes could be tried.'
120. *FR*, 356.
121. Add. MS 5495.
122. *HOF*, 11.
123. *ibid.*, 16.
124. Add. MS 5019.
125. *FR*, 37.
126. *ibid.*, 239.
127. Add. MS 4896 quotes from a speech of Clay in 1835, in which he deplores the development of the American Constitution to the point where, 'instead of having a balanced government with three co-ordinate departments, we have but one power in the State'.
128. Add. MS 5604, p. 11.
129. e.g. his treatment of Robespierre (*FR*, 286), and explicitly, with reference to Condorcet (*ibid.*, 270).
130. Add. MS 5019.
131. Add. MS 5552, p. 11 (1877?).
132. *HOF*, 65.
133. Add. MS 4898 (1819).
134. It is interesting to note in this context the Whig *hauteur* which the young Acton showed his Carlow constituents when he was their M.P. See J. J. Auchmuty, *Acton as a member of the House of Commons* (Farouk I University, Alexandria, 1949).
135. Add. MS 4955/89.
136. Add. MS 5466.
137. Add. MS 5466.
138. Add. MS 4956/187.
139. Add. MS 4907.
140. Add. MS 4942/380.
141. Add. MS 5466.
142. Add. MS 4907.

Notes to Chapter 5

1. T. Appel, *Life and Work of John W. Nevin*, (Philadelphia, 1899).
2. cp. Lionel Kochan, *Acton on History* (1954), in the appendix, pp. 149–51, where he writes, 'Acton's support of the American Revolution is more of a tribute to his heart than to his head. The hyperbolical terminology alone indicates the emotional factors at work.' Kochan, however, was not aware of the teleological context in which Acton saw the Revolution, and therefore misses the point of Acton's enthusiasm.
3. Himmelfarb and Kochan both agree that 1875 is the division in dating the earlier and the later cards of the Acton MSS collection. Conzemius puts it at 1878.
4. 'The late Lord Acton', *Edinburgh Review* (April 1903), p. 502.
5. *HOF*, 329 (1861).
6. 16 Feb. 1861; *ASC* II, 122.
7. *ibid.* II, 193, 202.

8. Acton chose to review a large number of books about the American Civil War in his successive journals.
9. *HES*, 142 (1866).
10. Lady Blennerhasset to Döllinger, 6 Feb. 1866 (*DB* IV, 68.
11. *Home and Foreign Review* (1864), pp. 718–19. It is interesting that at this time he spoke of 'the most legitimate and glorious revolution recorded in modern history. I mean the revolution of Brabant [in 1830].' (*DB* III, 437.)
12. *HES*, 126 (1866).
13. *ibid.*, 142 (1866).
14. *Home and Foreign Review*, pp. 656–9.
15. *ibid*, pp. 322–4.
16. *HES*, 136 and 140.
17. *Home and Foreign Review* (1864), pp. 718–19.
18. *Letters from Rome*, Quirinus, 108.
19. His copy of it is marked by a slip from *The Times* of 24 Oct. 1876.
20. Add. MS 5408/58.
21. A. M. Schlesinger, Jr., *The Age of Jackson* (London 1946).
22. cp. Gasquet, *Lord Acton and His Circle* (1906).
23. M. A. de Wolfe Howe, *The Life and Letters of George Bancroft* (1908), I, 223.
24. *History of the United States*, II, 337.
25. *HOF*, 84.
26. It is notable that Bancroft's *History of the United States* figures largely in the bibliographies in Vol. VII of the *Cambridge Modern History*.
27. This is made more probable by the fact that there is a group of boxes, Add. MSS 4894–8, which are labelled *America* and which appear to be organised (though incompletely) on the basis of the sequence of Acton's note-making, rather than according to the type or chronology of events.
28. Neither could he have obtained it from the other books on America, e.g., Laboulaye and Holst, which he was reading in these years. These were anti-Democrat, even where they were not anti-democratic. It is hardly likely that Acton would have been much influenced by the rising general interest in Quakerism in the 1880s. (See *Edinburgh Review*, July 1891.) It was chronologically later and concerned with the mystical rather than political aspects of Quakerism.
29. Acton appends here a note referring to Tocqueville and, significantly, to Leibnitz's theory of free will.
30. *LMH*, 10.
31. Bancroft, *History of the United States*, II, 337. The section 'To Locke ... in the soul' is lined by Acton. The great issue of colonial political thinking had been on what basis were the American colonists to stand in claiming the precious traditional rights of Englishmen, e.g. as enshrined in Magna Carta as well as in custom, when they no longer lived in the land to which those rights were related and limited.
32. Add. MS 4895/127.
33. Bancroft, *op. cit.*, II, 339.
34. *ibid.*, II, 352.
35. Add. MS 4895/126.
36. Schlesinger, p. 381.
37. Acton's early horror of unicameral government had given way to a preference for it in his review of Bryce in 1889. This, too, may be due to Bancroft's influence.
38. See Edith Philips, 'Pennsylvanie: L'age d'Or', *Am. Hist. Rev.* (1930) for an account of the 18th century French image of Pennsylvania.

39. Though Henri Peyre, 'The Influence of 18th Century Ideas on the French Revolution', *Jnl. of Hist. of Ideas* (1949), seems to give weight to the position Acton adopts in the opening chapters of *FR*. It is noteworthy that the Quakers were granted special privileges under the Girondin government.
40. Add. MS 5440/100.
41. Add. MS 4944/341.
42. *HES*, 31.
43. *LMH*, 6.
44. *HOF*, 410 (1890).
45. *LMH*, 11.
46. *HOF*, 84 (1878).
47. Add. MS 5392/236.
48. Add. MS 5392/234.
49. Add. MS 5392/61.
50. *ASC* II, 203.
51. Letters of May and June 1882, *DB* III, 257–82.
52. cp 15 June 1882: 'Gewissensfreiheit war längst amerkannt in Theorie und Literatur, wo nicht vom Pöbel, doch von der geistigen Aristokratie. Bei ganzen Kirchen war es fast Dogma, in ganzen Ländern Gesitz. Ich denke an Socinianern Arminienanern. Independenten. Quakers.' (*DB* III, 281.)
53. Add. MS 4954/20.
54. Add. MS 4895/182.
55. Add. MS 4902. It is interesting to compare (in the *CMH* I, p. 48) the account of a French Huguenot expedition to Brazil in 1555: 'God ... looked down from heaven and saw that the corrupt Christians of Europe had utterly forgotten both Himself and His Son. He therefore resolved to transfer the Christian Mysteries to the New World.'
56. 'Conscience, understood in this way, supplied a new basis for freedom. It carried further than the reign of Whiggism. The deeper Quakers perceived the consequences. Penn drew the consequences in the constitution of Pennsylvania. It was the standard of a new Party and a new World.' (Add. MS 4960/299.)
57. *Corr.* 276.
58. Add. MS 4960/299.
59. Add. MS 5392/184.
60. Add. MS 4952/204.
61. Add. MS 4952/205.
62. Add. MS 4951/204.
63. J. Stoughton, *Life of William Penn* (1882), p. 302. This book is in the Acton Library and is much lined.
64. Add. MS 4948/264, a quotation from Moncure Conway, *Life of Paine* (1892).
65. *FR*, 22.
66. Add. MS 4921/331 (1890s); cp. his comment in 1862 that it was the French which was the first real revolution (*HOF*, 271).
67. *Contemporary Review*, Dec. 1952, p. 353, an article by G. Fasnacht entitled 'Acton's Notes for a Romanes Lecture'. These notes were begun in Nov. 1900, but his health broke down before he was to deliver the lecture at Oxford.
68. *HOF*, 578.
69. Add. MS 4949/294. Smith admired America so much that he went to make his home there. In 1862, Acton had written, 'he [Smith] discusses the morality of man and actions far oftener than history ... either requires or

tolerates.' (*HOF*, 234.)
70. e.g. Add. MS 5602, p. 41.
71. cp. *LMH*, 311, Add. MS 4954/82 and Add. MS 4954/19.
72. Add. MS 4897.
73. Add. MS 4954/70.
74. Add. MSS 5553, 5554, and 5605.
75. Add. MS 5605 (1878), p. 18.
76. *LMH*, 206.
77. Add. MS 4944/109.
78. Add. MS 4965/35. It is an important question to Acton. He referred to it in the Cambridge lectures: 'the real enemy was the House of Commons. The old European securities for good government were found insufficient protection against parliamentary oppression. The nation itself, acting by its political representatives, had to be subjected to control' (*LMH*, 309). In card Add. MS 4895/265 he attributes the moral impotence of the Parliament to George's success in suborning it.
79. *LMH*, 303–4.
80. Add. MS 5605, p. 56.
81. Acton's relation to Burke is almost as complex as the history of his relation to Döllinger. Miss Himmelfarb's article, 'The American Revolution in the Political Theory of Lord Acton', *Jnl. of Modern History*, XXI (1949), pp. 293–312, treats this topic very much in the light of Acton's relation to Burke. She shows no awareness of the change in Acton's attitude to America, nor of the special importance he attached to the Quakers. She writes that Acton was aware that Burke's advocacy of the American case was based on pragmatic, and not moral, grounds. This, as we shall show in the next section, is patently untrue.
82. Add. MS 4953/238.
83. *LMH*, 276.
84. This is directly stated in Add. MS 4949/127.
85. Add. MS 4898, cp. also Add. MS 5611, p. 24 (1880), Add. MS 4895/196, and Add. MS 4945/167.
86. Add. MS 4945/166.
87. e.g. Add. MS 5611, p. 47 (1880).
88. Add. MS 5467.
89. Crane Brinton, in 'Lord Acton's Philosophy of History', p. 108, *Harvard Theological Review* (Jan. 1919) pp. 84–112.
90. *LMH*, 217.
91. Add. MS 4895 (1878?).
92. *HOF*, 56.
93. Add. MS 4945/111 (1894?).
94. *LMH*, 311.
95. Add. MS 4953/111.
96. cp. Add. MS 4954/50, Add. MS 4945/288, Add. MS 4965/61 and *LMH*, 308
97. Add. MS 4953/239.
98. Add. MS 5643 (1890–5).
99. This experience of powerful moral movements of political action against one's own national or material interests is perhaps a feature of modern British and American history that is in world terms unusual, to say the least, e.g. in America the anti-Vietnam War agitation, in Britain the Lancashire millworkers support for the northern states in the American Civil War, and the opposition to the Boer War in South Africa.
100. *LMH*, 217.

101. Add. MS 5611, p. 20.
102. Add. MS 5608, p. 18.
103. Add. MS 4954/228.
104. Add. MS 5602, p. 6.
105. Crane Brinton remarks (*op.cit.*, pp. 95–7) on a similarly over-intellectual and altruistic approach to the motives of the Confederate rebels in the younger Acton.
106. Add. MS 4960/138. The alternative conclusion is that very few non-ideological people are revolutionaries – certainly George Eliot was not.
107. Add. MS 5604, p. 4.
108. See David Newsome, *Godliness and and Good Learning* (London 1961).
109. *HES*, 483 (1888); and cp. Add. MS 4893/60 and Add. MS 4921/173.
110. Add. MS 4960/75.
111. Add. MS 4898.
112. Add. MS 4945/168.
113. Add. MS 4898.
114. It is interesting that Acton, as a young man at Munich, followed the conservative Burke from 'catholic' principles, and yet that, when he began to interpret Burke as a 'scientific' revolutionary, he could still claim that these ideas were 'catholic' by identifying them with St Thomas.
115. A card which is clearly a draft for this (Add. MS 4954/232) runs, 'under the name of natural law, hidden away in Latin folios ....'
116. *HOF*, 55.
117. It is significant that it was at this time Gladstone began his appeals to the moral sense of the nation about Turkish atrocities over the heads of Parliament.
118. *FR*, 78, cp. *HOF*, 86 (1878). 'The most novel and impressive lesson taught by the fathers of the American Republic was that the people, and not the administration, should govern .... Authority submitted to public opinion, and left to it not only the control, but the initiative of government.'
119. Add. MS 4953/84.
120. Add. MS 5606, p. 38.
121. Add. MS 5602, p. 58.
122. Add. MS 4897.
123. Add. MS 5602. p. 3.
124. Add. MS 5611, p. 30.
125. Crane Brinton (*op. cit.*, p. 108) has pointed out Acton's 'scientific' ambiguity very clearly. He writes that he 'tends to categorise the matter of history and falls into that very *a priori*-ism he seeks to avoid .... We have a feeling that Acton's liberty would only transfer the individual from the authority of external political power to that of a historically-determined conscience.'
126. Add. MS 5602, p. 44.
127. Add. MS 4915 (1890–5).
128. Of Switzerland. Acton could imagine no possible revolution against this presumably ideal constitution (it is interesting that it arose from an anti-Catholic *Kulturkampf* context). In this respect, as in so many others, he is a Platonist.
129. *HOF*, 586 (1889).
130. *ibid.*, 585 (1889).
131. Add. MS 5602, pp. 48–9 (1877) and cp. Add. MS 5608, p. 16.
132. Add. MS 4895/289 (?1878).
133. cp. Add. MS 5602, p. 29 and 'No army, no navy, no debt. No troubles from foreign neighbours .... No great party questions. Independence, prosperity,

liberty so secure as never before in world' (Add. MS 4895).
134. Add. MS 4945/165.
135. Add. MS 4942/333. Laboulaye used America as an Ideal State. His biographer, Boutmy, compared his vision of America to Fénelon's Salente in *Télémaque*.
136. Even before Acton came to admire the Revolution, Hamilton shared with Calhoun a high place in his thought. In Acton's copy of Jefferson's *Anas*, Hamilton's part in the constitutional discussions is intensively marked. Add. MS 4896.
137. Acton's dictum is one conclusion from the premise that social structure determines the limits of possibility in relationships, language, and knowledge. Marx shared a variant of the same perception.
138. Add. MS 5019.
139. Add. MS 4897.
140. Add. MS 4949/151.
141. Add. MS 5602, pp. 31 and 45.
142. *DB* III, 357.
143. Add. MS 4895/167.
144. Add. MS 4921/165.
145. cp.*HOF*, 296 (1862) and *HES*, 272 (1871).
146. cp. his essay on 'Nationalism', *HOF*, 270–301 (1862) and the note: 'Catholic politics – Notion of a checking power – That is the essential element. Therefore opposes Democracy. Promotes Federalism' (Add. MS 5611, p. 4l (1880)).
147. *LMH*, 314.
148. Add. MS 4897.
149. Add. MS 4916/141.
150. Add. MS 4895/284.
151. Add. MS 4895 (?1878).
152. Add. MS 4897.
153. Add. MS 5552, p. 11.
154. Add. MS 5392/66.
155. Add. MS 5604, p. 11 (1879)
156. Add. MS 4960/318.
157. Add. MS 4954/205.
158. *LMH*, 10.

Notes to Chapter 6

1. Sept. 1882: 'I wish to omit everything that has not been, somehow, a force in the progress of Liberty, or that does not illustrate the law of its growth.' (*DB* III, 311.)
2. cp. Add. MS. 5395/5: 'Conscience unknown, unrecognised in the religions of the East. They taught virtue, punishment, etc. But they never knew that the test of what is right is within. Reigning authorities were suffered to determine it. China, India, Persia, Egypt, Assyria. There was no God, or their God was their king, or their God was the Devil.'
3. In the '100 Best Books', for instance, he spoke approvingly of the tolerance of Buddhism, and mentioned Schu-King and the Vedas for their influence, while Avesta 'taught the purest religion unrevealed'. March-Phillips and Christian, pp. 154 and 187.
4. Add. MS 4871.

5. Add. MS 5394/44.
6. Add. MS 5395/46.
7. Add. MS 4901/97.
8. *HOF*, 71.
9. *ibid.*, 4.
10. Add. MS 4915.
11. Add. MS 5392/239.
12. Add. MS 5395/54.
13. Add. MS 5392/100 and 102.
14. Add. MS 5392/134.
15. cp *HOF*, 4 and Add. MS 5611.
16. Add. MS 5392/90.
17. *Jer.* 31, 33.
18. G. F. Moore, *Judaism in the First Centuries of the Christian Era*, II, p. 82.
19. A. Schweitzer, *My Life and Thought* (London 1955), p. 115.
20. Add. MS 4871.
21. Add. MS 4871.
22. *HOF*, 27 (1877).
23. *ibid.*, 29 (1877).
24. *The History of the Popes* I, 10. This is quoted by Newman in his *Letter to the Duke of Norfolk*.
25. *HES*, 503 (1887).
26. *Edinburgh Review*, April 1903, p. 504. There are several references to Lasaulx in the Acton MSS. He was a mystic (Add. MS 5641, p. 74). He was 'full of grace and nobleness and distinction, in company with the best men – a certain sterility, in spite of richness – inefficient, with all his elevation — syncretism – Socrates and Christ' (Add. MS 5643, p. 28).
27. Add. MS 4913.
28. *Corr.* 255.
29. *Corr.* 263.
30. Add. MS 5643, p. 67.
31. *Butler's Works*, I, p. 126.
32. Add. MS 5640/55; cp. Add. MS 4912.
33. Add. MS 5552, p. 2.
34. Add. MS 5392/85.
35. Add. MS 5392/65.
36. Add. MS 5608, p. 33.
37. There are several references to the Essenes in Add. MS 5019 (which is labelled 'George Eliot') especially in connection with Eliot's novel *Daniel Deronda*. It appears that she found what was then known of the Essene religion attractive.
38. *HOF*, 26 (1887), cp. Add. MS 5392/145.
39. Acton had read about the Essenes in Philo of Alexandria and Josephus. There was discussion of them in the 1860s through the popularising work of Venturi. Lightfoot, in his *Epistles of St Paul* (1875), connects them with Zoroastrianism rather than with Christianity. Modern scholarship has been revolutionised by the discovery of the Dead Sea Scrolls, with evidence of their community life and their connexion with the groups among whom Christianity took shape.
40. March-Phillips and Christian, *loc. cit.*
41. Add. MS 5392/245; cp. also 238 and 31 of the same box.
42. Add. MS 5605 (1878).
43. Add. MS 5019.

44. *HOF*, 73 (1878).
45. Add. MS 4901/178.
46. It is difficult to see in what sense Acton uses the phrase 'voice of God' of Stoicism: particularly if it is supposed to 'dwell' in human souls. The Stoic was accustomed to use the word 'logos' for God. Acton was presumably using it as equivalent in this case for the 'voice of reason'. But, in this case, it cannot 'come down' to 'dwell' in our souls. The Holy Spirit which has traditionally been spoken of as 'voice' is transcendent, and cannot be confused with any human moral faculty.
47. *HOF*, 24–5. This last sentence is Acton's conventional conflation of William Penn and Kant, and it is interesting that Schweitzer, *op. cit.*, p. 178, also brackets together the Stoics and late 18th-century rationalists.
48. Add. MS 5392/60 and 174; Add. MS 5019.
49. cp. Add. MS 5392/237.
50. Add. MS 4943/200.
51. Add. MS 5392/43.
52. Add. MS 5392/217.
53. Add. MS 4944/73.
54. e.g. Add. MS 5552, p. 20; Add. MS 5392/173, /1, and /264.
55. Add. MS 5392/262.
56. Add. MS 5605, p. 26.
57. Add. MS 5392/79.
58. Add. MS 5392/38.
59. This passage is quoted by Newman, and lined by Acton, in his article 'On Consulting the Faithful in Matters of Doctrine' (*Rambler*, July 1859, p. 212). The intention of this article was to establish the authority and orthodoxy of the Catholic people as a whole, and was the cause of Newman's precipitate withdrawal from the journal.
60. Add. MS 5553, p. 6.
61. Add. MS 5392/62.
62. Add. MS 4983/116.
63. Add. MS 5611, p. 5.
64. Add. MS 5392/108.
65. In the note Add. MS 4901/194, there is a transcript of Tertullian in a hand that is not Acton's with the note, 'He is the only ancient writer who uses the word *conscientia* in a psychological sense, corresponding with our consciousness.'
66. Add. MS 5392/1488; cp. also Add. MS 5392/166 and /92.
67. *HOF*, 28 (1877).
68. Add. MS 5392/268.
69. Add. MS 5392/127.
70. It is probable that he meant Chrysostom when in 1887 he wrote to Creighton (*HES*, 503) 'Progress in ethics —. There is little of that between St John and the Victorian era.'
71. Add. MS 4901/16.
72. Add. MS 490l/161.
73. Add. MS 4979/100.
74. *Hom.* 54 (as quoted by Acton from his German edition): 'Niemand also wende vor, dass er Unwissenheit der Tugend vernachlässige, oder weil er niemanden habe, welcher ihm den Weg zu derselben zeige. Denn wir haben einen völlig ausreichenden Lehrer, das Gewissen, und es ist unmöglich, dass man der von da ausgehenden Hilfe beraubt werde?'
75. Add. MS 4901/203, commenting on *Psalms* and *II Chron.*

76. Add. MS 5596, p. 35.
77. *Corr.* 211, dated Cannes, 11 April 1888. This correspondence began as a discussion of the theistic novel *Robert Elsmere* and went on to deal with the whole question of the world into which Christianity was born, its relations with Judaism in the 1st and the 2nd centuries and the hunger of contemporaries.
78. cp. C. Spicq, OP, 'La Conscience dans le Nouveau Testament' in *Revue Biblique* (1938); A. N. Wilder, *Eschatology and Ethics in the Teaching of Jesus* (New York, 1939); C. A. Pierce, *Conscience in the New Testament* (1955); and the article by J. P. Thornton-Duesbury, 'Conscience', in *A Theological Word-Book of the Bible* (1950).
79. H. A. Hodges, *The Pattern of Atonement* (London 1955), p. 90.
80. *vide* 'Tolerance of the early Church – Lasaulx – did not pass as legacy to the Middle Ages.' S. Augustine (Add. MS 5552, p. 20); 'Möhler's dread of great names, particularly of St Augustine. Fully shared by Döllinger, led to his assiduity in looking up lesser lights' (Add. MS 4913); and 'He did not like ... St Augustine' (Add. MS 5401, labelled 'Döllinger').
81. Add. MS 4911, 'D[öllinger]. Augustinianism. Es ist in seiner äussersten Consequenz gegen das sittliche Selbst bewusstseyn indem es mit der Freiheit unverträglich ist, und gegen die Idee von Gott, dessen Gerechtigkeit und Barmherzigkeit in Widerspruch mit einander gerathen.'
82. 'St Augustine and the Christian Idea of Progress', Theodor Mommsen, *Jnl. of the Hist. of Ideas* (1951), pp. 346–74.
83. Mommsen, pp. 365, 372. Augustine goes back behind the Fathers to seek authority in the Scriptures.
84. Add. MS 5403/29 *bis.*
85. e.g. Add. MSS 4949/110, /145, /177 and 5403/72.
86. Add. MS 5392/74.
87. Add. MS 5392/119.
88. Add. MS 5392/148, also /128.
89. Add. MS 5392/142.
90. Add. MS 5552, p. 13.
91. Add. MS 5395/31.
92. Add. MS 5606, p. 10, and cp. Add. MS 5392/146.
93. Add. MS 4901/5.
94. Add. MS 5392/69.
95. Add. MS 5392/78.
96. Add. MS 5604, p. 18 (1879).
97. Acton was always astonished that eleven tracts of Priscillian, discovered at Wurzburg in 1885, had never been noticed by Döllinger, under whose care they had been.
98. Add. MS 4901/8.
99. Add. MS 5392/194, cp. 5392/179.
100. Add. MS 5392/19.
101. Add. MS 4979/197.
102. *Augustine: Later Works*, ed. J. Burnaby (London 1955), p. 183.
103. *ibid.*, 192.
104. It is clear from Add. MS 5416, labelled 'Fénelon', that Acton drew a close connection between him and Rousseau, both of them stressing the undogmatic and ethical character of religion. cp. also Add. MS 4921/341 and 'Fénelon' in the '100 Best Books'.
105. *Works* I, 87; *Works* II, 250; and *Works* I, 104.
106. Add. MS 4906.

107. *HOF*, 336 (1861).
108. cp. Add. MS 4921/303.
109. cp. Add. MS 4912: 'We assume each man is good until the contrary is proved. Then we condemn. Döllinger – less charitable before, was more charitable after. Found no end of excuses. Inconsistent with free will. Tending toward determinism. Strange for an admirer of Semi-pelagians.' (a) NB. Add. MS 5392/230: 'Guilt implies free will – principle of Pelagians. S. Augustine insists on original sin, which is apart from our will, and justifies punishment. So we have no claims of our own. — Idea that a man has no rights, that he is condemned at starting, that what he enjoys is understood.'
110. Add. MS 4908.
111. *inter al.* Add. MS 4942/9.
112. Add. MS 5395/45, cp. Add. MS 4901/5.
113. Add. MS 5019.
114. Add. MS 5395/28.
115. Add. MS 5395/10.
116. Add. MS 4901/19.
117. March–Phillips and Christian, *loc. cit.*
118. Add. MS 4908: 'No priest, accustomed to the confessional, and *a fortiori* no historian, thinks well of human nature'; and the series of which this (Add. MS 4960/87) is characteristic: 'Understand what the historian refuses to tell: the degrading misery of the poor — the horrors of the battlefield, the smallness, selfishness and cowardice of great men.'
119. Add. MS 5395/55, also Add. MS 4901/242.
120. Add. MS 5392/271.
121. Add. MS 4939/157.
122. In the *Dictionnaire de Théologie Catholique* (art. 'Quakers') (1936) L. Cristiani writes of their attitude to original sin: 'Contraire aux autres sectes protestantes, les quakers ne veulent pas admettre la corruption radicale et incurable de l'homme par le péché originel. Pour eux le péché d'Adam n'est imputé à personne jusqu'à ce qu'on le fasse sien par de semblables actes de désobéissance. Il y a donc corruption initiale, mais non imputation de culpabilité. — Aucune thèse de Barclay, dans son *Apologie*, ne porte directement sur la personne ou l'oeuvre de Jésus rédempteur. Ce n'est qu'incidemment qu'il atteste sa foi en la divinité du Christ et à son intervention dans l'oeuvre du salut de tous les hommes.'
123. 'Yet this corruption of unregenerate man is, it must be added, no hindrance to his possession of true moral virtues and his performance of good actions in his civic life, actions which spring from a good principle, without any evil intention, and without mixture of actual sin. Wherein I hope I shall be forgiven, if I have dared to diverge from the opinion of S. Augustine, who was doubtless a great man, of admirable intelligence, but inclined sometimes, as it seems, to exaggerate things, above all in the heat of his controversies.' (*Theodicy*, ed. Farrer, 70.)
124. *ibid.*, 9.
125. *Temporal Mission of the Holy Ghost*, quoted in Add. MS 5463.
126. Quirinus, 832, n. 1. Newman wrote to defend the priority of the individual Christian conscience over against the Pope in his *Letter to the Duke of Norfolk*.
127. Add. MS 4906. cp. *Corr.* 154, where Acton writes, 'the way out of the scrape will yet be found in insisting on the authority of tradition as the only lawful rule of interpretation'. Acton's lifelong confidence in the Vincentian canon

of tradition was reinforced by the fact that he could see Lérins from the window of his house at Cannes. *DB* III, 365 (1887)

128. cp. Acton's instruction to his son (1890) (Add. MS 4871) – and its politic refusal to conclude the argument: 'The token which convinces us of the authority of a sacrament or an institution which is scarcely to be traced in the NT is when we see that institution existing at the same time in different and distant cities –. For then we understand that the said institution received apostolic sanction before the preachers of Christianity had dispersed. This is the operation of Tradition. In upholding it, we have to contend with two enemies. With the Protestants who allow it to be devoured by the all-importance of the NT, and with those foolish Catholics whose belief in it drowns their ....' (sic)

129. Add. MS 5463.

130. 'A Catholic historical divine. The interpretation of (the) past thoroughly – the ascertaining of it – is all he has to do.' Add. MS 5641, p. 33.

131. cp. Cristiani in *Dict. Theol. Cath.*, *loc. cit.*: 'C'est surtout dans le latitudinarisme de leur conception de l'Église que les Quakers ont innové. Ils admettent une *Église Catholique* hors de laquelle il n'est point de salut, mais qui est aussi bien entre les paiens, les Turcs, comme entre toutes les diverses sortes de chrétiens. Cette Église est donc une Église invisible, formée de toutes les âmes sincères et de bonne foi.'

132. Add. MS 4979/57: 'Papacy. It began about 500 with forgeries to prove that the papacy was not to be judged by any authority, and could alone call Councils.' And Add. MS 4911, which quotes Döllinger as saying the 'sich erstreckende Reihe von Falschungen und Fictionen' began in the 5th century.

133. cp. Add. MS 5392/63 and /152: 'After Constantine, influx of heathen, not quite sincere. Made it hard for Christianity to work out its own thoughts. This happened only when the Germans came.'

134. Add. MS 5392/2. It seems the non-appearance of resistance and division before the 5th Century was Acton's major objection to the Anglican Church, and the authority it gave to the first four centuries. See Add. MS 4954/116.

135. Add. MS 5392/216.

136. Add. MS 5392/157.

137. Add. MS 5392/64.

138. Zschimmer published an account of Salvianus at Halle in 1875, which may well have brought this obscure figure to Acton's notice at this time.

139. Add. MS 5395/80.

140. cp. e.g. Add. MSS 4939/2, 4942/395, 4941/49, 4916/22.

141. Add. MS 5751 (May 1857): 'true monarchy – the creation of the Middle Ages – of Christianity acting on the German race and institutions.' cp. *HOF*, 203, 211 (1859).

142. cp. G. P. Gooch, *History and Historians in the Nineteenth Century* (1952).

143. *HOF*, 200 (1859).

144. Add. MS 5550, p. 20.

145. Add. MS 5392/162. In Add. MS 4916/140, labelled 'Ethics of Politics', he notes, 'the first notion in law of monarch's duty towards the constitution in 9th century.'

146. In Add. MS 5642, p. 66, he writes, 'Theory of the seed planted by God immemorially – in the breast of barbarians – nursed and matured by providential history – is welcome – gives unity to Western civilization ....' cp. Add. MS 4938/214, 'That we have been aiming the same way ever since Solon. Never all along the line. Not even in America. Grundrechte', and the

conclusion of Add. MS 4960/190, 'Unity – leading to America'. It is not uncommon to find Acton justifying power and force in a cause of which he approves. In Add. MS 5641, p. 20, he writes, 'Virtue succeeds in preserving, seldom in creating.'

147.   cp. Add. MS 4979/127.
148.   Add. MS 4957/197.
149.   Add. MS 5611, p. 12 (1880).1

Notes to Chapter 7

1.   cp. Add. MS 4948/213, following a quotation from *Bracton's Notebook* ed. Maitland 1887: 'A constitutional theory not yet embodied in definite institutions found expression for a while in the glittering paradox that submission to self-imposed law is the supreme feat of God's omnipotence.'
2.   Add. MS 4960/206.
3.   Add. MS 4960/205.
4.   The uniquely cesaro-papal government of the old papal territories had, in Acton's opinion, contributed to the difficulty exeprienced by the curia in comprehending the conventions of modern societies.
5.   *LMH*, 31.
6.   Add. MS 4907. cp. e.g. Add. MSS 4940/293 and 5552/6. Add. MS 5552/7 has a list, headed by St Thomas, of 'Revolutionary theory among divines'.
7.   Add. MS 4960/263.
8.   Add. MS 4901/8; the reference to St Paul occurs also in the other box labelled 'Conscience', Add. MS 5395/33.
9.   Jahnel was almost exactly of Acton's generation (b. 1835). I have not been able to discover what was his later career. Acton had much respect for Trendelenburg who (with Sir William Hamilton) he once said was the first man to 'know history' (Add. MS 4909).
10.   The article 'Conscience' in the *Dict. Theol. Cath.* by M. Chollet takes all its illustrative material from the works of Bonaventure and Aquinas. He writes, 'Les deux grands docteurs du 13ème siècle ont admirablement exposé ce rôle de la conscience.' H. Meyer, in *The Philosophy of St Thomas Aquinas* (St Louis, 1944), says that Aquinas, like the Stoics, maintained that a certain beginning of knowledge about the first principles of ethics is given us by nature, and, 'Synteresis, not a habit obtained by repeated actions, but a primitive original power innate in our minds. Thus, S. Thomas developed a potency into a full-fledged faculty' (p. 337).
11.   Add. MS 4901.
12.   Add. MS 4941/354, cp. Add. MS 4941/352, 'The world was monarchical. Aristotle was republican. S. Thomas married the two ideas. In all this, he innovates. In the Church he is not free. He strives to cover all that subsists. There he is conservative, apologetic.'
13.   Add. MS 4942/394.
14.   I have not been able to find any other writer who speaks of this Commentary and particularly this verse of it as particularly significant.
15.   The card with this characteristic tag of Abelard's follows directly after Acton had said 'Idea of Conscience after XIII Century. Found S. Thomas on that'. (Add. MSS 4960/263–4.) That Acton lays much less stress on Abelard than on Aquinas is mirrored in Jahnel's treatment, where, similarly, Abelard is brought in only to compare with Aquinas.
16.   Add. MS 4960/327, and Add. MS 4960/259, which again is a quotation from

the *Commentary on Romans*. Although not an especially novel thought, it is interesting to see that Neander (quoted in Jahnel), and Kirchmann, editing the edition of Leibnitz's *Theodicy* which Acton possessed, speak of Aquinas as 'the greatest figure in the development of ethics since Aristotle' and the root of 'the concept of natural religion' respectively. Both passages are lined by Acton. (Jahnel 95, and Kirchmann II, 9.)

17. See Meyer, 197. 'Thus man possesses an inner light by which he is guided, an inner law of his actions, the self-legislation of his practical reason which is indeed independent of his subjective attitudes because the moral order is based on the order of being, and the moral goodness of our acts is judged by comparison with this objective order.'

18. Add. MS 4969/262.

19. He wrote to Gladstone in December 1874 that Döllinger accepted his view that, 'Ultramontanism should be attacked in the root and stem, rather than in the flowering top' (*Corr.* 49), which probably refers back to the letter he wrote Döllinger in September, 'Diese Entwicklung (wie der Kirche Ultramontan wurde) bis zu ihren feinsten Wurzeln zurück zu verfolgen, wäre jetzt das wichtigste aller Werke.' (Add. MS 4914.)

20. *HOF*, 573.

21. Add. MS 4957/238.

22. *HOF*, 556.

23. Add. MS 4906.

24. It is probably true to say that Acton's acquaintance with the Middle Ages is generally undervalued, for the bulk of his published work comes from the early journalism, prior to 1870, when his interests were not in this area. In the earlier period, it is common to find him laying the principal emphasis on St Bernard in his estimate of medieval ideas of conscience.

25. Add. MS 4960/244.

26. Add. MS 4960/270. This is the only clear case known to me where Acton shows himself conscious of the fact that he is identifying 'conscience' with 'synteresis'. Acton is mistaken in ascribing the invention of the concept of 'synteresis' to Alexander of Hales.

27. St Bonaventure is quoted in the article 'Conscience' (*Dict. Theol. Cath.*) as saying, 'La conscience est comme le héraut et le messager du Dieu; ce qu'elle dit, elle ne l'ordonne pas de son propre droit, mais elle l'ordonne de la part de Dieu.'

28. Acton quotes Bonaventure, *Comp. Theol. Veritatis*, Add. MS 4960/300, 'Synteresis vis est animae motiva ... et in istis numquam errat, neque secundum synteresim est peccare.'

29. Add. MS 4960/185, cp. Add. MS 4960/180.

30. The phrase 'for the poor' recurs constantly in Acton's writing about the essence of Christianity (e.g. Add. MS 5392) in the late 1870s. It is curious that he apparently took so long to admire the Franciscan tradition. His early work contains so many disparaging comments on the Order that one must suspect they were unpopular at Munich.

31. Add. MS 4979/149, cp. Add. MS 4960/332. As one would expect, Acton believed the tension between Church and State in the 13th century contributed to produce 'conscience'. Add. MS 5403/17 compares Spain in 1260 with Northern Europe. In Spain, 'the papal tyranny promoted the political, just at the time of S. Thomas and Simon de Montfort. That is an example of what would have happened if there had been no collision.'

32. cp. Add. MS 4960/271, where Acton identifies 'conscience' with 'synteresis' in a typical way: 'Conscience. The Fathers thought it might perish. The

Scholastics from XIII century maintained that it cannot. They mean, in a mind that is not insane.' A quotation from Billuart, *Cursus Theologiae*, in the same box, gives the orthodox scholastic view. 'Synderesis est regula morum infallibilis sed remota, quia legem tantum generaliter et in communi proponit. Conscientia autem est regula fallibilis, sed proxima, quaternus explicat et applicat legem ad actus particulares.'

33. Add. MS 4960/283.
34. Add. MS 4960/268.
35. *LMH*, 171.
36. Meyer, *op. cit.*, 488.
37. *ibid.*, 404.
38. Add. MSS 4960/329–30.
39. Add. MS 5395/7.
40. cp. for example, *HES*, 503 (1887), 'the high absolutist theory of the papacy was the real cause of the breach with Luther', and, Add. MS 4945/34, 'Inheritance of the Middle Ages. Wherein they failed, How far beyond antiquity. Failure in religious liberty. No more than a feeble aspiration. In this respect the undivided reign of Christianity had gone back. Union of Church and State the cause of it all. Distinction of powers, mutual control and balance is the Christian idea. So the Reformation had the mission to accomplish this, by division. That was the main thing that remained to do. NB. How the Reformation began with that declared purpose.'
41. *HOF*, 325.
42. *ibid.*, 40.
43. Add. MS 5643, p. 11.
44. Add. MS 5611, p. 11 (1880); Add. MS 5413/88.
45. Add. MS 5395/43.
46. Some later research has tended to show the Canon Law at the root of the Conciliar, as well as the hierocratic, movement, e.g. B. Tierney's *Foundations of the Conciliar Theory* (1955).
47. Add. MS 4960/314.
48. Add. MS 4960/310.
49. March-Phillipps and Christian, *loc. cit.* cp. also Add. MS 5019, 'Kempis the most adequate and characteristic expression of the Catholic idea.'
50. Add. MS 4960/281.
51. *Edinburgh Review* (April 1903), p. 504.
52. Add. MS 5019.
53. *LMH*, 73.
54. cp. Add. MS 5604, p. 29 (1879), 5626, p. 9 (1881) and 5605, pp. 15–6 (1878).
55. Note Acton's commendation of the anti-dogmatic character of mysticism, e.g. in Add. MS 5641, p. 14 (1894): 'Mystik. Its disciplinary value. A priest has one constant temptation. to detect error. Study of mystic cultivates the opposite faculty. So much at first appears meaningless, exaggerated, loosely figurative, fantastic – get eyes used to the twilight.'
56. Add. MS 5395/74.
57. Add. MS 4979/179.
58. *Edinburgh Review* (1903), p. 528.
59. See especially *HES*, 440, and Add. MS 5613, p. 24 (1873). cp. *HES*, 429 and 30, *HOF*, 52, Add. MS 4960/121, and Add. MS 4904. 'Indeed a considerable liberality grew up under the Catholic unity – expressed by Sir Thomas More and his contemporaries. The fires were nearly extinct ....'
60. See Add. MS 5626 (1881), pp. 8 and 49.
61. Add. MS 4960/190.

62. Add. MS 5413/46. This box is labelled 'Erasmus'.
63. Add. MS 5413/64.
64. Add. MS 5413/115. cp. also /5, /10, and /39.
65. Add. MS 4960/282, cp. Add. MS. 5395/29, 5413/68, and Add. MSS 4960/93, /279, /285, /319, /325.
66. Add. MS 5413/9.
67. Add. MS 4960/288.
68. Add. MS 5413/21. Acton's final attitude is clear in *LMH*, 104, cp. with Add. MS 5413/42.
69. Add. MS 5604, p. 27 (1879), 'Humanists. They would have come to a breach with Rome,' and p. 30, 'When Luther rose up, unity was already gone – wide divergences.'
70. Add. MS 5604, p. 16.
71. Add. MS 5395/25.
72. Add. MS 5403/4
73. Add. MS 5642, p. 5.
74. Add. MS 5532, p. 18.
75. Add. MS 5626 (1881), p. 8, and p. 19, where he speaks of Calvinist doctrine of Grace making religious compulsion useless, and therefore as eventually encouraging Toleration. It is curious that Acton never spoke of Polish toleration in the 16th century, which was by far the most systematic and complete in Europe. Neither did he mention Acontius, who in W. K. Jordan's *The Development of Religious Toleration in England*, pp. 303–64, is given the prime place in the history of toleration.
76. *HES*, 503. The prominence of the early friars in the Cambridge lectures may indicate that the medieval foundations of Acton's scheme were only established in his thinking in the early 1890s.
77. Add. MS 4944/108.
78. Alfonso de Sarasa was a Flemish Jesuit of the 17th century. J. C. Fischer in *Vita Sarasae* (Jena 1741) describes him as 'hodie obscurum'. In the edition of *Les Ecrivains de la Compagnie de Jesus* (ed. de Backer 1876) in the Acton Library, he is mentioned only in passing, but it is clear that his main work, the *Ars Semper Gaudendi*, which is a collection of sermons, was republished frequently – and especially in Germany – until the latter part of the 18th century. Fr. Bosmans, in an article in the *Biographie Nationale de Belgique*, comments that many of these editions were poor and misleading. The edition used by Acton (Frankfurt 1750, ed. Fischer), is inaccessible in England. Fischer's belief that Leibnitz owed a large debt to Sarasa's ideas for his *Theodicy* seems to have been widespread, for the copy of the *Ars* in the Jesuit Library, Mount St., London W1, bears a note to that effect in a 17th-century hand. In his own day Sarasa appears to have been known chiefly for his eloquence and his mathematical work.
79. Add. MS 4945/33.
80. The Quakers have never had a strong sense of an objective corpus of revelation. Bancroft, in his famous chapter on the Quakers, draws the connection between Cartesianism and Penn. (See *History of the United States* (London 1849), II, 329, 337–8.)
81. Add. MS 5644, p. 58.
82. Add. MS 5644, p. 49.
83. cp. Add. MSS 4955/55, 4960/76, and 4953/242. cp. Add. MS 5602 (1877?), p. 58, 'Liberty founded on doubt is not liberty at all.'
84. Add. MS 4946/259.
85. cp. Add. MS 5395/53, and Add. MS 4901/350, 'Das Gewissen, Triebfeder des

Fortschritts [Conscience, the mainspring of progress]. So it was recognised only after it. Now conscience, feeble to the end of the 16th century, is the occupation of the 17th. Perkins, Ames, Sanderson, Taylor, Clarendon, Sarasa, Basnage.' Add. MS 4901 (labelled 'Conscience') is conspicuously full of quotations from 17th-century writings and sermons on conscience.

86. Add. MS 5602 (1877?), p. 39.
87. Add. MS 5602, p. 43, 'After Grotius said that law is not from Revelation. The next step was to say that the seat is in our own minds, irrespective not only of revelation and inspiration, but of all divine influence. We carry its source in ourselves; we draw it from no deeper source than human nature and human reason.'
88. Add. MS 4893/121.
89. cp. Add. MS 4941/208. 'In conflict with Calvinism, Socinus developed freedom of C[onscience]. They were in a perpetual minority. Soc[inus], Castallio, Coornhert, Milton, Locke, Bayle, Penn. Independency came to it by principle, not by necessity.'
90. Acton, like Döllinger (Add. MS 4907), made much of the English Catholic writers of *c.* 1660 (cp. Add. MS 4954/76).
91. cp. Add. MS 5602, p. 41, and Add. MS 4916/62.
92. Add. MS 4954/207. cp. *LMH*, 142, 'Whereas Henry ... could change religion at will ... there were some among the Puritans who enforced, though they did not discover, the contrary principle, that a man's conscience is his castle, with kings and parliaments at a respectful distance.'
93. *ibid.*, 206.
94. e.g. Add. MS 4901/256, 'Conscience was a thing appealed to by the destroyers of Church and State, by enthusiasts and fanatics. At the Restoration it was disparaged and denounced as a plea for revolution and regicide. South. Hobbes. Locke.' cp. also *LMH*, 208 and Add. MS 4949/262.
95. Add. MS 4950/58.
96. Add. MS 4901/259.
97. cp. Add. MS 5643, p. 22 and Add. MS 5551, p. 3, which gives a thumbnail sketch of the history of conscience, 'Rise in 13th century. Retarded by Casuists – another conscience than one's own. Outgrown in Terillus and Sarasa. Decline of notions of authority. Theory of erroneous conscience .... Sufficiency and infallibility.'
98. Add. MS 4954/44.
99. At one time Döllinger was to have written a biography of Innocent XI, and vide Add. MS 5645, p. 19.
100. J. La Placette was the French Protestant pastor in Copenhagen, and an antagonist of Bayle.
101. Add. MS 4960/300, /301. See also Add. MSS 4960/246 and 5395/51.
102. *LMH*, 116.
103. Add. MSS 4960/303–5.
104. *Corr.* 79–80.
105. cp. Add. MS 4901/264 and Add. MS 4944/110.
106. *FR*, 3.
107. Add. MS 4942/17.
108. Add. MS 5416 (labelled 'Fénelon').
109. Add. MS 4901/338, cp. Also MS 4901/231.
110. Add. MS 4901/355.
111. cp. *LMH*, 232, ' ... a time came, under George III, when [English traditions] were exhausted. It was then that another and more glorious Revolution, infinitely more definite and clear-cut, with a stronger grasp of principle,

and depending less on conciliation and compromise, began to influence England and Europe.'

112. Add. MS 5626, p. 7. References to the Quakers are quite frequent in Acton's notes on George Eliot, which were largely composed between her death in 1880 and his article in 1885.

113. Add. MS 4953/88, 'Innocent XI. At the turning point of history. Protestantism risked being put down [if the Glorious Revolution had failed] and absolutism secured.'

114. Add. MS 4949/306.

115. Add. MS 5602, p. 48.

116. Add. MS 4954/13.

117. *LMH*, 231.

118. Add. MS 4953/79. Other references to Innocent XI's position in liberal history include Add. MSS. 4953/76, 4946/230, 4953/88, and *LMH*, 226–7. Add. MS 5605 (1878), p. 25, describes 1688 as 'S. Thomas without Rome'.

119. Add. MS 4951/281. cp. also Add. MS 5605, p. 18, 'What they wanted was the wisdom without the narrowness [i.e. of the Sects] the politics apart from the religion and the national law. To dissociate what was permanent in these ideas from what was temporary and local and transient. How this was done in the Whig doctrine between 1670 and 1690.' Algernon Sidney is especially interesting in this context. He is transcribed by Acton (Add. MS 4948/7) as saying, 'The great and fundamental axiom of ethics is: So act that thou mayest be able to will, that thy maxim should be the law of all rational beings.' This is the Kantian essence of Acton's position, and it is important that Sidney was a close friend of Penn.

120. In the 'History of Liberty' box, Add. MS 4947, there are two transcripts from a *Letter against restraining the Press* (1698), which point the direction of thought that Acton regarded as significant (/57 and /176.) The most important sentence runs, 'So that profaneness and immorality cannot be destroyed but by all sects doing as they would be done unto; which must establish an entire and universal liberty, since they have all the same right to judge for themselves, and are equally obliged to act according to that judgment.'

121. Add. MS 4901/20. Other cards which speak of the 'full development of Conscience' in the 18th century are in Add. MS 5395.

122. Add. MS 4901/182, cp. Add. MS 4901/330, 'Theory of conscience led up to its supreme development in Vinet – Catholic, Protestant, Deist, Rationalist, Sceptic – all co-operated to make it supreme among the divisions and the ruins of churches and authority.'

123. This equation was made principally by C. Wolff, the dominating figure in 18th century German philosophy, who was a disciple of Leibnitz. Acton quotes from him for the Cambridge lectures (Add. MS 4960/307), 'Lex naturae est lex conscientiae.' Acton ascribed considerable importance to him, for he kept together the link between conscience and progress that Acton saw going back from Leibnitz to Sarasa. 'Law of Nature was Wolff's theory, filtered through Neufchatel. Progress towards ever higher perfection: The strongest of all ideas at one time, came from Wolff's master, Leibnitz.' Add. MS 4921/304.

124. See Add. MS 5606, p. 38 (1878), 'Do to others as you would be done by. And Kant's formula. This is the leading precept of politics. Put yourself in his place. Invert the position.'

125. Add. MS 5602, p. 3 (1877). In Add. MS 5626, (1881), p. 6, he takes medieval Catholicism as an example of this deprivation, and in Add. MS5604 (1879)

he writes of the Catholic revival being 'liberal so far as it was sincere'.

126. Add. MS 5611 (1880), p. 30.
127. Add. MS 5495 (labelled 'Vinet').
128. Add. MS 4901/282.
129. March–Phillipps and Christian, *loc. cit.*
130. Add. MS 4901/53.
131. Acton quoted S. T. Coleridge on the Quaker teaching about the conscience in Add. MS 4901/96, 'the existence and sovran authority of that voice. In the essentials of their faith, I believe as the Quakers do.' Coleridge was much read by Döllinger, and his kind of mystical thought had much in common with that of Vinet. A discussion of the details of the Quaker doctrine is to be found in Rachel King, *George Fox and the Light Within* (Philadelphia 1940). See also J. Coulson, *Newman and the Common Tradition* (Oxford 1970)
132. In his *Christianisme et Romantisme—Alexandre Vinet* (Paris 1925), Ernest Seillière devotes much space to Vinet's reading. The following passage in Pressensé, *Alexandre Vinet* (Paris 1891) is marked by Acton in his copy, 'Vinet a exercé sur notre théologie une influence égale à celle de Schleiermacher sur la théologie allemande, avec cette notable différence, qu'au lieu de se rattacher à un vague spinozisme, il s'est, par son inspiration generale, rattaché à la tendance de Kant, dans lequel nous voyons de plus en plus l'immortel precurseur de notre rénovation théologique' (p. 232).
133. *La Manifestation des Convictions Religieuses* (1837), p. 355.
134. See *Études sur la Litt. Francaise*, III, 428.
135. *Essais de Philosophie Morale*, (Paris 1837), xix.
136. *La Manifestation*, pp. 52–3; 'plus un homme redescend vers son conscience, plus il est probable qu'il se trouvera d'accord avec un autre homme, qui s'est également recueilli dans la sienne ... quand nous pressons le devoir de chercher et de dire la verité ... c'est à la conscience, c'est-à-dire a un principe d'unité.'
137. cp. *Jnl. of the Hist. of Ideas* (June 1955), pp. 356–75, 'Hutcheson's Moral Sense Theory', W. Frankens. In the boxes labelled 'Conscience', Acton describes Hutcheson's 'moral sense, as imperative as Kant's ... impartial and incorruptible' (Add. MS 5395/62) and that he and Hume 'push the absolutism of conscience as far as Rousseau' (Add. MS 4901/164).
138. *La Manifestation etc.*, p. 192.
139. *ibid.*, p. 441.
140. *Liberté des Cultes* (1826), p. 124.
141. Add. MS 5392/27.
142. Add. MS 4921/328. cp. Add. MS 4921/160 and *HOF* 585 (1889).
143. Add. MS 4947/192.
144. Add. MS 4901/20.
145. Add. MS 5395/9.
146. *HOF* 417 (1890). cp. Add. MS 4898: '[The Americans] fought at Lexington, not only for their own liberty but for England and all the old world. Extinct [already] in England, it would have been extinguished everywhere.'
147. Add. MS 5395/52.
148. See the extremely interesting letter that Acton wrote Gladstone in 1895 (*Corr.* 79), setting out points for the latter to bear in mind in his edition of Butler: '1. To bear in mind that the doctrine of the *Sermons* on the infallible conscience is not only borrowed from Sarasa, but is also indefensible. 3. To view Butler in connection with his immediate predecessors, Leibnitz and

Notes

especially Malebranche .... 4. To examine his relations with Kant ....' When Acton declares Butler 'indefensible', he is probably referring to Courtney's *Constructive Ethics* (1886) which is frequently referred to (e.g. Add. MS 4901/327) for its criticism of Butler. This can be compared to Acton's reference to an essay by Hartmann which 'pulverised the ethics of Kant'. It is nonetheless true that Acton continued to honour both figures, but the weakening of his passion for the infallibility of conscience, which appears to have led to changes of emphasis in his sytem in the 1890s, may have sprung from this source.

149. 'Kant stands on the shoulders of the *Analogy* when he elevates the probability into a substitute for proof; and on those of the *Sermons* when he makes the infallible Conscience the basis of certainty and the source of the Categorical Imperative. And my point is that he hails really from Butler, directly or indirectly and not as they say, and he himself seems to imply, from Rousseau.' (*Corr.* 226 (Oct. 1892))

150. *Corr.* 225 (Sept. 1892). cp. Add. MS 5395/81, 'Conscience. The 18th century tendency to exalt it culminates in Kant. He believes that Conscience proves God, where reason cannot', and Add. MS 5602, p. 7 (1877?).

151. March-Phillipps and Christian, *loc. cit.* It is interesting that the phrase 'reign of conscience' – Acton's preferred definition of liberty – forms part of this epithet.

152. *Corr.* 276 (1887) to Lady Blennerhassett.

153. Add. MS 4955/110.

154. Especially for Baader and Görres: see *Political Thought of the German Romantics*, Reiss (Oxford 1955), pp. 1–43.

155. Reiss, *op. cit.*, p. 22.

156. Add. MS 4901/167.

157. Add. MS 4960/254.

158. Add. MS 4901/165.

159. Reiss, *op. cit.*, p. 17.

Notes to Chapter 8

1. The present writer has prepared an article on this subject to be published in *St Luke's Journal of Theology*, University of the South, Tennessee.

2. The project as set out by Acton in 1896 is reprinted in *Longitude 30 West*, published to celebrate in 1969 the 20th anniversary of the establishment of the American branch of the Cambridge University Press in New York.

3. cp. Ernest Gellner, *The Psychoanalytic Movement*, London 1985, who makes the point that the official picture of the dynamics of human psychology at the end of the 19th century bore no relation to the general human *experience* of greed, self-delusion, exploitation, confusion, jealousy, etc. Acton is a notably apt target for this observation. His 'conscience' is a natural rational-mystical competence to know 'ethical science' within whose exercise the person engages with God. It acts, however, in a world overwhelmed with historical evidence of 'insincerity' and self-aggrandise-ment. Gellner sees Freud as offering the immediately post-Acton generation a marvellously well-tailored release from this tension. Perhaps, however, 'conscience' has been overshadowed by the Freudian concept of 'super ego' for too long. An empirical psychological treatment is in G. M. Stephenson's *The Development of Conscience* (London 1966).

4. See *DB* III, 302 (Sept. 1882) where Acton comments on the unbelief of the

literary classes since 1850. *see also* W.O. Chadwick, *The Secularization of the European Mind in the Nineteenth Century* (Cambridge 1975).

5.   *HES*, 303.

6.   cp. *DB* III, 348, June 1885, where Acton ranks her literary stature as second only to Shakespeare, and comments on her having developed a system of morals that is equal to the contemporary church's. Yet she was systematically atheist. She is a phenomenon of cultural history.

7.   'The fruits of the death of Christ, ripening for the world. Effects on society more than on men. S. Bernard or S. Francis, Mahomet or William Penn. Hardly a place for S. Anthony – for the inner, inward life.' (Late card from Add. MS 4907)

8.   W. H. McNeill (ed.), *Lord Acton: Essays in the Liberal Interpretation of History* (Chicago 1967), p. xviii.

9.   'That the same principle, the same cosmic, elementary force, was working to abolish negro slavery, the Penal Laws, the Corn Laws, and the old regime abroad, he [Döllinger] understood. But he would not believe that men's motives were the same. He thought that they were not conscious of it.' (Add. MS 4912)

10.   Add. MS 4921/309.

11.   Add. MS 4908.

12.   A large number of cards list the prerequisites of liberty, and in 1877, he spoke of liberty needing to be 'pregnant with culture; cp. 'cogito ergo sum – useless in the 5th century....Cicero on printing. Aristotle on machinery. All this was of no use' (Add. MS 4960/239).

13.   Add. MS 5628, p. 30.

14.   *LMH*, 317.

15.   The 1880s were a time when mystical and even occult thought was much in vogue. Acton used the phrase 'rational mysticism' with particular (though not exclusive) reference to two Scots divines associated with the University of St Andrews: John Tulloch, Principal of St Mary's College and writer on the Cambridge Platonists of the 17th century; and Robert Flint, author of the *History of the Philosophy of History* (Edinburgh 1893).

16.   cp. the 'divine seed' in *I John* 3.9.

17.   An example from the 1890s is Add. MS 4960/73, headed 'Stages of Revolution': 'Milan, Tyrannicide; Reformation and Bauernkrieg; Counter-Reformation. Ligue; Puritans; Whigs and the Revolution; The Colonial system; America. Naturrecht. Rousseau; French Revolution. Brabant; Spain. Ireland. Belgium. Greece; Poland. Italy; 1830. 1848. 1859.'

18.   Add. MS 5602 (1877?), p. 24.

19.   Add. MS 4960/186.

20.   cp. the frequent references to liberalism being the spirit, even if it may not be in the letter, of Christianity.

21.   eg. Add. MS 4965/5, *LMH*, 51, and Add. MS 4950/126.

22.   McNeill, *Lord Acton: Essays* ..., p. xiv. There is something unattractive about Acton as a collector of manuscripts and books: he congratulated himself too warmly on his plums: e.g. in 1877 he wrote, 'even they [German scholars] would be rather astonished at my library [at Aldenham]' (*DB* III, 180), and *passim* in his paper, 'Notes on Archival Researches 1864–1868' given to the Eranus Society at Trinity College after 1895, printed in McElrath, *Decisive Decade*, pp. 127–40.

23.   cp. *DB* III, 231, 11 Feb. 1881: 'Die H[istory of] L[iberty] soll zwar keine Weltgeschichte sein, aber doch eine Art Philosophie der Geschichte.'

24.   cp. Add. MS 4908.

Notes

25. Add. MS 4916/7 and cp. *LMH*, 12, 'History is the true demonstration of Religion' and 'the historian usurped the place of the prelate' (Add. MS 5463).
26. *HOF*, 473.
27. Add. MS 5463, quoting this passage from Molitor, 'Wo wir eine ununterbrochene Führung Gottes und eine wirklich genetisch fortschreitende Entwicklung der Göttliche Offenbarung erblicken, konnen wir gewiss sein, die wahre Religion gefunden zu haben.'
28. Add. MS 4906.
29. Döllinger did not share this view. '[He] would reply ... that the ways of Providence are not inscribed on the surface of things, that religion, socialism, militarism and revolution possibly reserve a store of cogent surprises for the economist, utilitarian and whig.' (*HOF*, 392 (1890))
30. Acton believed he had derived the 'scientific' criterion of success from his German training. The German historians had needed a 'standard that does not vary' and found it in the 'fixed standpoint of manifest destiny'. The events of history were 'the verdict of the power that governs the universe .... The judgment of ages impresses and imposes itself alike on royalist and republican, Christian and pagan, whose several sympathies have nothing to do with the manifest facts of science.' (*HES*, 500 (1890); cp. Add. MS 4960/104 (1893) and *HES*, 382 (1886))
31. Add. MS 4960/88.
32. *LMH*, 19.
33. cp. Add. MS 4945/164. 'Society is the sphere of constancy. State is the instrument of progress .... Progress depends on its [the State's] superiority over the inert mass. Object of Civilization: to increase that superiority.'
34. Add. MS 4960/37.
35. *LMH*, 202, cp. *ibid.*, 11.
36. *HOF*, 19, and in 1878, Acton wrote, 'Progress consists in this – that man should be governed by authority rather than by force, by opinion rather than authority, by conscience rather than by opinion.' (Add. MS 5605, p. 28)
37. Add. MS 4914, dated 22 Sept. 1882. Döllinger's 'Es freut mich von Herzen dass Sie es als eine Art Theodicée fassen' (Add. MS 4911), of 27 September, which Acton said referred to 'my work', was a reply to this. Acton's confession to Lady Blennerhassett in 1890 that his theodicy was that of the Whigs refers back to this correspondence as well as to Leibnitz.
38. Add. MS 5552, p. 9, cp. Add. MS 5467, 'Providence not manifest in history of the Church .... Inferiority of division .... Include the state – and profane history is more religious' and, of Newman, in Add. MS 5463, 'He would have recoiled from a theory which makes orthodoxy depend on politics, puts the State above the Church. He would (not) have said: [Adam] Smith a better Christian than [Samuel] Johnson. The final conclusion of which would be that only Whigs believe in God.'
39. *Études sur la Littérature Française*, III, 428.
40. In 1861 it is the denial of the unity of the human race which is 'the greatest objection' against Christianity (*ACS* II, 162). In 1872, the unity of his work is becoming visible: it will be what links together the dawn in the 15th century of personal moral responsibility with Döllinger's ethic of historical truth via the evil ultramontane doctrine of murder 'to the glory of God' (*DB* III, 82). In 1878 he has found the 'unity' in the history of English constitutionalism from feudal absolutism via Reformation ideas (*ibid.* 198). In 1882 he has found the 'grand unity in the history of ideas', its theodicy (*ibid.* 312). If, as planned, Acton had written the first chapter of the

Cambridge Modern History, vol. I on 'The Legacy of the Middle Ages' and his friend Flint had written the last chapter of vol. XII on 'The Philosophy of History', the ideological message of the project would have become far more explicit: Acton's '[Liberty] is almost, if not altogether, the sign and the prize and the motive in the onward and upward advance of the race for which Christ was crucified' is from his review of Flint in 1895. In the event, the final chapter, in a distinctly lower key, was 'The Growth of Historical Science' by G. P. Gooch.

41. Add. MS 5467.
42. Add. MS 4912.
43. *DB* III, 222, 30 Dec. 1880: 'Konnte mich aber mit ihrer [George Eliot's] Auffassung der neueren Kirchengeschichte nicht befreunden, da ich eben die Herrschaft der Sünde für viel weiter halte, und nicht anders darin erblicke als ein Kampf für und gegen dieses Reich auf Erden.'
44. D. Bonhoeffer's concept of 'religionless Christianity' was widely influential in such books as E. R. Wickham, *Encounter with Modern Society* (London 1964), Harvey Cox, *The Secular City: secularization and urbanization in Christian perspectives* (London 1965), R. Gregor Smith, *Secular Christianity* (London 1966), and is expressed in the title of e.g. S. W. Phipps, *God on Monday*.
45. Acton to Marie, May 1865: 'You know that the one supreme object of all my thoughts is the good of the Church; and I wish to arrange all things so that this may be accomplished as well as my means allow' (McElrath, *Decisive Decade*, p. 64).
46. *DB* III, pp. 64, 429, 447.
47. McElrath, *Decisive Decade*, p. 48; cp. also *ASC* II, 58 and 195.
48. McElrath, *Decisive Decade*, p. 23.
49. K. Rahner, *I Remember* (London 1985).
50. See J. C. Murray, *We Hold These Truths: Catholic reflections on the American proposition* (New York, 1960) and F. Burgess, *The Relationship between Church and State according to John Courtney Murray* (Düsseldorf 1971).
51. *Ecumenical Review* 17, 1966, p. 81.
52. *America*, 114, 1966, pp. 592–3.
53. John XXIII had been much influenced by his contact with the Orthodox churches. It may be relevant that the most fervent of Acton's allies at Vatican I, Bp Strossmayer of Djakovo, placed the policy of ecumenical unity with Orthodoxy at the heart of his episcopate among the South Slavs.
54. 'Reward in this world positively opposed to the notion of Christianity – which expects all men to be tried to the breaking limit – and therefore good men more severely' (Add. MS 4907 (?1890–5)).
55. *LMH*, 32.

Select Bibliography

I The unpublished Ph.D. dissertation (1957) on 'The Idea of Conscience in the Work of Lord Acton', by J. S. Nurser in the University Library, Cambridge (England) contains a survey of the Acton papers used for that work. These were principally notebooks and boxes of cards, catalogued in 1903 as Additional Manuscripts. The bibliography (pp. 261–75) also contains (a) a list of Acton's published writings – to which must now be added *DB* and *ASC*, and also E. Campion (ed.), *Lord Acton and the First Vatican Council: a journal*, Sydney, 1975; (b) selected secondary works: (i) obituaries, (ii) articles and papers, and (iii) books; and (c) an appendix analysing the works and authors cited by Acton in the two card-boxes labelled 'Conscience'.

The conclusion of the survey in this appendix is that Add. MS 5395 is the earlier; and there is reason to suppose that the cards date from before 1885. The Add. MS 4901 has numbers of cards dated in the 1890s, and probably dates from after 1885. It is possible Add. MS 5395 was the box in use at Aldenham. Acton's librarian, H. R. Tedder, remarked in his obituary notice on the notable shift in Acton's reading after 1885; it became more concentrated on British 19th-century works, and he normally bought only current books. His magnificent collection at Aldenham had ceased to be his working library some years before the financial crisis that led to its purchase by Andrew Carnegie (*vide* Owen Chadwick, *Acton and Gladstone*).

There is a difference in character between the two boxes. Add. MS 5395 has a high proportion of 18th-century names, deists and anti-clerical rationalists; while Add. MS 4901 has a large number of Cartesian and Platonist names of the 17th and 19th centuries, many of the second and third class. In both boxes, however, there is a concentration of interest in representatives of the two periods 1680–1710 and 1780–1840.

II There are admirable bibliographies relating to Lord Acton in V. Conzemius, *Ignaz v. Dollinger. Briefwechsel*, vol. I, pp. xxxv–xlv, and D. McElrath, *Lord Acton: the Decisive Decade*, pp. xi–xvi.

III   Titles referred to in the text and notes

Alatri, P., *John Emerich Acton: Cattolicesimo Liberale*, Florence, 1950
Albarnoz, *see* Carillo
Altholz, J. L., *The Liberal Catholic Movement in England: 'The Rambler' and its contributors (1848–1864)*, London, 1962
Altholz, J. L., and D. McElrath, *The Correspondence of Lord Acton and Richard Simpson*, vols. I–III, Cambridge, 1971–75; vols. II and II with J. Holland
Appel, T., *The Life and Work of John W. Nevin*, Philadelphia, 1899
Auchmuty, J. J., 'Acton's Election as an Irish Member of Parliament', *English Historical Review*, 1946
— , *Acton as a member of the House of Commons*, Alexandria, Egypt, 1949
Ben-Israel, H., *English Historians and the French Revolution*, Cambridge, 1968
Blakiston, N. (ed.), *The Roman Question: Extracts from the despatches of Odo Russell from Rome 1858–70*, London, 1962
Blennerhassett, Charlotte Lady, 'The late Lord Acton', *Edinburgh Review*, April 1903
Brinton, C., 'Lord Acton's Philosophy of History', *Harvard Theological Review*, Jan. 1919
Burgess, F., *The Relationship between Church and State according to John Courtney Murray S.J.*, Düsseldorf, 1971
Butterfield, H., *The Whig Interpretation of History*, London, 1931
— , 'Journal of Lord Acton at Rome 1857', *Cambridge Historical Journal*, 1945
— , *Lord Acton* (Historical Association Pamphlet), London, 1948
Butterfield, H. and A. Watkin, 'Gasquet and the Acton-Simpson Correspondence', *Cambridge Historical Journal*, 1950
Burnaby, J., *Augustine: Later Works*, Cambridge, 1955
Cambridge Modern History (eds. A. W. Ward, G. W. Prothero, and Stanley Leathes), Cambridge, 1903 onward
Campion, E. (ed.), *Lord Acton and the First Vatican Council: a journal*, Sydney, 1975
Carillo de Albarnoz, A., 'The Ecumenical and World Significance of the Vatican Declaration on Religious Liberty', *Ecumenical Review*, Geneva, 1966
Chadwick, [W.] O., *Acton and Gladstone*, London, 1976
— , review of Conzemius, *Döllinger. Briefwechsel*, vol. I, *Journal of Ecclesiastical History*, 1965

— , *The Secularization of the European Mind in the Nineteenth Century*, Cambridge, 1975

— , *The Popes and European Revolution*, Oxford, 1981

Collini, S., D. Winch, and J. Burrow, *That Noble Science of Politics*, Cambridge, 1983

Conzemius, V. (ed.), *Ignaz v. Döllinger. Briefwechsel*, vols. I–III (*mit Lord Acton*), Munich, 1963–75. *see* also W. O. Chadwick

— (ed.), *Ignaz v. Döllinger. Briefwechsel*, vol. IV (*mit Lady Blennerhassett*), Munich, 1981

— , 'Lord Acton oder das freie Wort in der Kirche', *Herrnsheim 771–1971*, Worms, 1971

Coulson, J, *Newman and the Common Tradition*, Oxford, 1970

Cowling, M, 'Mr Woodruff's Acton', review article in *Cambridge Journal*, Dec. 1952

Cox, H., *The Secular City: secularisation and urbanisation in Christian perspective*, London, 1965

Cupitt, D., *Taking Leave of God*, London, 1980

Dessain, C. S. (ed.), *the Letters and Diaries of J. H. Newman*, London, 1961—

Döllinger, *see* Conzemius

Farrer, A. (ed.), *Leibnitz: Theodicy*, with Introduction, London, 1951

Fasnacht, G. E., *Acton's Political Philosophy*, London, 1952

— , 'Acton's notes for a Romanes Lecture', *Contemporary Review*, Dec. 1952

Figgis, J. N. and R. V. Laurence (eds.), *Lectures on Modern History*, London, 1906

— (eds.), *The History of Freedom*, London 1907

— (eds.), *Historical Essays and Studies*, London, 1908

— (eds.), *Lectures on the French Revolution*, London, 1910

— (eds.), *Selections from the correspondence of the 1st Lord Acton*, vol. I, London, 1917

Frankens, W., 'Hutcheson's Moral Sense Theory', *Journal of the History of Ideas*, 1955

Gasquet, F. A. (ed.), *Lord Acton and his Circle*, London, 1906

Gellner, E., *The Psychoanalytic Movement*, London, 1985

Gooch, G. P., *History and Historians in the Nineteenth Century*, London, 1952

Gregor Smith, R., *Secular Christianity*, London, 1966

Herzberg, W., *Catholic, Protestant and Jew*, New York, 1955

Himmelfarb, G. (ed.), *Essays on Freedom and Power*, Glencoe, Ill., 1948

— , 'The American Revolution in the Political theory of Lord Acton', *Journal of Modern History*, 1949

— , *Lord Acton: a study of conscience and politics*, London, 1952

Holland, J. *see* Altholz and McElrath

Hodges, H. A., *The Pattern of Atonement*, London, 1955

Janösi, F. Engel de, 'The Correspondence between Lord Acton and Bishop Creighton', *Cambridge Historical Journal*, 1940

Jordan, W. K., *The Development of Religious Toleration in England*, London, 1932

King, R., *George Fox and the Light Within*, Philadelphia, Pa., 1940

Kochan, L., *Acton on History*, London, 1954

Lally, F. E., *As Lord Acton Says*, Newport, R. I., 1942

Longitude 30 West, New York, 1969

MacDougall, H. A., *The Acton–Newman Relations*, New York, 1962

— , *Lord Acton on Papal Power*, London, 1973

McElrath, D., *The 'Syllabus' of Pius IX: some reactions in England*, Louvain, 1964

— , *Lord Acton: the Decisive Decade 1864–74*, Louvain, 1970

— , *see* also Altholz

McNeill, W. H., *Lord Acton: Essays in the Liberal Interpretation of History*, Chicago, 1967

Magnus, P., *Gladstone*, London, 1954

March Phillips, L. and B. Christian (eds.), *Some Hawarden Letters*, London, 1917

Mathew, D., *Acton: the Formative Years*, London, 1946

— , *Lord Acton and his Times*, London, 1968

Meyer, H., *The Philosophy of St Thomas Aquinas*, St Louis, Mo., 1944

Mommsen, T., 'St Augustine and the Christian Idea of Progress', *Journal of the History of Ideas*, 1951

Moore, G. F., *Judaism in the First Centuries of the Christian Era*, 3 vols., Cambridge, Mass., 1927

Murray, J. Courtney, *We hold these Truths: Catholic reflections on the American proposition*, New York, 1960

Newsome, D., *Godliness and Good Learning*, London, 1961

Noack, U., *Geschichtswissenschaft und Wahrheit*, Frankfurt, 1935

— , *Katholizät und Geistesfreiheit*, Frankfurt, 1936

— , *Politik als Sicherung der Freiheit*, Frankfurt, 1947

Nurser, J. S. 'The Religious Conscience in Lord Acton's Political Thought', *Journal of the History of Ideas*, Jan.-March 1961

Bibliography

Paul, H. (ed.), *Letters to Mary, daughter of the Rt Hon. W. E. Gladstone*, London, 1904; new and expanded edition 1913

Peyre, H., 'The Influence of 18th century Ideas on the French Revolution', *Journal of the History of Ideas*, 1949

Philips, Edith, 'Pensylvanie: l'Age d'Or', *American Historical Review*, 1930

Pierce, C., *Conscience in the New Testament*, London, 1955

'Quirinus', *Letters from Rome on the Council*, London, 1870

Rahner, K, *I Remember*, London, 1985

Reiss, H. S., *Political Thought of the German Romantics*, Oxford, 1955

Rothblatt, S., *The Revolution of the Dons: Cambridge and society in Victorian England*, London, 1968

Schlesinger, A., Jr, *The Age of Jackson*, London, 1946

Schweitzer, A., *My Life and Thought*, London, 1955

Seillière, E., *Christianisme et Romantisme – Alexandre Vinet*, Paris, 1925

Spicq, C., O.P., 'La Conscience dans le Nouveau Testament', *Revue Biblique*, 1938

Stephenson, G. M., *The Development of Conscience*, London, 1966

Thornton-Duesbury, J., *A Theological Word-book of the Bible*, London, 1950

Tierney, B., *Foundations of the Conciliar Theory*, Cambridge, 1955

Underhill, E., *Mysticism*, London, 1930

Wickham, E., *Encounter with Modern Society*, London, 1964

Wilder, A., *Eschatology and Ethics in the Teaching of Jesus*, New York, 1939

Wolfe Howe, M. A. de, *The Life and Letters of George Bancroft*, vols. I & II, New York, 1908

Woodruff, D. (ed.), *Essays on Church and State*, London, 1952. *see* also Cowling

Index

Abelard, Peter (1079–1142), 37, 135.
absolutism illegitimate, 102.
abstract ideas, 81, 92, 94, 97.
Acton, Charles (later Cardinal; 1803–47), 1.
Acton, Sir Ferdinand Richard Edward (1801–37), 1.
Acton, Sir John (1736–1811), 1.
Acton, John Edward Emerich Dalberg, 1st Lord (1834–1902); A. and Donatists, 120; A. and Luther, 144; A. and Pelagianism, 123–66; A. as Regius Professor, 4; A. at First Vatican Council, 8–9; A. elected to Commons, 5; A. on English historians, 4; A.'s anxiety for truth, 11; A.'s break with Döllinger, 14–15; A.'s catholic apologetic, 47–48; A.'s characteristic concerns, 164, 175; A.'s diplomatic missions, 2; A.'s dissatisfaction with Jesus of history, 116; A.'s education, 1–4; A.'s Germanic 'system', 95; A.'s history an apologia, 167; A.'s correspondents, 7; A.'s orthodoxy, 125; A.'s peerage, 8; A.'s religious experience, 32; A.'s sense of vocation, 4, 171, 181 n.23; A.'s *Times* apologia, 11–12; A.'s view of America formed 1877–82, 83–4; A.'s writing and influence, 19–20.
Acton, Mamy, 7.
Acton, Marie (née Arco-Valley; 1841–1923), 6.
Acton, Richard, 108.
Adams, Henry (1838–1918), 78.
Adams, John (1735–1826), 96, 156.
Adams, John Q. (1767–1848), 72.
Adams, Samuel (1722–1803), 96.
'adult' education, 58.
Aegidio di Viterbo (1465–1532), 143.
Aldenham, 1, 6.
Alexander of Hales (1170–1245), 137.
Ambrose, St (339–97), 113, 118, 120, 123, 155.
American bishops, 82.

American Civil War, 75–6, 81.
American Constitution, 77, 83, 157; Am. Const. as limit and guarantee of liberty, 102–5.
American example dangerous, 83.
American Revolution, 66, 89, 92, 94, 96.
American revolutionaries, 130.
American whiggism scientific, 96.
American War of Independence, 130.
Ames, William (1576–1633), 153, 200 n.85.
Anabaptists, 144, 146.
anti-Infallibilists, 82.
Antonelli, Cardinal Giacomo (1806–76), 8.
Arco-Valleys, 6.
Arianism, 127, 129.
Aristotle, 69, 113.
Arnold, Thomas (1795–1842), 33, 98.
Assassins, 34.
Athanasius, St (296–373), 118.
Augustine, St (of Hippo; 354–430), 37, 87, 115–28, 134; A.'s admiration for slavery, 121; A. changes Christian conscience, 121.

Baader, Franz (1765–1841), 44, 204 n.154.
Bacon, Sir Francis (1561–1626), 145, 147.
Bagehot, Walter (1826–77), 75.
Bancroft, George (1800–91), 63, 84, 89, 150, 200 n.80.
Barclay, Robert (1648–90), 150.
Baronius, Cardinal Cesare (1538–1607), 56.
Basnage, Jacques (1653–1723), 200 n.85.
Baur, Ferdinand (1792–1862), 113.
Baxter, Richard (1615–91), 44.
Bayle, Pierre (1647–1706), 89, 201 n.89.
Beccaria, Cesare (1738–94), 97.
Benson, Archbishop Edward W. (1829–96), 161.

213

Index

Berger, Peter, 161.
Bernard, St, of Clairvaux (1090–1153), 38, 134, 198 n.24.
Bismarck, Otto (1815–98), 9.
Blennerhasset, Lady Charlotte (née von Leyden; 1843–1917), 8, 81, 113, 142, 153.
Bohemian Brethren, 38, 142.
Bonaventure, St (1217–74), 32, 134–7, 140, 143.
Borromeo, St Charles (1538–84), 14.
Bossuet, Bishop Jacques (1627–1704), 117, 127.
Bourdaloue, Louis (1632–1704), 154.
Bovillus, Charles [de Bovelles] (1470–1553), 143.
Bracton, Henry (d. 1268), 132.
Bridgnorth, 11, 40.
Bright, John (1811–89), 159.
'British Israelites', 164.
British Museum, 18.
Brownson, Orestes A. (1803–76), 84.
Bryce, James, Viscount (1838–1922), 16, 17, 83, 100, 102.
Burke, Edmund (1729–97), 3, 5, 60, 73, 75, 84, 93–4, 97, 155, 190 n.114; B.'s scientific whiggism, 96.
Butler, Bishop Joseph (1692–1752), 26–7, 31, 48, 63, 66, 113, 124–5, 145, 151-7; B. and Sarasa, 149.
Butterfield, Sir Herbert, 13.

Calhoun, John (1782–1850), 52, 191 n.136.
Calvin, John (1509–64), 43.
Calvinism, 153.
Cambridge ethos, influence of, 163.
Cambridge Historical Tripos, 19-20.
Cambridge Modern History, 12, 19, 25, 38, 165.
Cambridge University Library, 21.
Cambridge University Press, 160.
Camden, Charles Pratt, Earl (1714–94), 96–7.
Cannes, La Madeleine at, 6.
Carlow, 5.
Carnegie, Andrew (1835–1919), 18.
Castallio, Sebastian [Castellio] (1515–63), 201 n.89.
Cathari, 34, 122.
Catholic church, absolutism in, 47.
Catholic church in America, 81.
Catholic Congress, Munich, 6.
Catholicism and the Liberal state, 45.
Catholicism, reformed, 37.
Catholic reviews, 5-7.
Catholics, Old, 9.
Cavour, Camillo (1810–61), 17.
Celsus, 44.

century of conscience, 151–8.
Charlemagne (742–814), 130.
Charles I, King of England (1600–49), 139.
Charles V, Emperor (1500–58), 101.
Chatham, William Pitt, Earl of (1708–88), 96–7.
Chéverus, Bishop Jean-Louis (1768–1836), 26, 82.
checks and balances in democracy, 103.
Cherbuliez, Victor (1829–99), 102.
Christ and the Jews, 112; his ethical teaching, 112; his nativity and Amer Rev, 89; C. in the church, 112; work of C., 70.
Christendom, 42, 129, 132.
Christianity and conscience, 119; C. and killing, 122; coming of C., 112; C. forbids absolutism, 116; C. 'natural', 57; C. 'scientific', 44; should be politically committed, 59; Stoic and Essene sources of C., 114.
Chronicle, 6.
Chrysippus (405–79), 114.
Chrysostom, St John (347–407), 118, 120, 155.
church as 'given' tradition, 162; authority of c., 39; distinctive to Christianity, 112; in secular state, 105; Fathers, 117; c. 'of the future', 170; responsible for murder, 13; c.-state relations, 40.
Cicero, 115, 118, 120, 143.
Civil Rights, 174.
Civiltà Cattolica, 172.
Clarendon, Edward Hyde, Earl of (1609–74), 200 n.85.
Coleridge, Samuel T. (1772–1834), 58, 124, 153, 203 n.131.
Columbus, Christopher (1451–1506), 89, 109; his oppression of American Indians, 130.
commonwealth of nations, 163.
conciliar reform, 141–3.
Connolly, Bishop Thomas (1815–76), 82.
conquest beneficent, 66.
conscience, absolute value of, 60; c. and human rights, 97–8; c. and political federalism, 72; c. and revolution, 61; c., arguments against, 32; c., century of, 151–8; c. in early Christian church, 36; 'insincere' c., 169; c. in Victorian period, 25; sovereignty of c., 55, 77–8; c. key to secular liberalism, 57; c. of Quakers, 87; c., perversion of by Augustine, 120; c. proactive, 62; c. the fruit of

214

Index

Old Testament, 154, 160.
Old Testament history, 13.
'one world', 164.
Orestes, 110, 134.
original sin, 111, 123.
Orthodoxy, Eastern, 34, 207 n.53.
orthodoxy, liberalism the only, 101.
Oscott, 1.
Otis, James (1725–83), 96, 99.
Oxford Movement, 4.

Pacem in Terris, 174.
'pagan' element in church, 128.
Paine, Thomas (1737–1809), 91–2, 100.
papal aggression, 2.
Parmenides, 110.
Pascal, Blaise (1623–62), 145, 154.
Paul, St, 62, 111, 119-120, 135.
Paul VI, Pope, 171.
Pelagius, (*fl.* 400–18), 115, 120, 123,
  125–7; P. on side of conscience, 121.
Penn, William (1644–1718), 32, 36, 60,
  85–7, 89, 93, 100, 110, 134, 145–50,
  156–7, 167, 201 n.89; P. a 'great
  man', 88; contrast with Locke, 63;
  his golden rule, 122; his radical
  reformation, 88;
Pennsylvania, 43, 72, 86-87, 106, 128–
  9, 171; P. a new age, 89; P. Quakers,
  90; P. 'undeveloped Christianity',
  88.
Perkins, William (1558–1602), 153,
  200 n.85.
persecution, 37, 124, 140; Acton's
  intolerance of, 100.
Philadelphia Yearly Meeting, 91.
Philo, 115.
Pietism, 150.
Pius VII, Pope (1740–1823), 46.
Pius IX, Pope [Pio Nono] (1792–1878),
  7, 27, 35, 132, 168, 172–3.
Plato, 69, 87, 113.
political freedom, definition, 52.
political importance of establishment
  of church, 112.
political science secular, 56–7, 98;
  ethical fruits of, 57.
politics, as ethics of public life, 100; p.
  as 'science', 53; p., 'intentional', 74;
  p., spiritual basis of, 63; p.
  transcend religion, 124.
Politiques, 124, 144.
poor, care for the, 49, 116, 118, 175.
Postel, Guillaume (1510–81), 143.
power of the dead, 74.
pre-Christian philosophy, 107.
prejudice, 79.
'Preparation of the Nations', 109.
'primitive revelation', 113.

Priscillian, Bishop (*d.* 385), 123; P.
  invents Christian persecution, 122.
privatising of religion, 162.
progress, 73–4, 163, 166–9; p., Acton's
  belief in, 91; p. and conscience, 149;
  p. and liberty, 65; p. and 'the best',
  79.
Propaganda Fide, 45.
prophetic inspiration, 109.
Protestantism, 143.
providence, 170.
Pseudo-Clementine books, 117.
Pseudo-Dionysius, 132.
'public opinion', 66.
Puritans, 106, 147.
Pym, John (1583–1643), 92.

Quakers, 84–9, 88, 126-127, 147, 150,
  153–4, 169; creation of
  Pennsylvania, 114; notion of
  conscience, 86; 'sense of the
  meeting', 87; non-violence of, 89.
Quarterly Review, 5.

Rahner, Karl, 172.
Rambler, 5, 51.
Ranke, Leopold (1795–1886), 29, 112,
  169.
rationalists, 155–6.
rational mysticism, 166.
Raymond of Pennaforte [Penyafort]
  (1180–1275), 136–40.
Raynal, Guillaume (1713–96), 80, 87.
recent Acton scholarship, 21–3.
Reformation, 128, 140, 142, 144–5, 147;
  sects of, 143.
reign of conscience, 51, 56, 65, 71, 103,
  106, 114, 126, 146, 156, 171.
religion a watch-dog for liberty, 69.
Renaissance, Stoic philosophy of, 143.
'Render unto Caesar', 40, 112.
Renouf, Sir Peter (1822–97), 34.
renovatio, 172.
repentance, 54.
'resident aliens', 72.
responsibility, individual, 69; to God,
  64.
Restoration, 148.
revolution, 67, 73, 92, 95; r., abstract,
  101; r., Acton's doctrine of, 99–100;
  r. a medieval idea, 132; r.
  conservative, 80; r., element of
  Christianity, 116; liberal r., 76.
Rhode Island, 97.
Ritschl, Albrecht (1822–89), 150.
Roman Catholic church, Acton and the,
  5.
Roman Catholics, English, 4.
Romans 14: 23, 119, 122, 130, 134–5.

218